An introduction to cognitive education

Cognitive education brings together the disciplines of cognitive psychology and education. This book provides a clearly written introduction to this field and explains:

- concepts commonly found in the cognitive psychology and cognitive education literatures;
- theories and models of human thinking and intelligent behaviour;
- how these have been applied to psychoeducational assessment, instruction and the adaptation of student behaviour.

The book includes numerous examples to explain the concepts, theories and applications together with supplementary reading lists and study questions.

Adrian Ashman teaches at the Fred and Eleanor Schonell Special Education Centre at the University of Queensland. **Robert Conway** teaches at the Special Education Centre at the University of Newcastle, New South Wales.

An introduction to cognitive education

Theory and applications

Adrian F. Ashman and
Robert N. F. Conway

London and New York

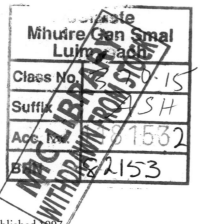

First published 1997
by Routledge
11 New Fetter Lane, London EC4P 4EE

Simultaneously published in the USA and Canada
by Routledge
29 West 35th Street, New York, NY 10001

© 1997 Adrian F. Ashman and Robert N. F. Conway

Typeset in Garamond by
Solidus (Bristol) Limited
Printed and bound in Great Britain by
TJ International Ltd, Padstow, Cornwall

British Library Cataloguing in Publication Data
A catalogue record for this book is available from the British Library

Library of Congress Cataloguing in Publication Data
Ashman, A. F. (Adrian F.)
An introduction to cognitive education: theory and applications/
Adrian F. Ashman and Robert N. F. Conway.
    p.   cm.
Includes bibliographical references and index.
1. Thought and thinking – Study and teaching. 2. Cognition. 3. Educational
psychology. 4. Learning, Psychology of.   I. Conway, Robert N. F., 1949– .
II. Title.
LB1590.3.A74 1997
370.15–dc20   96-27652
                                               CIP

ISBN 0-415-12839-0
ISBN 0-415-12840-4 (pbk)

Dedication

After a professional career that has spanned forty years, J.P. Das retired from the University of Alberta in Edmonton, Canada, at the end of 1996. We dedicate this book to him as a very modest acknowledgement of the substantial influence he has had on our academic careers over the past twenty years.

He has been our academic adviser, mentor, and collaborator. He remains an inspiration to us, and to his many colleagues around the world, who have been, and continue to be, captivated by his intellect, wit, commitment, and gentle nature. He has contributed significantly and generously to the literatures of neuropsychology, cognition, and disability, and has been a vigorous advocate of the application of cognitive theory to education.

In friendship and gratitude.

A.F.A. and R.N.F.C.

Contents

List of illustrations

TABLES

Preface

For a large part of our academic lives, we have been involved in the field of cognitive psychology. Our interest in this area developed through the 1970s and has endured for twenty years. Over much of that time we have been involved in teaching students at both undergraduate and graduate levels and we have endeavoured to pass on to them a knowledge of, and interest in, the application of cognitive theory to education.

This book developed as a result of a number of influences. First, it has come from our desire as teachers to demystify the complex field of cognitive psychology for both undergraduate education and psychology students. Since the 1940s there has been a prodigious growth in the number of terms being used in the professional literature, and a parallel construction and deconstruction of terms as researchers have built a comprehensive knowledge of cognitive concepts. We have attempted to deal with the major innovations and some of the subtleties in this book.

Second, the book developed from our own involvement in the young field known as cognitive education. In the early 1980s, we worked together to build a model of classroom teaching called Process-Based Instruction that integrated our academic and practical knowledge and our skills as school and tertiary educators. As part of the development process, we gained considerable insight into the teaching-learning process. Perhaps through the hundreds of hours we spent together talking, arguing, and model-building, we clarified our own and our collective view of the various influences that affect the processes of learning and problem-solving. We recognised the need for the systematic introduction of cognitive concepts within school classrooms and to teach children and adults about the processes of planning and decision-making.

Third, we have been involved in international efforts to disseminate information about the application of cognitive concepts to education. We have been aware of the growing interest in the field since the mid-1980s and the burgeoning of many approaches that have the same conceptual bases and, in many cases, the same historical roots. To our knowledge there has never been a compilation of the major programmes, procedures, and techniques.

Hence, this book is concerned with a systematic exposition of concepts, procedures, and programmes that can be grouped together as members of the same 'intellectual community of ideas' called cognitive education. In general terms, cognitive education refers to the application of cognitive theory and principles to assessment, instruction, remediation, and clinical practice within the field of education. We have also tried to place cognitive education within the context of formal and informal education, not only the instruction that takes place during the years of compulsory schooling.

The book is aimed at students in education, psychology, and related disciplines predominantly at the undergraduate level, and their instructors. In a book such as this which has been prepared as an introduction to the field, we have had to make some difficult inclusion-exclusion decisions. The mammoth cognitive psychology literature can not be summarised in its entirety in a book of 100,000 words without making compromises. We have presented our own views in a number of places, being careful to substantiate our claims from published material. We have not included descriptions of every assessment or instructional method that can be found in books and professional journals. We have endeavoured to include those that have been publicised widely and have included references to others that we believe deserve notation, if not elaboration. We have excluded some that colleagues might have expected to see in these pages, and included others that some researcher and writer colleagues might dismiss. We have attempted to be international in our coverage, and also as even-handed and objective as possible in our descriptions and evaluations.

Finally, we recognise that cognitive education has traditions and a heritage that extend back over a hundred years. However, the application of psychological concept to regular education, regular classrooms, and inter-active education processes is relatively new. It is our hope that this book may stimulate the interest of young scientists and scholars to the extent that they will join the growing body of researchers and practitioners concerned with the improvement of teaching and learning.

The book is divided roughly into three segments. The first third provides an introduction to cognitive concepts and their traditions. The second third deals with ways of assessing intellectual skills, and the final third concerns instruction and remediation.

Numerous people have assisted us during the preparation of this book and we must recognise the valuable contributions they have made. We are especially grateful to Carl Haywood, Jack Naglieri, Kathy Greenberg, Donna Wilson, and Randy Hays, who have generously provided information on a range of topics. We are especially indebted to Deb Selway, Louise Young, Susan Wright, and Pam Tupe who have worked on the manuscript with us. Without their commitment to this project it would not have come to fruition.

Chapter 1

Education and learning

Almost every aspect of our daily lives involves learning and problem-solving. Whether we are at work, studying, playing sport, engaging in a hobby, watching TV or listening to music, we are continually adding to, and applying, our ever-expanding store of knowledge. The process of acquiring information and using it to our advantage (or disadvantage) begins at birth – and possibly before – and continues until death. Learning takes place in the family home, in schools, school playgrounds, with peers out-of-school, at colleges and universities, and at work and during leisure activities.

Not surprisingly, most of the research dealing with learning and problem-solving has concentrated on the period of compulsory education. Relatively few investigators have examined the process of learning in the workplace or during recreation or leisure activities. Some writers have proposed an intriguing argument that children may learn more outside school than they do in the classroom. This is perhaps not surprising since they spend three times as many hours away from school than they do at school (J.S. Brown *et al.* 1989; Hawkins *et al.* 1987; Whitaker 1995). In this chapter, we begin our exploration of education and learning in a general way to emphasise the common aspects of learning across settings and, in later chapters, turn our attention to the school and classrooms.

Before we go too far, let us define two key terms you will encounter throughout this book: learning and problem-solving. Learning refers to the acquisition of knowledge through interactions with, and observations of, the physical world and the creatures that inhabit it. For example, we learn about cause and effect, social and interpersonal skills, laws and rules, and information about science, technology, and business. Problem-solving refers to the application of knowledge to achieve a desired outcome. For example, we use our problem-solving skills to get an extra serving of ice-cream after the Sunday meal; fix a broken toy; make friends; get through our exams at school; and generate an income to satisfy our needs. So, in general terms, learning refers to obtaining knowledge, and problem-solving refers to using it.

We must also consider how effectively and efficiently learning occurs.

Four general agents interact to produce successful (or unsuccessful) learning outcomes. These agents are the learner, the teacher, the physical setting, and the curriculum (i.e. the information to be learned) and together they comprise the teaching-learning environment.

THE TEACHING-LEARNING ENVIRONMENT

Every setting in which learning takes place involves a learner, a teacher, a setting, and information to be learned. For a very young child, a parent sibling, or grandparent may act as the teacher, the home is the setting, and knowledge about the world is the curriculum. In the classroom, there is a student, a teacher, the classroom environment, and the various curricula to be mastered. At work, there is an employee (the learner), an expert or supervisor (the instructor), the workplace, and the specialist knowledge required for the job. In some situations, the teacher may not be a person. For example, if you are studying at home using a textbook, there will be no teacher present, but the textbook represents the implicit teacher to facilitate learning.

The influence of each of the four agents on a student's learning varies constantly. At one time all the agents may be in equilibrium, contributing to effective learning. At other times there may be an imbalance, or a deficit that reduces the effectiveness of the teaching-learning process. For example, the student may feel unwell, the teacher may assume prerequisite knowledge which the learner does not possess, there may be loud disruptive noise in the learning environment, or the curriculum may not be structured in a form that develops knowledge in a systematic way.

A list of just some of the factors that affect learning is given in Table 1.1. Can you add to the list?

Learning, therefore, occurs in an ecosystem in which there is a series of inputs, a series of teaching and learning processes, and a series of outputs. The concept of ecology is a very useful one as it focuses on the interaction of all influences, rather than isolating one agent as a potential problem source. The idea of a learning ecosystem was introduced by Doyle and Ponder (1975) and, although it has not been widely used, it fits nicely with the notion of four interdependent agents. In the following section, we discuss each of the four agents and the ways in which they contribute to learning.

Gordon et al. (1996) extended the concept of ecology to include both a personal ecology and a classroom ecology. At a personal level they listed personality; family variables; historical variables (e.g. home, friends, school); beliefs about oneself (e.g. self-concept); beliefs about others; and needs satisfaction. At the classroom ecology level, they included potential for needs satisfaction; classroom climate; group interaction patterns; level and type of class organisation; mechanisms for conflict resolution; teaching style (e.g. instructional methods, teacher's personality); physical environment; relevance of content; and the wider school ecology. While Gordon et al. focused

Table 1.1 The agents and their characteristics that lead to successful, or unsuccessful, learning outcomes

The learner

Genetic endowment	Perception and reaction to the teacher
Prior learning experiences	Accessible learning strategies
Personality	Adaptability to the learning setting
Motivation to learn	Creativity
Previously acquired knowledge	Interest in content and learning
(e.g. content, strategies)	

The teacher

Teaching experience	Confidence
Familiarity with the content	Emotional state
Ability to communicate/rapport	Physical well-being
Interest in meeting student needs	Pressures from the school administration

The setting

Light conditions	Available equipment
Weather	Teaching resources
Noise (e.g. interruptions, disruptions)	Physical size and structure
Number of learners present	Number of teachers present
Time of day	Layout

The curriculum

Simplicity/complexity of content	Structure of the knowledge base
Dependence on previously acquired knowledge	Outcome requirements (e.g. repetition and understanding)
Number of units to be completed	Assessment requirements
Strategies needed/provided	

on behavioural aspects of the classroom, they clearly acknowledged the importance of the interaction of a wide range of variables in determining both the cause of behaviour problems and corrective procedures.

The learner

Each learner (or student) in any teaching-learning setting is unique in that each has a singular learning history comprised of knowledge, a mental disposition toward learning (called affect), and a set of problem-solving strategies (Figure 1.1).

There are two forms of knowledge. The first refers to specific detail (called declarative knowledge) such as science or history facts. The second relates to information about how to perform a task (called procedural knowledge). Procedural (or process) knowledge may include, for example, how to read or decode a word, how to recall a telephone number, or how to get from home to the nearest video shop. The accumulated total of all these pieces of knowledge form the knowledge base on which the learner operates. For some learners, this knowledge base may be largely composed of facts, while for

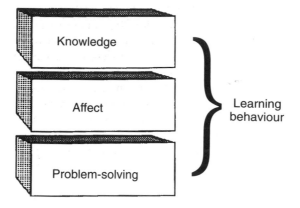

Figure 1.1 Three factors involved in student learning

others, it may contain a balance of facts and procedures.

Affect is important in any learning context because the disposition one brings to the teaching-learning process will determine the learner's level of involvement. Affect includes motivation which is linked to past experiences, and to the willingness of the student to attempt similar tasks or new activities. When students have experienced success, there is an increased likelihood that they will be willing to engage in similar or new learning activities. When the student has experienced repeated failure, there may be little motivation to attempt either previously unsuccessful tasks or new ones. This is common among students with learning or behavioural difficulties and can lead to the student becoming trapped in a failure cycle (i.e. there is a pattern of academic failure, followed by further misbehaviour, followed by failure to learn, followed by misbehaviour). The cycle can be broken only by altering both the students' motivation to learn and their level of success.

Problem-solving strategies refer to the learner's ability to adapt to new and novel learning experiences. These strategies include setting priorities, making decisions, and planning with a particular outcome in mind. These organisational skills, therefore, are vital to effective and efficient learning. When students are able to plan and make decisions, their ability to work independently is increased and their reliance on teacher direction is reduced.

The teacher

The person responsible for the implementation of a curriculum is the teacher or instructor. The teacher decides how learning will occur. Even in those situations in which the teacher passes control of some or all aspects of learning to the student, the underlying operational control remains with the teacher.

Hence, teachers can substantially determine the quantity and quality of students' learning. When a teacher is confident, supportive, and enthusiastic, the learning experience and the outcomes can be positive. Students can be motivated and reinforced for their learning, and the curriculum can meet their learning needs. When the teacher fails to motivate the students or provide learning experiences that are aimed at satisfying their learning needs, comparatively little productive learning may occur. In a sense, teachers have a pivotal influence on learning as they manage themselves and the other three agents involved in the learning environment.

In some situations the teaching role can be taken by peers. In a school classroom, for example, a student may be asked to demonstrate skills or procedures. When this occurs, students typically describe the learning process in their own words (we call this student language). Not only does this allow students to reflect their understanding of the content and process but also it requires them to express their knowledge in the student's rather than teacher's frame of reference. Student language can be seen in many informal learning situations: children teach games to each other and pass on their culture; a supervisor in a manufacturing setting can explain a technical procedure to a co-worker over lunch without reference to a complicated technical manual; a television documentary on the Kruger National Park in Africa teaches us about animals, their habitat, and survival of the fittest.

The setting

The physical environment also has a major impact on the way in which we learn. In any environment, appropriate levels of noise, light, temperature, and physical facilities are necessary to maximise concentration and minimise disruption. Suitable resources, teaching materials, time, and space are also needed. While teachers and learners can adapt or habituate to adverse conditions, some naturally occurring and human made phenomena may have a serious impact upon their capacity to do so. For example, extremes of heat or cold can reduce the student's ability and willingness to learn because their attention is focused on maintaining homeostasis rather than the task. Less extreme conditions can also have an effect on both teachers and students. For example, Conway et al. (1991) found that misbehaviour levels by secondary students were significantly higher on wet, windy days than on dry, windless days.

How the setting is arranged or used can affect the students' view of the importance of learning. The differences between infants, primary, and secondary classrooms illustrate this point. Infants and primary classrooms are often 'alive' with activity and colour. Children discover that their classroom is not only a place where they gain knowledge but also a gallery for their art and other learning achievements. In contrast, many secondary school classrooms are sterile and colourless, appearing to function only as a space in which students congregate. While there are reasons for dull classrooms (e.g. the lack of home rooms for teachers or students), there appears to be little enthusiasm for enhancing the physical environment of many secondary schools and this may adversely affect both high and low achievers.

Social factors also play an important role in learning such as the cultural and socio-economic circumstances in which the learner lives. For example, a number of investigators have demonstrated that students from different cultural groups have different approaches to learning in the classroom (see McInerney and McInerney 1994). Where the language of instruction differs from the students' home language, difficulties arise not only in the actual process of instruction, but also in communicating with family and friends, and gaining support for education within the home. While debate continues between those who advocate that students must learn within the language of the dominant culture, others argue that students should be allowed to learn in a bilingual environment, using all the social, cognitive and language skills available to them. Certainly, many countries have wrestled with the questions of whether assimilation, cultural integration, cultural pluralism or some other approach is the most effective in terms of meeting the needs of the majority population and cultural minorities.

The effect of culture is important as each group and sub-group within a society places different emphases on learning and thinking. Partington (1995) warned of the dangers of assuming that all students in a cultural group will have common learning or cognitive styles. Studies with ethnic minority students in a number of countries have shown that erroneous measures of performance can be used to 'demonstrate' cultural deficits that have been the basis of arguments of cultural superiority and inferiority. A number of investigators have attempted to show cultural difference rather than the supremacy of one culture over another. For example, studies of Australian Aboriginal and non-Aboriginal rural students have consistently shown the visual-spatial preference of Aboriginal people (Kearins 1986; Klich and Davidson 1984). This disposition may have come from a cultural history based on the ability of Aboriginal communities to live in remote areas where knowledge of the environment and geographic locations is essential for survival.

The curriculum

Finally, what we teach determines learning outcomes. The term curriculum can have a number of meanings. It can encompass all learning regardless of the age or ability level of the students. An example of this broad definition is provided by the National Board of Employment, Education and Training (NBEET) in Australia, which defines curriculum as an umbrella concept – comprehensive in scope and complex in practice. In broad terms it has to do with the teaching and learning of knowledge, skills and attitudes, and embraces issues such as subject matter, pedagogy, assessments/evaluation, and related resources involved in the organisation, delivery and articulation of educational programs.

(NBEET 1992: 1)

An alternative general definition was given by York *et al.* (1992: 3), who define curriculum as simply 'everything children learn in school'. Here, the focus is on acquisition of knowledge by the student, rather than the broader NBEET focus on teaching and learning and the instructional cycle. York *et al.* acknowledge, however, that learning can occur in three overlapping areas: learning to be part of the community; learning skills that can be used across learning situations; and learning skills that are content specific.

The curriculum in the context of school education can also operate at multiple levels. Conway (1996), for example, suggested that the term can describe a national curriculum, a regional systemic curriculum (e.g. state curriculum for primary schools), a specific regional subject curriculum (e.g. mathematics), a school district curriculum, or a school-level curriculum which may be developed by teachers to meet the specific needs of the students in that school.

In countries such as the United Kingdom, the curriculum is determined at a national level and incorporates a set of standards and national assessment. Such an approach is not always popular because it is 'fixed, heavily prescriptive and rests on a strongly normative model of progress in learning' (Gold *et al.* 1993: 56). Furthermore, Whitaker (1995) commented:

> The National Curriculum reforms build on an assumption that if only we get the definition of content right then standards of learning will rise. It is important to challenge this assumption and to claim that the practical means by which the learning process is transacted between teachers and learners is also of vital importance. In recent years attention to pedagogy [the science of teaching] and methodology has been sacrificed in the struggle to write programmes and install new content.
>
> (Whitaker 1995: x)

In several countries, there has been widespread disaffection with national curricula because schools have had difficulties in implementing them for students with special needs. A mismatch between the content and students' readiness to learn may occur because curriculum content is too difficult (or too easy) for the students, irrelevant to their needs, poorly presented through inappropriate textbooks, manuals, or activities, or not reinforced by the teacher. In many cases, curriculum content is fixed, and there may be few chances for the teacher to select topics or activities that are motivating for both high and low achieving students. In many secondary schools, for example, teachers must cover a prescribed curriculum regardless of the interests or specific characteristics of the learner group (e.g. predominant cultural or socio-economic background).

An alternative approach is to have a national curriculum which has a set of agreed key learning areas and national profiles of student progress for each area, while leaving the decisions about content to lower levels in the educational process such as state/territory departments of education, school districts, and individual schools. This approach has been proposed in Australia, with limited success, partly because compulsory school education remains a state/territory responsibility with each jurisdiction having somewhat different philosophical views and educational models.

The resolution of curriculum formulation, and the level at which it occurs, remain an issue for each education system. As important as it is, however, the curriculum is only one factor that contributes to successful learning and problem-solving outcomes. Teaching and learning involves bringing the four agents into balance through a systematic cycle of instruction. Within these constraints, the actual teaching and learning of the classroom can be determined to meet the needs of individual students.

THE INSTRUCTIONAL CYCLE

To be effective, teaching and learning must be systematic. In other words, what is to be learned, how it will be taught, and how learning will be measured, must be clearly defined and understood. This approach can be described as an *Assessment, Preparation, Instruction, Evaluation* model and the four components should be evident in any teaching context. Whether the teacher elects to provide strong direction and control learning, or to use a student-oriented method, there is still a need for thorough organisation at each stage of the cycle.

Assessment

A wide variety of assessment techniques are available to establish the student's existing knowledge in a predetermined domain, although the context in which learning takes place will dictate, to some extent, the assessment methods that a teacher may adopt. Two assessment forms are common. The first includes norm-referenced tests that have been administered to a large group of children (the norming population) so that typical performance on the test can be established for that population. Norm-referenced tests have been popular in schools, especially in reading, mathematics, and a number of other curriculum areas for many years. The second form includes criterion-referenced tests that are often teacher-made. Criterion-referenced testing, also commonly known as curriculum-based assessment, has an advantage in that each sub-section of the curriculum can be identified and an individual's performance can be assessed on those tasks. Theoretically, students are assessed only against their individual mastery of the content and not against each other, and certainly not against a norm established for a population.

Three advantages of criterion-referenced tests are: (a) they provide practical information that can guide instruction; (b) they can be linked directly to teaching and evaluation of performance; and (c) they can be used to demonstrate mastery of learning (Biehler and Snowman 1990). In addition, criterion-referenced assessment can permit students to assess and evaluate themselves by working through the items in an assessment databank.

There are, however, some disadvantages to this form or assessment. Criterion-referenced testing can, for example, lead to the division of content into small, finite units that are assessed in isolation from others. This may mean that the student never perceives the broader picture of knowledge within a specific section of the curriculum, or across the curriculum. As Beane (1995) argued, we have already compartmentalised education far too much in terms of teaching knowledge in discrete units (such as in science, mathematics, or history). Criterion-referenced and curriculum-based assessment methods exacerbate these distinctions and prevent assessment of knowledge applications across tasks.

This situation can be avoided, in part, through the use of teaching units that focus on a theme across a number of content areas. For example, a theme on 'The Greenhouse Effect' can draw from English, mathematics, science and technology, human society and its environments, the arts, and physical and health sciences. This approach can encourage students to see relationships across content domains and to apply their knowledge and process skills broadly.

Preparation

The preparation phase includes the selection of content, teaching methods, and resources. In determining the content to be taught, it is often important to have a clear, unambiguous statement of the desired learning outcome. In some situations, a very specific description of outcomes may be written. This may divide what is to be taught into very clearly defined segments of knowledge, rather than providing a broad overview of the interrelated aspects of learning. One difficulty with this approach is that outcomes are often listed in ways that focus only on knowledge, leaving process – procedural knowledge – and attitude to learning unaddressed. Some educators believe that explicit instructional statements about objective outcomes are at odds with an emphasis on the development of the learner's thinking skills. Rather than having a specific statement of outcomes such as, 'Name three types of energy', the outcomes may be expressed as, 'Understand the differences between types of energy'. These two statements emphasise factual knowledge alone, and facts and process respectively.

A second aspect of the preparation phase is the selection of teaching methods and materials. Two options are available.

1   The teacher may select methods which are intended to be teacher-controlled such as a remediation programme taught to a student with a severe learning difficulty on a one-to-one basis. Such an approach may also be appropriate, for example, when teaching first aid or a procedure which is highly prescriptive and which must be followed explicitly.

2   A teaching approach may aim to link declarative (content) and procedural (process) knowledge and allow students to be in control of the learning process. Discovery learning exemplifies this method where it is important to describe the learning skills that students are to acquire in addition to content knowledge. For example, learning a complex word processing package on a computer involves learning about the terms or icons used, plus the sequence of steps needed to operate the package efficiently.

Instruction

The instruction phase extends from the decisions made during the preparation phase. Teaching may follow a prescriptive sequence which involves teaching, testing, teaching, and testing. In this approach, the instructor models the desired behaviour, the student practises the skill and then completes a short test on the content (this short test is sometimes called a probe). This approach is often known as 'teaching to the test'. There is an excellent chance that you have been involved in such a learning process. For example, if you took a written test for your driver's licence, you will have studied the rule book and then taken a test that dealt only with your knowledge of road rules as described in the book. If you failed that test on your first attempt, you would have simply repeated the process until you passed.

Proponents of this prescriptive approach argue that the aim is to gain mastery of knowledge or skills and each test (or probe) is a measure of how well that knowledge or skill has been learned during that instructional session. Generally, probes used in this way do not require the application of knowledge or skills, and what is learned may not be retained over a long period. See if you can still recall some of the information you would have learned when you wrote your driver's licence test. How far away from an intersection are you permitted to park your car? If you are travelling at 80 kph (50 mph) what distance is required to stop your car on a dry, bitumen road? Tough?

When there is only one teacher and one student, it is comparatively easy to write an instructional objective and work progressively toward its achievement. When there are many students involved – as in a regular school classroom or university lecture group – achieving an instructional objective is difficult unless all students are working toward the same goals. In some subjects, such as mathematics, the content can be easily structured because they are highly sequential in nature. Other subject areas (e.g. in the social sciences) may seek a number of largely unrelated outcomes (such as the development of values, attitudes, and understanding) that do not lend themselves to goals that are objectively defined. In these cases, it may be appropriate to consider a two-pronged instructional approach that has both academic content outcomes (e.g. learning about the causes of the Vietnam War), and outcomes that relate to how one learns (e.g. learning about note-taking).

Evaluation

Evaluation may occur at three levels in an instructional cycle. First, it may be included during instruction to 'inform' later programming decisions (this is called formative assessment). It is seen most clearly in mastery teaching approaches where there is a measure of performance at the end of each teaching session. Evaluation may also occur at the completion of the unit or topic to determine the knowledge that the learner has acquired (this is called summative assessment). This is the most common form of assessment and is used at the end of units (e.g. semester or term exams), subjects (e.g. end of year examinations), or the end of a programme of study (e.g. an oral defence of a thesis or dissertation at university level). The third approach (called meta-evaluation) refers to the evaluation of a whole unit or curriculum, and is designed to measure the effectiveness of the programme and its teaching, together with an assessment of teacher and student performance. While there is usually no resistance to evaluating student performance, there is often a reluctance to ascertain whether the unit, syllabus, or curriculum met student needs and whether the teacher had achieved the curriculum or unit goals.

Teachers in a wide range of instructional settings use mastery learning methods, particularly when teaching has been expressed as a series of instructional objectives. In this case, evaluation can be clearly linked to teaching as the student must master the content at a specific level before moving on to the next curriculum task. Other common evaluation methods include the use of checklists, direct teacher observation of the learner's on-the-job performance, and the use of performance measures that draw from a broad range of student activities such as essays, problem-solving exercises, individual worksheets, and short curriculum-based tests.

Some assessment methods are called authentic assessment (McInerney and McInerney 1994). The term 'authentic' refers to a belief that the best way to judge a learner's progress is to collect ongoing information drawn from a range of sources. These might include diaries, portfolios, work samples, and observation of an individual's performance while alone or in small groups.

These assessment methods judge what the learner is actually doing rather than relying on a single indication of performance, such as an examination result. All too frequently, however, the focus of assessment is on the content (or declarative knowledge) rather than the process (or procedural knowledge). When knowledge is assessed on content alone, there is no indication of whether the learner can apply that knowledge to real-life situations and problems (Waugh 1995).

CLASS AND STUDENT NEEDS

While many learning events occur when a person is alone or in a small group setting, education in most formal settings is more likely to occur in a class group. In schools and tertiary education institutions around the world, the most typical instructional setting is the classroom. It is often only when practical skills need to be developed that individual or small group instruction occurs. Large group instruction creates a number of problems for the teacher and the students. What happens in secondary schools may make this clear.

Secondary teachers interact with a large number of students during any school day, across a wide range of grades and, in some faculties, a range of subject areas. There is an implicit expectation that students will complete units of work (syllabus topics) in preparation for external examinations. Secondary teachers argue that with the pressure on students to complete work, there is no time to allow them to interact in groups, to discover and think about learning processes, or to dwell on topics that are of interest. In addition, in some educational systems, students are promoted on age rather than ability. Hence, failure on one topic does not preclude the student from moving on to the next without the prerequisite skills. As a result, classes will contain students who may not have the skills to complete topics successfully, let alone attempt new ones.

For this reason, many secondary teachers favour the practice of streaming students (Conway 1996), placing the brightest children in the top class and then streaming (or tracking) students who are the least academically capable, into what soon becomes known as the bottom class, stream, or track. The lower groups commonly include students from the lowest socio-economic areas and cultural minorities. While this may appear a suitable solution from the teacher's perspective, a number of researchers have shown that streaming has little educational benefit (Gamoran and Berends 1988; Good and Brophy 1987). While teachers prefer to work with high ability students, and have difficulty catering for those of less ability, the impact of inadequate programming on students in lower streams is often overlooked. Morale may suffer and the students' desire to learn may be reduced by mundane, uninteresting activities that are only appropriate for their more capable peers. In these situations there can often be major discrepancies between the learner's level of competence and the level at which instruction is presented (see Box 1.1).

One way of ensuring that the 'giving' aspects of teaching and the 'receiving' aspects of learning remain congruent is by moving away from the restrictive notions of pedagogy (teaching children) and embracing the principles of andragogy (the art and science of helping people to learn). This transition requires an approach to instruction in which the teacher encourages and supports learning. It implies that students come to the learning setting with many skills acquired through earlier experiences. In other words, they are not empty vessels to be filled with knowledge by teachers. What schools must do, Whitaker (1995) claimed, is to light the fire of learning and use school experiences to increase students' independence in learning and problem-solving activities.

Students can be encouraged to participate in this process by enabling them to become aware of the ways in which they think, learn, and problem-solve. Several technologies have been suggested, among them, learning diaries, thinking aloud procedures, and self-disclosure (McInerney and McInerney 1994). Learning diaries require students to record their reflections on, and reactions to, learning activities. Revisiting these diaries after a unit of work is completed can highlight changes in the student's thinking, attributions about the successes or failures met, and changes in the interactions with others including the teacher. The use of the thinking aloud technique also attempts to involve students in the teaching-learning process through evaluations of what is taking place during learning, and can provide a window into the student's thinking processes. Self-disclosure occurs after the event. Through interviews, questionnaires, and discussions with the student, the teacher can assess the student's understanding of what has been learned and how it has been learned.

EDUCATIONAL REFORM IN SCHOOLS

Since the mid-1980s, there has been a growing awareness of the need to move away from the traditional focus on teaching content and student re-presentation of that content in examinations (Paris 1995). In support of this view, Gardner (1990) stated:

> Students dutifully learn the symbolic, notational and formal conceptual accounts that are presented in a scholastic setting; when the identical eliciting circumstances appear, they can spew back the correct answers. . . . By and large, knowledge acquired in school helps one to progress in school, but its relation to life outside school is not well understood by the student, and perhaps not even by the teacher. The credentials provided by the school may bear little relevance to the demands made by the outside community.
>
> (Gardner 1990: 93)

Box 1.1

Dealing with students of differing abilities

This hypothetical example relates to a lowest streamed Year 9 class, with the following characteristics:

- The textbook is written at a readability level of Year 12.
- The teacher is using a Year 7 level oral instructional language level (the lowest level taught by the teacher).
- Students' performances vary, but the average is about Year 5 – just above the level required for survival level comprehension.

The result is a teaching programme with:

- A seven-year gap between student written-word comprehension level, and the teaching resource.
- A two-year gap between the teacher's oral instructional level and the students' general oral comprehension level.

Where the teaching in this classroom is of content knowledge alone, with no coverage of issues that deal with how to learn or how to solve practical problems, there can be no expectation of learning.

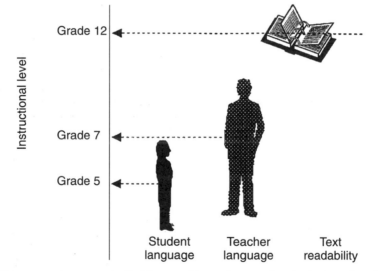

	Student language	Teacher language	Text readability

This scenario suggests that few positive outcomes for students or teachers in low-ability classrooms in the middle high school can be expected. In a study of Grade 8 and 9 English classes, Gamoran (1993) found that where quality programmes occurred in these classes, they were characterised by:

- High expectations that students would cover the normal academic curriculum.
- A focus on the use of oral discussion in class.
- A practice of not assigning weak or inexperienced teachers to the classes

All three characteristics represent good teaching practice and may be effective because of the willingness of teachers to persist with students.

These comments help to remind us that schools – and many other learning situations – are a reflection of the broader society in which we live, and survival in that society depends upon our ability to apply and adapt what we have learned to new situations. To do this we must perceive links in our knowledge storehouses and solve problems without relying on others to provide the information or help.

Whitaker (1995) viewed the changes urged by Gardner as requiring a paradigm shift in learning that would require acceptance of the principles of andragogy and result in a wide variety of new outcomes. Some of these are listed in Table 1.2.

The emphasis, therefore, is on broadening the concept of education from a lock-step approach that

1 is based on a predetermined set of topics
2 is taught at specific grade levels
3 emphasises content assessment measure to one in which learning
   • is based on student needs
   • extends students' abilities
   • is facilitated by a variety of techniques
   • stimulates students' interest
   • encourages participation in the teaching-learning process.

Table 1.2 The paradigm shift in learning

Old paradigm assumptions	New paradigm assumptions
Emphasis is on content, and acquiring a body of right knowledge, once and for all.	Emphasis is on learning how to learn.
Learning as a product, a destination.	Learning as a process, a journey.
Learning processes have a relatively rigid structure, and there is a prescribed curriculum.	Learning processes have flexible structures, varied starting-points, mixed learning experiences.
Learning is age related.	Learning is not age specific and there is an integration of age-groupings.
There is a priority on performance.	A priority is given to self-concept as a key determinant of successful learning.
Emphasis is on the external world. Inner experiences considered inappropriate in the school setting.	Use of students' inner experiences provide contexts for learning.
Education is seen as an age-related social necessity.	Education is a lifelong process and only partially related to schools.
The teacher is the instructor and imparter of knowledge.	The teacher is a learner too, one who learns from the students.

The change in approach can be exemplified by an analysis of some specific curricula, such as science. The movement away from knowledge supplied by teachers toward a talking, reflecting and explaining approach was described by Chi *et al.* (1994) as a 'talking' science rather than a 'hearing' science. Talking science involves understanding the organisation of science, through participation in science discussions and, as a result, increasing awareness of the way in which learning occurs, and how science knowledge and skills can be applied. In this way science becomes much broader than a series of facts learned for the purpose of examination. In a similar vein, Magnusson and Palincsar (1995) argued that science education must have, as its primary objective, student understanding of scientific problem-solving developed through ownership of learning goals. They suggested that this might occur through guided inquiry which is analogous to the stages of map-making (i.e. students need to be aware of the terrain or the relationships between the information available on the topic, and then use this information to build up the knowledge of the topic to form a 'map' of the topic).

The characteristic changes from a teaching focus to a learning focus can also be seen in Table 1.3, which is adapted from Montgomery (1994). The consequences of this shift can be felt across all aspects of teaching, not only in the goals of instruction, but also in terms of the input of information, the processes adopted, and the outcomes of learning.

In this chapter we have drawn attention to some general principles and characteristics of education and human learning. We focused much of our attention on the four agents that operate within any teaching-learning situation: the learner, the teacher, the setting, and the curriculum. We also considered the instructional cycle – assessment, preparation, instruction, and evaluation – and the need for a change in the belief structures of those involved in the teaching-learning process. We urge, as others have, that education:

Table 1.3 Consequences of a focus shift in education

	Teaching-orientation	Learning-orientation
Focus	Teachers	Learners
Learner's involvement	Mostly passive	Mostly active
Learning	Teacher responsible	Jointly responsible
	Context-independent	Context-related
Desired learning outcome	Retention	Reflection and application
Teacher's attitude	Experts	Coaches or facilitators
Teacher's roles	Good presenters	Good facilitators
Educational outcomes	Production or solution	Process learning
	'Tool kit'	Increased skill in applying 'tools'

- becomes a joint activity in which teachers and learners work inter-dependently to achieve their personal and collective goals
- is an activity in which knowledge and the processes of learning are emphasised equally.

The remainder of this book deals with the development of teaching-learning methods that adhere to the fundamental premises we have suggested immediately above. In Chapter 2, we trace the theoretical and practical bases in the behavioural approaches to assessment and teaching, and then chart the development of cognitive education that has grown in popularity since the mid-1970s.

STUDY TASKS

1.1 In note form, list the main points covered in this chapter. Pay particular attention to the four agents and the four stages in the instructional cycle.

1.2 Refer to Table 1.1. Select two points under each heading (e.g. creativity, genetic endowment, and so on, under 'The Learner'). List ways in which learning can be advantaged or disadvantaged by each.

1.3 Collect information about the way in which the curriculum is designed in your region or locality. What aspects of the curriculum will need to be carefully managed to ensure that students learn effectively?

1.4 Consider your own learning situation. List the four agents and the four stages of the instructional cycle and describe the way in which these eight components are operating to maximise or minimise your learning and problem-solving.

ADDITIONAL READING

Elliott-Kemp, J.E. and Elliott-Kemp, N. (1992) *Managing Change and Development in Schools: A Practical Handbook*, Harlow: Longman School Management Resources.

Page, R.M. and Page, T.S. (1993) *Fostering Emotional Well-being in the Classroom*, Boston, MA: Jones & Bartlett.

Rogers, C.R. and Freiberg, H.J. (1994) *Freedom to Learn*, 3rd edn, New York: Merrill.

Steiner, D.M. (1994) *Rethinking Democratic Education: The Politics of Reform*, Baltimore, MD: Johns Hopkins University Press.

Chapter 2

Developing models of cognition

In the introduction to a book of readings on curriculum and learning, V. Lee (1990: 1) reflected on the constantly changing approach to teaching in schools: 'Ideas that seem elegant to one generation seem less compelling to the next'.

To understand the reasons for the current orientation to the study of thinking and learning, it is important to have an appreciation of the two major traditions that have influenced instructional theory and practice. The first, behaviourism, began in the early years of the twentieth century in Russia and the United States and dominated American psychology until the middle of the 1960s. While much behavioural research focused on animal learning, behaviourism spread its influence into education and was advocated as a means of understanding the nature of human learning. Behaviourism also provided teaching techniques that led to marked changes in students' academic performance.

The study of human learning was also influenced by a second tradition that coexisted with behaviourism, namely, human memory. Memory research began in the late 1800s and has led to an understanding of the complex mental processes that constitute the fabric of human cognition.

In the first section of this chapter, we introduce the concepts associated with behaviourism and the adaptations that occurred when that view of human behaviour was thought to be an oversimplification. In the second half of the chapter, we explore memory, memory research, and the origin of the field called cognitive education.

A BEHAVIOURAL FRAMEWORK FOR LEARNING

The behavioural approach to teaching has played a crucial role in the education process since the mid-1960s, most particularly in special education, but also in regular education. Although many teachers and parents have seen its application in the management of social behaviours – often called behaviour management – it has also had a major influence on the teaching of academic skills. The impact on social behaviour, including discipline, will be examined in Chapter 9. Here we focus on the general principles of the behavioural approach and its role in the teaching-learning process.

Behaviourism has at its core the belief that behaviour is influenced by the environment in which learning occurs. The role of association is important because we link certain events to what has happened in a specific situation, or in a similar situation on a previous occasion. For example, if a child gets the correct answer to a numeration exercise by using a particular strategy, it is likely that the same strategy will be used in a similar lesson with the same degree of success. In other words it is the success or failure that will govern future behaviour.

The behavioural approach to instruction has its roots in the work of Thorndike, Pavlov and Skinner, although the term 'behaviourism' was originally used by Watson (1913). Thorndike and Pavlov both studied the influences of manipulating environmental conditions on animal behaviour. Thorndike's (1913) 'law of effect' was based on teaching a hungry cat to press a bar in order to escape from a box and obtain food. While trying to escape confinement the cat originally discovered by chance that the bar would release a door in the box. Each time the cat accidentally pressed the bar, the door opened and it was fed. The law of effect then came into play when the cat made the link between bar pressing and food. Thorndike (1931) argued that the same pattern of behaviour could also explain human learning. Giving the correct response to a question would lead to reinforcement and learning would occur. Thus, early work on the 'law of effects' was translated into what we now call 'reinforcement'.

Pavlov (1927) performed his classical experiments on dogs, training them to respond to a stimulus that had no previous impact on the animal's behaviour. The natural (or unconditioned) response to showing a dog food is salivation. However, when Pavlov rang a bell just prior to putting food powder in front of the dog, the animal associated the sound of the bell with food and soon began salivating when the bell rang, even before the food was presented (see Figure 2.1). The bell became a conditioned stimulus, an object to which the dog had not previously responded because it had no meaning. Pavlov also demonstrated that continuing to ring the bell without the presentation of food gradually caused the dog to stop salivating. This was a demonstration of what is now called extinction.

Although Pavlov did not use humans in his experiments, the same principles can be applied to the way in which humans deal with some situations. If a young child has a serious illness and is required to have numerous injections given by the nurse in a hospital, the sight of the nurse may trigger a pain reaction and fear in the child, even before the actual sensation of the needle is felt.

Watson and Raynor (1920) were the first researchers to apply conditioning principles knowingly to human subjects. Watson used a loud noise made by hitting a steel bar with a hammer to teach a child to become fearful of a

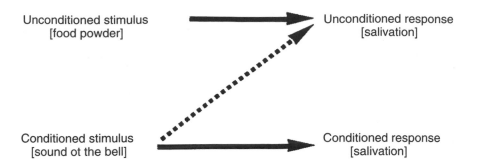

Figure 2.1 A schematic view of Pavlovian conditioning

white rat when it approached the child. The sound of the metal bar became the conditioned stimulus. Watson had to desensitise the child following this experiment as the boy became afraid of other white furry objects such as white rabbits and white beards. This experiment was also an example of how punishers (the loud noise) can be used to condition behaviour in addition to the reinforcers that had been used by Thorndike and Pavlov.

The result of these early experiments was the development of an approach to learning based on the concept of Stimulus-Response (S-R) Theory in which learning consists of acquiring new skills or responses as a result of manipulation by another person such as a teacher. The use of the word 'manipulation' here refers to structuring the learning environment, not the exploitation of the person. In S-R Theory, behaviours can be established, eliminated, increased or decreased, and also generalised by pairing reinforcement to a number of responses that might occur simultaneously or in a series.

From an educational point of view, the effects of the behavioural approach are most clearly seen in Skinner's work over several decades which began with animal studies and later involved humans. While the earlier work of Thorndike was termed instrumental conditioning, and Pavlov's classical conditioning, Skinner's methods became known as operant conditioning. Operant conditioning is based on sequences of learning in which each new learning step depends upon previously learned steps. In teaching terms, the selection of the learning step is synonymous with analysing the exact sequence of behaviour in a step-by-step fashion to reach a goal (this is called task analysis). Table 2.1 shows a sequence of arithmetic operations that conform to one section of a task analysis in mathematics. In other words, the student must learn Step 1 before Step 2, Step 2 before 3, and so on.

Terms introduced into the educational vocabulary as a result of Skinner's work include shaping, reinforcement, generalisation, and punishment. Shaping refers to the method of developing a behaviour by assisting the student

Table 2.1 An example of task analysis in mathematics

Step	Process
1	Single digit addition with addends less than 10 (e.g. $5 + 3 = 8$).
2	Single digit addition with addends less than 20 (e.g. $7 + 9 = 16$).
3	Double digit additions with no carrying from the units column, addends less than 100 (e.g. $25 + 11 + 52 = 88$).
4	Double digit additions with carrying from the units to the 10s column, addends less than 100 (e.g. $45 + 34 + 17 = 96$).
5	Double digit additions with carrying from the units to the 10s columns (e.g. $56 + 33 + 45 = 134$).
6	Multiple digit addition with carrying from the units to 10s column (e.g. $145 + 236 + 28 = 409$).
7	Multiple digit addition with carrying in several columns (e.g. $145 + 658 + 390 = 1,193$).

to work sequentially towards the desired behaviour. For example, in teaching a student to write an essay, the general steps are writing words, writing a sentence, writing a series of coherent sentences, writing paragraphs, writing a sequence of paragraphs, writing a coherent essay. Each step of the process is contingent upon the last, and each performance at each step is reinforced to ensure that it is learned. Generalisation occurs when writing at each level can be applied to tasks other than writing an essay, such as writing a diary or telling a story.

Skinner's impact on teaching was profound and often controversial (Skinner 1968; 1971). He argued that learning is the result of the reinforcement or punishment of behaviours within a context that is deliberately manipulated by the teacher. Hence, in learning mathematics the teacher defines the task to be taught and then structures the learning situation to reinforce the correct response. In some cases the teacher may also use punishers to ensure that the incorrect response is not given, or that the incorrect response does not occur again.

BEHAVIOURAL PRINCIPLES IN THE CLASSROOM

Early behavioural research had a significant effect on our understanding of how students learn and this influenced teaching practices in regular and special education settings. From those studies, three aspects of the behaviour were noted as being important. First, the behaviour itself is the major focus, as all teaching is aimed at altering the student's performance. Second, the consequences of the behaviour are important because they influence the likelihood that the behaviour will recur. Third, the antecedents are important because they are the factors that may also influence the recurrence of the behaviour. Hence, we can think of the links between antecedents→behaviour, and→consequences as follows:

$$A \rightarrow B \rightarrow C$$

Structuring antecedents and consequences can directly influence classroom behaviour.

The translation of conditioning theories into classroom practice was based on five guiding principles (Wheldall and Merrett 1984) and we comment on these in turn.

Teaching is concerned with the observable

The teacher is not concerned with the reasons for the behaviour, only its occurrence in the classroom at that time. This eliminates speculation about why the behaviour has occurred or concern about outside influences such as the child's home environment or personal problems. In this way, the teacher can consider the learning goal (i.e. the behaviour) solely as a classroom phenomenon. However, the behavioural goal must be defined as specifically as possible to ensure that there is no doubt about what is being measured and targeted for change, and this is typically achieved by defining the goal in terms of condition, behaviour, and criteria. The definition is called a behavioural objective and has three sections or characteristics:

- a statement of performance required
- the conditions under which the behaviour will occur
- the criterion – or level – at which the behaviour will occur.

(Mager 1990)

The final point is often also known as the mastery level.

Let us consider an instructional objective in mathematics using an example which involves the addition of two, single digit numbers which add to less than 10, such as 3 + 4 = ? The teacher would have already determined that this arithmetic operation was at the appropriate instructional level through an assessment that confirmed that the student had the prerequisite skills. The learning conditions then stipulate that the student will work through a set of relevant number sentences (e.g. 4 + 2 = 6; 6 + 1 = 7; and so on) and will complete as many as possible in one minute (as you will recall from Chapter 1, this work activity is called a probe). Importantly, the sheet must contain more examples than the student can complete in the time available. The criteria are the achievement of at least fifteen correct and no more than two errors in that one minute. In addition, the student must achieve the criteria on three consecutive occasions. Once this mastery level has been achieved, the child may be required to attempt the same task at a higher mastery level (e.g. getting twenty correct in one minute), or proceed to a new curriculum task. The attraction of such an approach seems clear; the performance standards are set, the criterion level is specified, and the student and teacher have an unambiguous programme. Table 2.2 provides examples of behavioural objectives for both an academic domain skill and a social domain skill.

If a behaviour is observable, it must also be measurable. Hence, the teacher can count the number of times that the behaviour occurs (e.g. how many times a child is out-of-seat), the length of time a behaviour occurs (e.g. how

Table 2.2 Behavioural objectives for an academic and a social skill

---

An academic domain behavioural objective
Given a one minute probe of single digit addition algorithms with addends of less than 10, Tom will complete at least fifteen correctly, with no more than two errors on three consecutive occasions.

The condition is:	a one minute probe of single digit addition algorithms with addend of less than 10	Tom is given pages of algorithms such as: 3 4+ — and is asked to do as many as he can in one minute.
The behaviour is: The criteria are:	Tom will complete at least fifteen correctly, with no more than two errors on three consecutive occasions	Tom must get at least fifteen algorithms correct and have no more than two incorrect in the one minute on three consecutive occasions when attempting the probe to achieve mastery.

A social behavioural objective
During the twenty minute reading time each morning, Jason will remain in his seat for at least 75 per cent of the time.

The condition is:	during the twenty minute reading time each morning	The time when the programme will take place.
The behaviour is:	Jason will remain in his seat	The behaviour Jason must display.
The criterion is:	for at least 75 per cent of the time	The per cent of observation times that Jason must be in his seat to reach criterion on one day. He must reach this level each day for one week to achieve mastery.

many times a pencil is tapped), or the number of correct or error responses (e.g. in a mathematics test). Measurements include duration, frequency, sampling behaviour across a specified time (i.e. momentary time) and the whole-of-interval sampling (whether a behaviour did or did not occur within the period of time) (Alberto and Troutman 1995). For the academic behavioural objective given in Table 2.2, the most appropriate method of recording behaviour would be a frequency count of the number of correct and error responses (i.e. arithmetic scores). For the social behaviour objective, the most appropriate method may be through momentary time sampling for which the teacher observes the child every fifteen or thirty seconds during the lesson and records whether Jason is in, or out of, his seat. The number of in-seat and out-of-seat responses are converted to a percentage of the total observations.

Almost all behaviour is learned

The behavioural model argues that academic and social behaviour is learned. While there is an acceptance that genetic factors determine certain behaviours (e.g. autistic responses), most behaviours of concern to classroom teachers are learned. Hence, students are not born unable to complete a reading task, or to remain in their seats during lessons. These behaviours have been learned through inappropriate teaching and/or reinforcement.

That behaviours can be learned also means that they can be unlearned. That is, more appropriate behaviours can replace inappropriate behaviours. While some may be firmly entrenched, the behavioural approach to instruction proposes that any behaviour can be increased, decreased, established, or maintained depending on the level of reinforcement and/or punishment provided by the teacher.

Learning involves change in behaviour

The role of a behavioural intervention is to produce change in each student's performance and to ensure that change occurs as a result of each lesson. This is often called the teach-test approach to learning. Again, let us take the behavioural objective given in Table 2.2. The aim of instruction is initially to ensure that Tom can achieve the goal and later to achieve a higher goal for that behavioural objective, or to achieve a specific goal on a more difficult task within the task analysis.

The behavioural approach emphasises the importance of measuring the level of a behaviour before a programme is started (baseline), measurement throughout the programme, and measurement at the completion of a programme. Quantifiable measures of behaviour gain or loss enable comparisons to be made between the baseline and end-of-intervention data levels. The ability to represent change graphically is one of the arguments most often cited as an advantage of the behavioural approach. In addition, daily measurements enable changes in the programme to be made on the basis of data, rather than on teacher feelings.

Figures 2.2a and 2.2b show the outcome of daily monitoring of a behavioural programme designed for young children on an academic task (recognising and sounding out vowel-consonant blends such as 'in', 'at', 'on') and a social skill (working without interrupting other children) respectively. The study involved four phases: Baseline (when the child's pre-intervention behaviour was recorded on the two skill areas); Token economy (when the child worked for counters that could be traded for preferred rewards such as a confectionery or time to work on a preferred puzzle); Token economy and praise (when the child worked for counters but was also praised generously by the teacher for good work); and Maintenance (when the child worked without the need to earn counters and with an amount of praise typical for a regular classroom). Notice the marked changes between the level of performance prior to the intervention (Baseline), during (Token economy, Token economy and praise), and at the end of the intervention (Maintenance).

Behaviour change depends mainly on consequences

If a behaviour is reinforced, then the likelihood of that behaviour recurring is increased. Conversely, if the consequences are negative, then the likelihood of a behaviour recurring is reduced.

The behavioural model suggests that unacceptable behaviour is the result of inappropriate reinforcement rather than any personal characteristic.

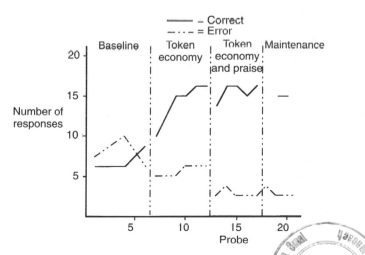

Figure 2.2a Correct and error responses on vowel-consonant blend probes

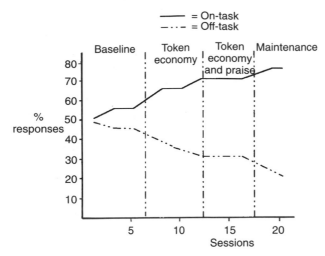

Figure 2.2b Mean percentages on-task/off-task behaviours over sessions

Academic failure could result from lack of teacher correction of errors, or from a failure to point out the errors. Poor social behaviour could result from increased attention to inappropriate behaviours – as with attention seeking behaviour – or through the teacher's inability to control a developing pattern of unacceptable behaviour.

Most behavioural programmes emphasise the importance of focusing on positive reinforcement, even using terms such as 'positive teaching' (Wheldall and Merrett 1984), particularly as the term 'behaviour management' has negative connotations for many education practitioners.

Behaviours are influenced by the contexts in which they occur

Where a behaviour occurs will influence its occurrence. Hence, it is important to consider the antecedents of the behaviour. For example, if a teacher saw John hit Mark, she would consider the behaviour to be unacceptable and may punish John. However, if the teacher had noticed the antecedents, she may have seen Mark prodding John with a pencil for five minutes before he retaliated. Changing John's behaviour would require a change in Mark's behaviour as well.

In a broader sense, the way we structure a classroom may also be an antecedent to a problem behaviour. Wheldall and Merrett (1984) reported that students seated at desks in small groups were more likely to talk than if they were seated in rows. By altering the antecedents (in this case, the layout of the classroom) it may be possible to alter behaviour without the necessity of introducing a specific behaviour programme.

BEHAVIOURISM AND THE CURRICULUM

While behaviour management programmes aimed at developing social skills have been the most common behavioural approach used in classrooms, they have also had a significant impact on content selection and teaching methods.

An example of a typical behavioural approach to instruction can be seen in a study by Stevens *et al.* (1991), who taught five students in Grades 5 and 6 to spell using a commercial computer software program. A spelling word would appear on the screen and, after a five-second delay, students would type the word on their keyboard within thirty seconds. If the word was typed correctly, one of ten confirmation statements would appear on the screen as reinforcement (e.g. 'Good on you'). If the word was typed incorrectly, a correction procedure would appear on the screen and come verbally from the computer: 'No. Check your answer and press return.' Over a series of sessions, students were taught to spell each word correctly on three consecutive occasions. Four of the five students in the study achieved the desired performance level. The students' ability to generalise their newly acquired spelling skills was measured by having them spell words given to them verbally by the teacher with reinforcement delayed until the end of the test.

Two important features that distinguish the behavioural approach from others discussed in later chapters are, first, the selection of content and teaching strategies without any direct student involvement, and second, the focus on domain-specific content (e.g. mathematics, reading, spelling) rather than on how individual students learn and problem-solve most effectively. This can be explained by a brief description of mastery learning.

The application of behavioural principles to instruction

'Mastery learning' emerged in the early 1970s largely through the work of Block (1971) and Bloom (1976). The approach was based on the premise that students could achieve mastery of curriculum knowledge if the instruction was organised, taught in a specific way, monitored consistently, and if students were given consistent feedback on their performance. More recently, Towers (1992) emphasised the need for structured, hierarchical, sequential units of material that were translated into clear instructional objectives. Students who failed to reach mastery on specific units were generally required to complete additional work before re-sitting the mastery test at the end of the unit, while those who succeeded in the mastery tests were encouraged to complete enrichment activities (e.g. the completion of more difficult examples).

Reviewers of the mastery learning approach (e.g. Block and Burns 1976; Guskey and Gates 1986; Kulik *et al.* 1990) have argued that students of high and low ability attain higher levels of performance, retain more knowledge, and show improved attitudes to instruction and content than when other approaches are used. Critics of mastery learning, however, point to the use of teacher-made tests which may be biased toward the mastery learning approach in experimental-control studies (Slavin 1990). Teachers may also teach to the mastery test which will inflate students' performance levels, and students may put little effort into the initial mastery test knowing that they will have another chance at a later time (Towers 1992). Another criticism is the failure of mastery learning approaches to give students an overview of the content of the subject making them unwilling partners in a narrow, behaviouristic, structured teaching situation (see Towers 1992).

Behavioural methods continue to influence teaching and learning practices especially in the early school years, although there have been several challenges to the principles underlying the methods. One notable criticism is the reliance on the teacher to select content, instructional strategies, and reinforcers needed to achieve the desired behavioural output. In a review of the evolution of cognition and instruction, Mayer (1992), for example, examined the three major influences on educational practice and research during the twentieth century. In his analysis of the behavioural approach, for which he used the metaphor 'learning as response acquisition', he argued:

> Within this behaviorist-inspired metaphor, the learner is a passive being whose repertoire of behaviors is determined by rewards and punishments encountered in the environment. The metaphor ... has straightforward implications for instruction, namely, creating situations that elicit responses from learners and providing appropriate reinforcement for each response. Drill and practice is the epitome of instruction within this view of learning.
>
> (Mayer 1992: 407)

Mayer argued that the behaviourist goal of instruction is to increase correct behaviours by ensuring a higher mastery level on the task on each attempt. Focusing on increasing response rates produces a teaching environment in which response is of greater concern than understanding. Regardless of the view that the behavioural approach 'has not fared well in the second half of this century' (Mayer 1992: 407), it can still be seen in operation in many classrooms and special education settings in the 1990s.

The development of the cognitive-behavioural approach

Teachers and researchers alike recognised that setting up a learning environment in which the student should work effectively and efficiently does not always result in effective and efficient learning. The student always has the 'power of veto' over learning. In other words, the student can decide not to be involved in a learning activity, or can engage in off-task or disruptive behaviour that will limit learning. Hence, there is a place for the organism (the person) in the behavioural (S → R) paradigm.

It was this recognition of personal control that led to the adaptation of the S→R view of learning to a Stimulus → Organism → Response (S → O → R) model. Hence, what the learner does within the learning environment and what (unspoken) dialogue occurs within the individual has an important effect on the teaching-learning outcomes. Researchers realised that it is the internal dialogue that assists or limits learning and this has become the focus of attention in cognitive-behavioural approaches to teaching and learning.

The concepts found in the cognitive-behavioural approaches seek to assist students to take greater control over their learning through the use of strategies that guide and monitor their thinking and actions.

Training is based on four core assertions:

1   The human organism responds primarily to cognitive representations of the environment.
2   Cognitive representations are functionally related to the nature and processes of learning.
3   Most human learning is cognitively mediated.
4   Thoughts, feelings, and behaviours are causally linked.

(Ashman and Conway 1993c)

These are important considerations because they emphasise the responsibility of the learner within the teaching process and, hence, the need for teachers to acknowledge and promote the need for student involvement in classroom decisions.

Verbal self-instruction

Cognitive-behavioural teaching is embodied in Meichenbaum's five step, verbal self-instruction training (VSIT) model (Meichenbaum 1977; Meichenbaum and Asarnow 1978; Meichenbaum and Goodman 1971) as shown in Table 2.3.

VSIT clearly draws from the behaviourism tradition through the use of modelling, the selection of content and self-instructional steps prepared by the teacher, and through an emphasis on guiding students' development from external prompts to internal self-control. The use of student language (i.e. of words and terms that a student, rather than a teacher, would use) was not present in the original VSIT model, instead, students needed to internalise the teacher-developed instructional steps. However, the clear link to current approaches which emphasise self-control can be seen in those learning steps that increase student responsibility for learning.

Cognitive-behavioural approaches have been used widely in many contexts. P.C. Kendall (1991) provided an extensive coverage of their use, not only in academic areas, but also in the management of children's behaviour

Table 2.3 Meichenbaum's verbal self-instruction training model

Step	Process
Cognitive modelling	The teacher models the self-instructions aloud while performing the task
Overt external guidance	The student performs the task while the teacher provides the self-instructions
Overt self-guidance	The student performs the task while saying aloud the self-instructions
Faded overt self-guidance	The student whispers the instruction while performing the task
Covert self-guidance	The student performs the task using internal language to work through the self-instructions alone

disorders, and for students with an intellectual disability or learning difficulty. In a review of academic applications of cognitive-behaviour modification (CBM), Wong *et al.* (1991) drew attention to the use of the procedures across a wide range of academic contexts. They emphasised the need to apply CBM to the development of social, emotional, behavioural, and academic skills of students with a learning difficulty.

One area of concern raised by Wong *et al.* (1991) was the lack of a review of learning processes at the end of the CBM sequence. The maintenance and transfer of learning strategies to novel tasks has become a major issue in the training literature since the earliest work on CBM. Wong *et al.* argued that having a self-control and self-monitoring orientation at the beginning and end of the training would assist the student to recognise the effectiveness of the strategy being taught and increase the likelihood of transferring its use to novel tasks.

The movement away from a behaviourist perspective toward a cognitive-behaviourist view acknowledges the value of the individual's involvement in the process of gaining knowledge. This emphasis on the individual's role in learning reflected an already substantial body of research that had developed about learning and the acquisition of knowledge. A major part of this research was based on an understanding of how we learn, remember, and recall information. Hence, regardless of the environmental constraints that might facilitate or hinder learning, there is a largely unseen aspect to learning that involves the storage and manipulation of knowledge. This leads us to an exploration of thinking processes.

A COGNITIVE FRAMEWORK FOR LEARNING

Cognitive psychology developed from a fusion of experimental psychology (the study of psychological phenomena using controlled, scientific methods) and psychometrics (the measurement of psychological variables including human performance). Research into thinking and knowing (i.e. cognition) rose in prominence in the 1960s when it was becoming clear that an explanation of thinking and learning using only behavioural terms was unsatisfactory. To understand cognition requires knowledge of what takes place in the brain, although obtaining this knowledge is problematic as there is no simple way to observe the activities that occur within the brain. Cognitive psychologists, therefore, turned their attention toward the careful observation and testing of human memory, learning, and problem-solving to explain the processes of thought.

The cognitive foundation of learning theory was based initially on the study of human memory. Memory is inextricably linked to learning. If there is no memory, there can be no learning and without learning, memory is an empty storehouse. How well we learn and collect information is generally an indication of how well we can retrieve knowledge from our memory. It should come as no surprise, therefore, that researchers in the late 1950s and 1960s became interested in unravelling the mystery of memory, believing it to be the key to understanding people who have different intellectual abilities; in other words, those who can learn readily, and those who cannot.

Of course, memory and memory loss have been studied for hundreds of years. In 477BC, the poet Simonides attended a banquet given by a nobleman of Thessaly called Scopas. During the meal Simonides was given a message that two young men wanted to see him outside. He left the banquet but found no one waiting for him. While he was outside, the roof of the hall collapsed, crushing Scopas and all of the guests inside beneath the ruins. The people had been so mangled that those who came to remove the bodies could not identify their relatives. Simonides, however, was able to recall where each had been sitting, thereby providing one of the earliest examples of memory skills (Yates 1969). Later, Plato suggested that memories were like the impression made by a signet ring in wax and, in the mid-1700s, suggestion was made that the consistency of the wax was a crucial element in understanding the reception of images and their retention. In the late 1800s, a popular view was to liken memory to a great library. Even Sigmund Freud (the founding father of psychoanalysis) seized upon this comparison to assist his theorising.

MEMORY

What is memory and how does it work? If you consult a dictionary, you will find that the term 'memory' refers to the ability to remember or retain what has been learned. Memory also refers to the actual knowledge held in remembrance. In other words, memory refers both to the 'place' where information is held, and also to the stored information. Researchers in the fields of psychology and education have elaborated on these definitions and have also attempted to explain how memory operates.

It is a widely held view in psychology that the memory is not a specific, identifiable place inside our skull, but a metaphor to help us describe a complex brain function. In other words, we cannot lift the top off a person's skull, peer inside, and find a spot labelled 'Memory', and we cannot remove some small amount of brain matter that will destroy all of our recollections. Exactly how memory works remains a puzzle for neuroscientists. Certainly, we can map the patterns of electrical activity in the brain – predominantly in the cerebral cortex – that are associated with perception, thought, and problem-solving behaviour, and research since the mid-1980s has shown that various parts of the brain are involved in different aspects of memory. How electrochemical activities lead to the formation of memories, however, remains in the realm of speculation.

The idea of memory being linked to a chemical code in the brain has been discussed since the discovery of DNA (deoxyribonucleic acid). The notion is that when learning occurs, certain permanent physical changes take place in the associated cells in the brain, especially the nuclei of those cells. The changes create memory traces or engrams. While a large amount of research has focused on locating areas of the brain in which certain memory processes occur, more recent work has examined the long-term responsiveness (potentiation) of cells during memory events and the chemical changes that take place around cell extremities. Anderson (1990), for example, suggested that a nerve fibre (called a dendrite) might activate others close to it when sending high frequency impulses across the synaptic gap between the surface of two cells. In other words, the first fibre acts as a 'teacher' to the other 'pupil' fibres that are in close proximity.

The magnitude of the task facing researchers studying memory is, however, immense. First, neuroscientists often work at the level of physical structures and study individual cells or cell groups to understand the electrochemical events that occur during the process of thought. In other words, they are interested in what causes the communication between one cell and another. Others, such as neuropsychologists, have tried to under-stand memory by looking at the neural responses of individuals to stimuli in order to establish links between thought processes and behaviour.

One innovative neuropsychological theory of memory was described by Pribram (1986) following work on the visual system of monkeys. He found that information processing within the visual cortex was influenced by other brain structures in which previously learned information had been stored. Hence, perception and other thought processes involve a complex pattern of brain activity rather than the stimulation of any single location. Pribram's findings hinted at a memory structure that worked in much the same way as holography. He suggested that holography might be a useful metaphor to help in the comprehension of how memories are stored with the brain, with a hologram representing a memory (see Box 2.1).

Pribram (1986) suggested that electrical currents travel throughout the brain as memory traces (engrams) and intersect at various locations to form interference patterns of fibres that link the visual cortex to the retina. Hence, the reconstruction of a memory comes from the stored spectrum of information available at the time of learning. He stated that the phenomenon of holography accounted for clinical observations of limited damage to memory due to local brain lesions as information related to memory is distributed widely throughout the brain. While the holography metaphor has been used to explain other psychological phenomena (see Zinkin 1987), Pribram's speculations have not been universally accepted (see Wolfgram and Goldstein 1987).

Cognitive psychologists and neuropsychologists have faced an equally complex puzzle. To gain just a glimpse of the difficulty facing information-processing researchers, think for a moment about the words on this page. It is unlikely when you read along that you fixate on each word, determine the meaning of that word, and then pass on to the next. The sight of the words – and even phrases – stimulate electrical discharges in the brain that refresh recollections (about the meaning of words and phrases), and these in turn generate images or thoughts that allow for comprehension. For example, think about the word 'dog'. Does any image of a dog come to mind? Perhaps you immediately 'saw' your own dog in your 'mind's eye'. Perhaps you thought about a French Poodle, German Shepherd, or even an English Sheep Dog. You recall these dog-images because of the electrochemical activity that took place in your brain as you were reading the text. While these memories and images seem to be real, they are the product of the electrical and chemical activities. Precisely how these are transformed into thought and actions is beyond our knowledge. Consequently, cognitive psychologists have constructed models of memory and thinking using hypothetical constructs that explain phenomena inferred from behaviour.

Memory models

Research on human memory has been dominated by experimental, laboratory-based work for most of the 1900s. The tradition began with Ebbinghaus in 1879, when he used himself as a subject in the first documented experimental investigation of learning and memory (see Ebbinghaus 1913; Gregg 1986; Hoffman *et al*. 1987). The intensity of memory research reached a high plateau in the 1960s when teams of psychologists worked to develop models of human memory based upon experimentation that took into account the belief that memory is multidimensional.

Box 2.1

A schematic diagram of the way in which a transmission hologram is made

A hologram is created when laser light is directed at an object – a book, for example – and a holographic (photographic) plate. The beam passes through a beam splitter and reaches the book through a series of lenses and mirrors to illuminate the book from every angle.

Light that hits the book is scattered, and the rays intersect with the reference beam that is directed at the plate so that each light source interferes with the others producing a complex display called an interference pattern. This is recorded on photographic film as a blur, and is developed, washed, and fixed.

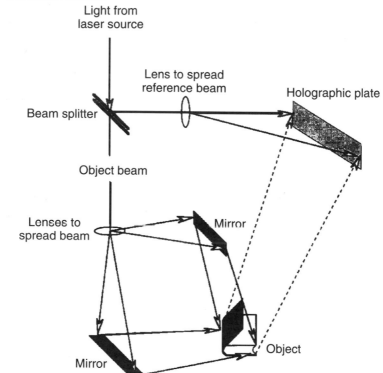

If the photograph is then lit by a laser beam, it reconstructs the image by applying the same transformation that produced the blur, but it creates a three-dimensional image of the book quite separate from the film. The amazing part of a holograph is that if only a part of the photograph is lit, you see all of the book, not just part of it. The image becomes less clear but the book is always visible.

Pribram (1986) argued that the image created by the interference pattern of light (the hologram) might explain the way in which memory traces intersect to create a memory which is stored throughout the brain.

The first unified model was developed by Atkinson and Shiffrin (1968) at Stanford University in California. They suggested a structural model of memory based upon the amount of time a unit of information is active within any memory component (Figure 2.3). In the model, information comes to the person via the various sense organs (e.g. eyes, ears, taste buds, and proprioceptors in the internal organs that are sensitive to movement) and is filtered at the sensory register (a metaphor for the first site in the brain on which information from outside the brain is projected). Atkinson and Shiffrin described the filter as something like a photographic trace that may last for several hundred milliseconds. It allows relevant information to pass through, and irrelevant information to be excluded. You might appreciate how effective the sensory register is if you stop reading for a short time at the end of this paragraph and allow yourself to become aware of events that are occurring around you. You might, for example, hear the wind rustling through the trees outside your room, or the electrical hum of a fluorescent tube. You might suddenly realise that you are hungry, or feel the pressure of the seat against your buttocks. All these stimuli coexisted with your reading, although they were (presumably) filtered out as a result of your fascination with the text! Information that is allowed through the sensory register passes into a component called the short-term store and is held there, active, for about five to thirty seconds. If it has importance, the information then passes into the long-term store where it may be retrieved at a later time, perhaps years later. As can be seen in Figure 2.3, at each point in the model, information can be lost as memories fade.

The evidence that supported the earliest models of memory was based upon studies within the verbal learning tradition. The tasks used in these studies included arrays of letters presented for only milliseconds, the recollection of nonsense syllables (e.g. WIK, WUS, QIV), the recall of pairs of words learned together (apple, eat; cart, pull), and stimuli that could be easily coded verbally (e.g. photographs).

The structural model (Figure 2.3) – or adaptations of it – has persisted over the years and various components have been added, such as very short-term memory, intermediate-term memory, primary and secondary memories. However, it was not long after Atkinson and Shiffrin described their model in the literature that an alternative approach to memory was proposed. Craik and Lockhart (1972) argued that the characteristics of memory are linked to the relative importance of the information being processed. In other words, the more important the information is to a person, the more firmly it is stored away for later use. Consider the following example. Imagine an unlikely situation in which you are standing at a bus stop and a stranger next to you tells you the telephone number of a person who lives in the next town. It is 7 9 4 1 6 8 2 5. It is unlikely that you would pay much attention because the information has little significance for you. The chances are high right now, that you cannot recall the number you just read for exactly the same reason.

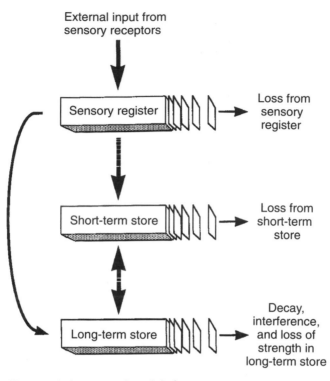

Figure 2.3 A structural model of memory
Source: After Atkinson and Shiffrin (1968)

It was processed at a very shallow level. If the stranger told you that a friend was looking to hire a bright young person for a very appealing job and gave you this phone number – 5 7 4 8 6 2 1 2 – you might put some considerable cognitive effort into memorising the information at a much greater depth than the stranger's phone number. Some numbers – like our parents' phone number when we were children – may have had great importance to us and consequently were processed very deeply and may be remembered after many, many years without use.

Describing memory in terms of the depth of processing – as Craik and Lockhart (1972) did – was thought to be an improvement over the earlier structural models because it placed emphasis on the importance of the cognitive activity that influenced the retention of information. Their conceptual framework for memory is shown in Figure 2.4.

Thinking about memory in terms of how information is processed, rather than as components of a memory system, implies that the person dealing with the information plays some active role in consolidating the information in the memory storehouse. It was not long, therefore, before researchers

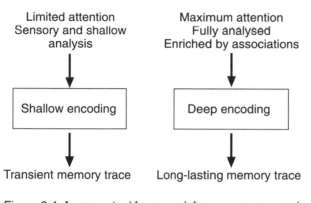

Figure 2.4 A conceptual framework for memory research
Source: Developed by Craik and Lockhart (1972)

turned their attention to a more systematic study of memory deficiencies and memory problems than had been undertaken previously.

The influence of early memory research

While many researchers focused their attention on the memory capacity of normally achieving children and adolescents, others sought explanations for the cognitive deficits of children and adolescents with severe learning problems or intellectual disability (still called mental retardation in the United States and, at the time of the initial studies, mental deficiency in the United Kingdom).

There was little dispute over the significant differences between the memory capabilities of those with and without severe learning difficulties. Of considerable significance among the early memory studies was a report by Butterfield *et al.* (1973), who argued that passive memory systems work about the same for all people regardless of age or intellectual ability. Passive systems refer to learning by non-rehearsing attention which leads to relatively impermanent retention in memory. When retrieval is important, adults usually adapt to the circumstances and employ effective ways of acquiring information through the use of various memory strategies (such as rehearsal). Butterfield *et al.* (1973) reported three studies to show how their adolescent and young adult participants who had severe learning difficulties differed from their non-disabled peers; they did not rehearse information presented to them spontaneously. When taught to rehearse, however, the performance of the participants with a disability improved dramatically. However, they did not adapt their learning pattern to meet the changing demands of the task. In other words, they failed to see that there was a link between the way they learned in the first place and the way they retrieved information from memory.

During the 1970s, numerous studies were undertaken to elaborate the problem-solving behaviour of people with learning difficulties or an intellectual disability. In general, it was shown that they could be taught to use efficient learning and memory strategies almost as effectively as non-disabled people, but they failed to continue using the strategies once the training ceased, and they were unable to adapt (or transfer) successful strategies to learning tasks other than those used in the training (see e.g. Kramer *et al.* 1980).

Over a number of years it became clear that there were substantial differences in the strategies used by people with and without a disability. It then became important to determine whether these differences were related to the structure (you might think of this as the architecture of the brain) or processing style (whether the person is able to identify and use memory strategies which they possess appropriately).

Early memory research was important for a number of reasons. First, it led researchers to consider the links between brain functions and observable behaviour related to the storage and retrieval of information. Second, it led to a close examination of the memory problems experienced by people with severe learning difficulties and this guided the development of teaching methods designed to improve their learning and problem-solving behaviour. Third, it provided a conceptual foundation for research into learning styles. Naveh-Benjamin (1990), for example, suggested that while much of the early work may not have provided clarification of the everyday use of memory, it gave direction to the study of human learning. In particular, he identified the work of Craik and Lockhart (1972) as the predecessor of educational research that has since focused on students' learning style preferences which involved the processing of information at a deep rather than surface level.

Certainly, since the mid-1960s, we have developed a considerable body of knowledge about human memory, not only in terms of the observable characteristics of memory, but also about brain functions. This has led to an impressive collection of memory terms, each of which is thought to play a part in human cognition (see Box 2.2). Whether we will ever fully understand the nature of memory and its operation is yet to be seen.

SUMMARY

In this chapter we introduced two traditions which have influenced the study of human learning and problem-solving. Behaviourism developed from the work of Pavlov, Watson, Thorndike and Skinner, and is based upon the belief that the links between an event and its consequence govern learning. Early behaviourists held the view that the environment controlled learning. Later, cognitive-behaviourists introduced the notion that the organism (the human) plays an important role in effective learning and problem-solving.

Concurrently, a second tradition in the discipline of psychology was growing. Studies of memory in animals and humans laid the foundation for investigations into the complex thought processes that occur within the brain. Researchers soon began to develop models of memory and thinking based upon their observation and inferences about the link between brain functions and behaviour, which became the field called cognitive psychology.

In Chapter 3 we continue with a discussion of the building blocks of cognition. We describe some of the basic concepts, discuss how successful

Box 2.2

A list of common memory terms and their meaning

Memory The ability to relive past experience through learning, retention, recall and recognition.

Memory trace A hypothetical neurological change that occurs when information is learned and accounts for the retention of this learned material (also called an engram).

Short-term memory (STM) The reproduction, recognition, or recall of a limited amount of material up to about 10 seconds. It is characterised by only a limited amount of information being stored at any one time, and there is rapid decay as storage is easily disrupted.

Long-term memory (LTM) The ability to practise a skill, recall an event, or reproduce information long after the original learning. It is characterised by substantial capacity and durability, relies on the deep processing of information, and has a slow rate of decay.

Working memory A hypothesised memory system that 'holds' the input while an interpretation or elaborate processing is undertaken.

Sensory memory system A memory system of extremely short duration (i.e. one or two seconds). After a stimulus is removed, its sensory representation is suspended in the mind for a brief time. Unless further processing occurs in the STM, the information will be lost.

Implicit memory The retention of material without conscious effort needed for its recall.

Semantic memory Long-term memory of objective, generic, and factual knowledge about the world in general.

Episodic memory Long-term memory of subjective information. It involves personal, autobiographical, and event memory derived from perception, and personal and life events.

Declarative memory Knowledge stored in the LTM through a variety of different representations, schemata, facts, and statements.

Procedural memory Knowledge stored in LTM about actions which are linked to conditions underlying our ability to do things.

Associative memory The recall of a past experience by remembering a fact or incident associated with it.

Memory span The greatest amount of material, usually six to eight units of information that can be recalled visually or orally after a single presentation.

research has been in explaining thinking, learning, and learning processes, and examine the relationship between intelligence and information processing.

STUDY TASKS

2.1 In note form, list the main points covered in this chapter.

2.2 Describe the differences between the early memory models of Atkinson and Shiffrin, and Craik and Lockhart.

2.3 Undertake an historical review of memory research, focusing attention on the 1960s and 1970s. Can you see any themes emerging in the literature? If so, what are they?

2.4 List some of the memory difficulties experienced by people with a severe learning disability.

ADDITIONAL READING

Anderson, J.R. (1995) *Learning and Memory: An Integrated Approach*, New York: John Wiley.

Frackowiak, R.S.J. (1994) 'Functional mapping of verbal memory and language', *Trends in Neuroscience 17*: 109–14.

Marshall, J.C. and Fryer, D.M. (1978) 'Speak, Memory! An introduction to some historic studies of remembering and forgetting', in M.M. Gruneberg and P. Morris (eds) *Aspects of Memory* (pp. 1–25), London: Methuen.

Mayer, R.E. (1992) 'Cognition and instruction: their historic meeting within educational psychology', *Journal of Educational Psychology 84*: 405–12.

Chapter 3

Cognition and cognitive concepts

Cognition refers to knowing and thinking. Hence, it involves taking in, storing, retrieving, transforming, and manipulating information that is obtained through the senses. It also involves perception, awareness, judgement, the understanding of emotions and, of course, memory and learning. Almost everything we do during our waking lives involves thinking (and perhaps while we are asleep as well!). Indeed, it is fairly difficult to identify aspects of our daily lives that involve no thinking. In this chapter we consider some of the more common concepts to be found in the literature on cognition that relate to thought, learning, remembering, and problem-solving.

Think for a moment about the last time you went to a supermarket to buy provisions. It seems like a relatively simple activity, but there are literally millions of decisions made prior to and during a shopping excursion. All of these decisions are enacted by the brain and influenced by previous learning. One way of gaining an overview of the factors that contribute to a successful shopping trip – or indeed any other activity – is to use a diagram that shows the interrelationship between key elements (see Figure 3.1).

Our knowledge base provides the building blocks for learning and problem-solving. We have thousands, if not hundreds of thousands, of pieces of information stored away inside our heads. There are

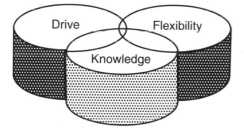

Figure 3.1 A schematic view of the relationship between factors that affect problem-solving behaviour

- *facts* such as the products to be found in the supermarket
- *knowledge* of how we deal with the world around us, using an array of *strategies* that help us remember what provisions we need
- complex routines (or *plans*) that relieve the cognitive burden of day-to-day activities. For example, you may take a predetermined route to the supermarket and have a particular way of doing your shopping, such as cruising the aisles, or beginning a systematic search from one end of the supermarket to the other.

Knowledge refers to declarative knowledge (i.e. the facts) and procedural knowledge (i.e. the processes we use to perform a task) and both are vital in any learning situation because what is learned, and how it is learned, is based upon what a person already knows. Furthermore, a person's ability to learn is dependent on the context in which the learning occurs.

Drive (see Figure 3.1) refers to motivation and other personality characteristics that affect the effort devoted to any task. Our enthusiasm is influenced by past experience and the emotional reactions we have to the tasks we must undertake. If you were anticipating an important phone call, for example, you may be less inclined to go shopping than if you had nothing else to do. You might also be reluctant to go to a particular store if a checkout person was rude to you the last time you were there.

Flexibility refers to the setting of realistic goals, making decisions, setting priorities, using strategies to advantage, and changing tactics if the problem is not being resolved. For example, you may decide that it is a busy time to go to the supermarket, so you choose a convenience store on the way home from work rather than search for an elusive parking space in your neighbourhood shopping centre.

Most (if not all) of the activities we undertake during a shopping excursion result from the way in which our brain is constructed. This involves acting on information being presented from the environment, integrating this information with knowledge stored in our brain, or retrieving and transforming information already held in memory.

Before we move on, it would be useful to clarify the relationship between several of these concepts, and we shall do this by using a metaphor to show the relationship between them. A telephone exchange is a useful metaphor to describe brain functions because it is a highly complex lattice of optic fibres, wires, and switches. The 'wiring' is the architectural structure of the exchange, like the cell systems in the brain. Assuming that there is no organic impairment, one person's brain is constructed in much the same way as that of another.

In the telephone exchange, certain equipment (such as switching equipment, transmitters, and receivers) allows for the passage of electrical currents along various pathways. The way in which this equipment operates is analogous to the way that cognitive processes work to allow information to be used in various locations within the brain. These processes enable thoughts, insights, dreams, the development of plans, and actions.

For it to be functional, we have to know how to use the telephone system. In other words, we must know how to get access to the exchange by pressing the buttons in a predetermined way to make the technology operate for us. In our brain, we use information-processing strategies to manipulate the information we receive from the environment. The use of these strategies provides the initial organisation that allows information to enter the brain and become stored in the most effective way. A strategy is a conscious or automatic cognitive act, or systematic routine that enables information to be stored in, or retrieved from memory. Strategies organise information into usable units that have meaning, although the repertoire of stored and available strategies may differ from person to person, in the same way that one person's recollections of an event will be different to another's. For example, the telephone number 2921292 may be organised as 292 1292 by one person, and as 292 1 292 by another, depending on the chunking strategy used (i.e. breaking up the numbers into familiar chunks).

STRATEGIES

As we have just indicated, strategies refer to the many ways in which we take in (encode), store and retrieve (decode) information – hence, in your reading, you may encounter terms such as memory strategies, cognitive strategies, coding strategies, and information processing strategies. These terms mean much the same. The main point here is to understand that a strategy is a way of organising information so that its complexity is reduced, and/or integrating information into the knowledge base that exists in the brain for later use.

As we grow and learn about the world around us, we begin to use and master a number of strategies which help us process (or deal with) information. For example, we learn as relatively young children that if we repeat a task or say something over and over again, it is more likely to be learned than if we do not. Saying a telephone number repeatedly is an excellent, simple way of remembering it for a short – or even long – period. This strategy is called rehearsal and it is best understood as repeating the information over and over again to keep it active in the working memory. For example, if you repeat the telephone number 4836 4690 – 4836 4690 – 4836 4690 – 4836 4690 – 4836 4690 – and so on, you will be able to recall it for a short period of time. Try it.

There is another form of rehearsal called cumulative rehearsal which is undertaken when a person is given (for example) a telephone number digit by digit, and then repeats each number set together with the next element. For the phone number immediately above:

> You would be given '4', you would say '4'
> You would be given '8', you would say '4, 8'
> You would be given '3', you would say '4, 8, 3'
> You would be given '6', you would say '4, 8, 3, 6', and so on until you held the complete number.

This strategy is excellent for small units of information (like telephone numbers) that have to be recalled over a relatively short period, and even for very complex knowledge that has to be rote learned, as in a script for a theatre production.

Rehearsal is not effective if there is complex information that is not readily coded in serial form. For example, have you ever asked for directions in an unfamiliar neighbourhood or city? If you have, you might have been told how to get to your destination in the following way:

> Well, you go down there to the 4th street and take a left. Then along to the supermarket, where you take the street to the right. Then after three blocks you go left, then take the first right. When you get on the freeway, take the fourth exit – I can't remember what it's called but it's the fourth exit – No wait, it's the fifth. So you get off there and go right immediately, then take the fifth street on the left. I think it's down there somewhere.

This is often not helpful. Usually after one or two changes of direction, you are totally lost, thank your informant graciously, and go off to look for a map!

So, some memory strategies may work well in some situations and not others. Researchers have gathered an impressive collection of these memory strategies (called mnemonics or mnemonic devices) which are used with varying degrees of proficiency depending upon our learning and problem-solving experience. Mnemonics allow personally relevant meaning to be assigned to incoming stimuli. Four of these strategies are described in Box 3.1.

The successful use of memory strategies requires a knowledge of when and how to apply them. As we become more experienced processors of information, we refine our use of strategies and develop more or less sophisticated ways of dealing with information provided to us. For example, few of us could listen to a lecture and remember all of the information given. Note-taking is a memory device that enables us to reduce the complexity of the information by removing perceived redundancies and organising it in a way that will facilitate our recall of the main ideas.

The impact of strategy research on educational practice

Early information processing studies described how children developed their memory skills with age and, in doing so, identified the role of memory (or coding) strategies in short- and long-term recall activities. This led to comparison studies using children with developmental disabilities. It came as little surprise that differences between the groups of children, with and without a disability, were primarily due to the effectiveness of strategy use (see e.g. Cohen and Nealon 1979).

The study of the representational system (i.e. concerned with organising, attending to, and interpreting information) and the effects of strategy training became a major research focus in the mid-1960s, and it remains an area of interest for some investigators today (see e.g. Kaniel 1994). Early projects concentrated on the development of memory aids (e.g. rehearsal), and the relationship between strategy use and memory performance. The most prominent characteristic of these research efforts was the use of a narrow range of training activities within a laboratory setting. While this approach provided for the isolation of specific training effects through tight experimental control, the application of training procedures was not especially successful in applied settings such as school classrooms.

Box 3.1

Four specific purpose memory strategies used to take in and store information

1   *Visualisation* involves creating an image in the mind so that it can be 'seen' and described. Some children's card games (like 'Concentration') rely on visualisation. Simonides' skill at the disaster in Thessaly (described in Chapter 2) was based upon his visualisation of the location of each guest in the room.

2   *Chunking* refers to the recoding of two or more initially independent pieces of information into a single familiar unit. Chunking is a knowledge-specific strategy that depends upon familiarity with the stimuli. Information presented in chunks (for example, 4,3,2,1 – 3,5,7,9, – 8,6,4,2) is more easily recalled by a learner than unchunked numbers (although not always at the first attempt).

3   *Verbal elaboration* also involves the recoding of material into meaningful units. This occurs by making up a sentence to help recall items, by asking questions about the information being presented, or by drawing implications or inferences about the stimuli. For example, if a person is given the words 'boot, hair, bus' to recall, making up a sentence, such as 'My boot had hair on it which I picked off when I got on the bus' might aid recall.

4   *Categorisation* is a method of expanding on, or integrating information into, an existing knowledge base. It is a chunking strategy that allows for the collection of elements into meaningful groups. For instance, 'bus, potato, truck, peas, car, aircraft' would be recalled more easily when collected under the categories of vehicles and food, than together. Think how difficult it would be to find things in a supermarket if they were not grouped by item type.

Notable among literature in the 1980s were studies of cumulative rehearsal, clustering, rote recall, and the self-interrogative activities of students with a mild intellectual disability (Belmont *et al*. 1982; Borkowski and Buchel 1983; G. Reid 1980; Turner and Bray 1985). Typically, early and even more recent studies have shown that students with a disability can make significant gains in recall through training in specific strategies. However, many may experience varying degrees of success in using their newly acquired skills once the 'experiment' has finished. In some cases, the strategy training did not help the students to improve their performance at all. Some continued to use the existing, less efficient strategies in preference to those taught to them. Clearly, these students saw little value in the teacher-imposed strategy.

There were a number of important issues raised by early research endeavours.

- First, some of the strategies related to very specific laboratory-type tasks (e.g. remembering lists of digits) and had limited apparent relevance to classroom lessons. In these situations it was not unreasonable for students to fail to recognise the importance of the strategy when no link was made to school-related activities.
- Second, early studies often focused on teaching students only one strategy, even though several tasks may have been used to show the students how the strategy could be applied. This practice sometimes led to the rigid application of the strategy to the training task only – called 'welding' (Shif 1969) – and that became an important barrier to be overcome in later strategy training projects.
- Third, some students continued to use their inefficient strategies even though they had been trained to use more efficient ones.
- Fourth, the results of some training programmes showed that students' performances decreased with the use of the strategy selected by the researchers. These findings suggested that students had preferred learning methods which were more efficient for them than strategies considered more appropriate by the investigators.
- Fifth, some students were unable to maintain their use of newly acquired strategies once the training programme finished. This suggested that they may have learned to use the strategy effectively but had no opportunity to apply it after the programme, or they failed to acquire the vital retrieval strategies necessary to link their new experiences with their newly acquired competence.
- Finally, many students failed to generalise the use of learned strategies to tasks that required the application of the strategy. This was often due to the researcher's failure to incorporate a 'bridging' or 'generalisation' component that explicitly taught the students to apply the strategy or strategies in a range of tasks or settings.

Many of the failures of early cognitive research mirrored the failures of behaviourist approaches discussed in Chapter 2.

While much of the early information processing research has not had extensive, direct application to classroom instruction, it is important because it has provided an understanding of the many ways in which people of different ages and abilities encode and decode information. Significantly, it drew attention to the fact that human cognition was not a simple process, and that overcoming processing difficulties was far from an easy task. It also led to considerations about the cause of learning problems: if due to a structural (architectural) deficit, an inability to develop the use of appropriate strategies (called a production deficiency), or an inability to use strategies which were provided by others (a mediation deficiency)? As it turned out, each of these reasons was implicated with inefficient learning and problem-solving.

EXECUTIVE FUNCTIONS OF THE BRAIN

If we had to act only like a land-based information sponge and soak up stimuli presented to us, we might survive by using only an extended set of strategies that allowed us to take in, store, and retrieve information. However, our life circumstances demand that we not only learn and memorise, but also react to the environment in an adaptive way. This means that our thinking processes are multidimensional. We recognise stimuli, make sense of them, store them, retrieve them, and then respond in a way that is required of us. In other words, information goes in, we respond to it, and we perform some action or complete some mental event to demonstrate that learning or problem-solving has occurred. Think about this simple puzzle. 'This person is my grandmother's brother's daughter. What is her relationship to me?' To complete this task, we read it, consider the family relationships, and then come to the answer, or say it aloud.

To solve the puzzle problem – as indeed any task we encounter during the day – we need to keep track of how our information processing performance is going. In other words, we perform some cognitive activity that keeps a record of what is being done, and how successful the learning or problem-solving activities are.

Most models of cognition include a component called the 'executive' which is a metaphor for a controlling agent capable of performing an intelligent assessment of the activities occurring within the brain. Consider, for example, what you are doing as you read this paragraph. The words are being translated into meaning and, as you progress, you will be ensuring that the words make sense. Brilliantly value the retrieve went don't only over now. Your brain right now should be saying, 'What? What's that last sentence doing there? It doesn't make any sense?' And that is right. The sentence is nonsense. You picked up the inconsistency and became alerted to a problem. You may have re-read it before going on, thinking that the proofreaders of this book must have slipped up pretty badly.

When you picked up the inconsistency in the text, your self-regulatory system (the executive) was brought into action. This cognitive mechanism plays an important role in all learning and problem-solving. The executive deals with the emotional side of your thinking as well. Let us assume that you are really keen to get a good grade in a course or subject for which this book is the prescribed text. You may be very motivated to learn as much as you can and know that this will maximise your chances of a good grade. As you read, you may be very sensitive to the information being presented. If you read a section that is not completely clear, you may stop, re-read it, and try to fit the information into the knowledge base already stored in your brain before you move on. Your executive will respond to your demands. Conversely, if you have had some negative experiences in the course or subject, find the instructor tedious, or think this book is boring and useless, then the way you read it will be quite different. You may skip this paragraph completely assuming that it contains nothing of importance. The executive responds according to your needs. In other words, it will integrate cognition and emotions, and help you make decisions about what is important, and how to deal with the activity while accommodating your needs.

So, the executive has several functions. It

- predicts performance
- predicts limitations in information-processing capacity
- maintains an awareness of the self-instruction activities
- checks progress against values
- maintains awareness of the problems being faced and strategies being applied to them
- monitors the problem-solving operations and outcomes.

Hence, the executive controls our information-processing activities, and operates via a range of cognitive 'tools'. Perhaps the most researched of these tools are the concepts of metamemory and metacognition.

Metamemory

One important executive process is an awareness of how we perform cognitive tasks (that is, our awareness of how we think). The concept was introduced into the psychology literature by Flavell et al. (1970). Their new term 'metamemory' described what we know about how we remember information. Flavell and his colleagues interviewed children about their memory span and their knowledge of how their memory worked. Not surprisingly, they found that the oldest children in their study (Grade 4 students) had a greater awareness of memory strategies than the younger children who were in nursery school, kindergarten, and Grade 2. Later, Kreutzer et al. (1975) were interested in how metamemory influences the quality of children's performance in memory activities. In other words, they wanted to know what the children knew, or could find out about memory as a function of maturation and experience. Through interviews, they discovered how children thought that they would go about the activity of remembering to perform tasks in their day-to-day lives. Here are two examples of the questions they asked:

> Suppose you were going ice skating with your friend after school tomorrow and you wanted to be sure to bring your skates. How could you be really certain that you didn't forget to take them to school in the morning?
> Suppose you were invited to a birthday party for one of your friends. How would you remember to buy him/her a present?

Take a few seconds here to think about what you would do it if you were asked.

As one might anticipate, the older children (in Grades 3 and 5) were more aware of how their memory worked than their younger peers who knew about forgetting, but not how to get their memory to work effectively for them. The children came up with a wide range of general strategies that could be used to ensure that they remembered their skates, or to buy a present. These fell into a number of categories. For example, they might write themselves a note and put it in a prominent place (e.g. on the fridge door, or beside their alarm clock) so they would not miss seeing it before they left the house. They might write the activity on the calendar or say 'skates, skates, skates, skates,' over and over again until they thought it was in their memory, or 'party, party, party, party'. Some children relinquished their responsibility for remembering what they were supposed to do and simply said that they would ask their mother to remind them.

Several researchers have conducted similar research using similar questions. Kirby and Ashman (1984), for example, studied the executive skills of Australian children. They administered a slightly amended version of the Kreutzer et al. (1975) task during a study aimed at elaborating the dimensions of planning. They suggested that the task may be an index of general cognitive development as students were not required to perform any task, but their performance was linked to achievement. In other words, high metamemory scores were related to high achievement.

In what was probably the first study of the metamemory of people with severe learning problems, Eyde and Altman (1978) also used a slightly adapted version of the Kreutzer et al. (1975) questionnaire to interview 5 to 16 year olds about their memory. They reported that children with a mild and moderate disability certainly had an understanding of how their memories worked, although it was not very sophisticated. They also found that the memory performance of their participants was related to chronological and mental age and to the richness of the individual's life experiences. Their results have important implications for how classroom teachers might explain awareness of cognitive activities when working with students with severe learning difficulties.

Researchers soon discovered a link between metamemory and memory recall and an argument was proposed that metamemory was not only important, but also vital for success in complex memory tasks (see e.g. Weinert and Perlmutter 1988). It has generally been assumed that metamemory is necessary to acquire and develop strategies that are tied to particular tasks and situations, and only after extensive experience with these strategies can this knowledge be generalised across tasks or situations.

The training of metastrategic behaviour

While some support for metamemory training was found in studies using regular education students, the same optimism was missing in studies in which students with low ability were involved. Indeed, there was little conclusive evidence to show the value of increasing children's awareness of their memory system alone. In other words, children's knowledge of the best way to remember information did not necessarily lead to improved performance.

Many of the early studies involving executive processes were based upon the presumed need to make the student's information processing more efficient through memory control processes (i.e. metamemory). Studies by Brown and her colleagues in the late 1970s saw some of the first attempts at metamemory training (A.L. Brown and Barclay 1976; A.L. Brown et al. 1979). A major feature of these interventions was the emphasis on general skills such as planning, checking, and self-monitoring. Hence, training focused on providing information about the activity and the effects of training. The results of these studies showed obvious age-related differences. For example, a comparison of students having mental ages of around 6 and 8 years demonstrated that the older children could incorporate general strategy training skills into their problem-solving activities, while their younger peers could not (A.L. Brown et al. 1979).

Metamemory training was soon viewed as the key to improving memory performance and numerous studies were conducted to train students to become more aware of their memory processes. The results across many studies, however, did not show consistent improvement in memory performance (C.R. Kendall et al. 1980; Kramer and Engle 1981; Tharp and Gallimore 1985).

Over the years, the term 'metacognition' has become more commonly used than metamemory. In the early 1980s, A.L. Brown et al. (1983) suggested that metacognition requires not only an awareness of cognition (that is, an understanding of the information processing involved in complex skills) but also competence in planning, monitoring, self-questioning and self-directing. Terms commonly associated with metacognition include 'planning to make a plan', 'stop and check', and 'knowing when, where, and how to remember'.

A model of metacognition has been described by Borkowski *et al.* (1989). There are three strategy components (Figure 3.2): general strategy knowledge (e.g. awareness of the importance of being strategic); specific strategy knowledge (e.g. organisation, verbal elaboration); and relational strategy knowledge (based on shared properties). In addition, there are components that involve selection and use of strategies appropriate for a task (strategy use), and components that monitor the strategy knowledge and its use (executive processes).

Hence, strategy and metastrategy knowledge is related to many aspects of the thinking process. The development of this knowledge would have begun, for example, from the time a child is taught to remember the alphabet using the rote-learning song 'A, B, C, D, E, F, G ... H, I J, K, elemeno, P ...' and so on, to the acquisition of higher order thinking skills such as self-regulating study and leisure time as an adult. Self-regulation is an important aspect of metacognition as it allows us to make decisions about:

- the existence of the problem in the first place
- the demands of the task
- the need for a strategy to solve it

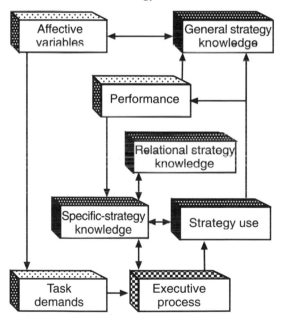

Figure 3.2 A model of metacognition involving affective variables

- past experience on the same or similar tasks
- the availability of an appropriate strategy to deal with the problem
- the success of the strategy as it is implemented
- whether to continue or try another strategy
- whether the task has been solved, or is insolvable under existing conditions.

Many of the early metacognition studies have historical importance as they reported students' failure to transfer training. They emphasised the need for students to be involved actively in learning, to be informed of the value of using the strategy, and to be given the opportunity to apply the strategy in alternative tasks (A.L. Brown and Palincsar 1982). Moreover, they led to a re-evaluation of teaching materials to be included in strategy training. Teaching materials such as stories, picture sequences, and expository text became more common as a consequence of the belief that strategy use would occur only if the student perceived the task to have practical relevance.

Contemporary studies have also examined the relationship between memory and metamemory. Short *et al.* (1993), for example, examined the notion that young and less skilled learners would have relatively more specific strategy knowledge at their disposal than well-developed general strategies. If specific strategy knowledge is acquired more quickly than general strategy knowledge, then task-specific metamemory should be more predictive of memory performance and more successful than general metamemory. They used task-specific and general measures of metamemory knowledge, arguing that performance difference may be due to limited strategy repertoires, children's inability to determine the value of known strategies, or some combination of both.

Short *et al.* (1993) found that average learners were superior to less skilled learners in their general metamemory knowledge. The average ability group improved over time while the less skilled learners showed no change in general metamemory knowledge across the four-year period of the study. This finding suggested that the latter group may be unable to use and manage strategies (which is called a 'production deficiency').

Overall, the study showed that highly structured tasks assisted memory performance in young and low-achieving children, and that structured material and contextual support is important if children are to demonstrate their competence and skills. For average ability children, there was a jump in their task-specific metamemory between Grades 2 and 4 implying that, during those years, children learn about their own memory processes at the same time as they learn about the world in general.

Metacognition and motivation

There have been numerous studies that have explored the many aspects of strategic and metastrategic behaviour. Outcomes, in general, show that there are good strategy users (a term used by Pressley *et al.* 1989a) who are self-confident, motivated by some personal desire to achieve (i.e. intrinsically motivated), and who are aware of the importance of task demands and strategy use for successful learning and problem-solving. Thus, cognitive, metacognitive, and motivational factors predict 'good' and 'poor' performance. Many of the early studies (i.e. in the 1970s) sought connections between memory awareness and memory behaviour with little success. Both the Borkowski *et al.* (1989) and Pressley *et al.* (1989a) studies suggested that results were due to the use of tasks that related to general metacognitive awareness rather than an awareness of knowledge of specific strategies.

Closely associated with motivation is one's beliefs about how successful one is in achieving goals (i.e. self-efficacy). Self-efficacy is established over a long period and comes from observations about how success is obtained. These attributions of success and failure are the consequences of strategy use and feedback that provide information to the individual about the importance of effort, the use of performance monitoring processes, and strategy use. The overall result is that some people are more strategic than others (i.e. in their use of strategies and metastrategies), and more flexible in how they learn and solve problems. In summary, self-efficacy is based upon detailed information about strategies, self-control procedures, and insights about effort and personal involvement in successful learning and problem-solving (Borkowski and Turner 1990).

Some general considerations

The concepts we have considered in this chapter are based upon inferences drawn from observable behaviour. Over the years, the definitions of many concepts have changed as the field continues to develop and new research leads to the refinement of terms. Schneider and Weinert (1990) drew attention to the general confusion that remains in the definition of cognitive concepts using examples from a seemingly straightforward area of knowledge. They stated:

> The long list of knowledge components addressed in the cognitive development literature ... includes terms like semantic knowledge, episodic knowledge, conceptual knowledge, the knowledge base, world knowledge or epistemic knowledge, content knowledge or domain-specific knowledge, procedural and declarative knowledge, and so on. Given this impressive flexibility and inconsistency in terminology, there is no doubt that even experts in the field get confused about possible denotations and connotations of the concept.
>
> (Schneider and Weinert 1990: 287–8)

Notwithstanding the confusion, Schneider and Weinert claimed that there have been numerous accomplishments. They suggested four are among the most prominent, namely:

- the clear understanding of how strategy-knowledge develops
- the development of comprehensive cognitive or metacognitive models that represent strategy-knowledge interactions, especially the finding that children may use several strategies when solving identical problems
- the inclusion of motivational, educational, and cultural factors in the analysis of strategy-knowledge interactions
- a tendency toward explicit consideration of individual differences and aptitude issues in the analysis of these interactions.

As we have seen, cognition and metacognition are fundamental to learning, problem-solving, and intelligent behaviour. At this point, however, it is timely to introduce another domain of psychology that has been closely linked to human cognitive performance, namely intelligence.

Up to this point we have not referred to intelligence for two reasons. First, it has typically been viewed as a more-or-less fixed human competence: you either have it, or you do not. Second, it refers to a set of abilities (generally related to cultural knowledge) but without reference to the underlying processes that enable the acquisition or use of knowledge gained through the person's interaction with the environment. This brief introduction to the 'traditional' approach to intelligence is important, however, because contemporary information processing theorists are using the term, intelligence, to describe general models of thinking. Two of these are outlined toward the end of the following section.

GENERAL MODELS OF THINKING

Modern views of the nature of intelligence stemmed from the theorising of Charles Spearman (1904). Upon his return from the Boer War, Spearman focused his attention on the problem of mental measurement. Spearman argued that all aspects of intellectual activity have one fundamental function (or group of functions) in common. He referred to this as 'g' or general intelligence. However, g did not account for a person's competence in all tasks and, hence, he suggested that each task must have a specific component of intelligence ('s') associated with it. Boring (1923) later described g as power, and the special ability, s, as a machine that uses the power for a particular purpose.

Spearman's deliberations mark a point in history where intelligence approached a metaphoric fork in the road. One direction continued along the way commenced by Spearman's speculation about the nature of intelligence (see Box 3.2), and the other to the assessment of intelligence. Modern views of the measurement of intelligence stemmed from the work of Alfred Binet (see Binet and Simon 1905) undertaken at about the same time as Spearman was developing his notion of g. The invariability of one's intelligence arose predominantly from the acceptance of the numerical Intelligence Quotient (IQ) as the 'true' and enduring indicator of ability.

Since 1980, the concept of intelligence has undergone a re-evaluation as different ways of testing skills and ability have emerged (which we shall consider in Chapters 5 and 6), and because of the growing – and seemingly heretical – belief that intellectual ability can be improved through effective instruction or remediation.

Like the notion of cognitive processes, intelligence is implied. It is a hypothetical construct. We refer to intelligence as though it exists, but we cannot touch it, feel it, or see it. We can, of course, measure it by inferring that intelligent behaviour has certain quantifiable characteristics. Its illusive nature, however, is exemplified by the many descriptions of intelligence such as those of Spearman (1904), Guilford (1959), Eysenck (1967), Vernon (1969), Cattell (1957), and Thurstone (1938) who wrote on the topic from the turn of the twentieth century to the 1970s.

Since the mid-1970s, a number of important advances have been made in describing the nature of intelligence. These are Howard Gardner's (1983) theory of multiple intelligences, and Robert Sternberg's (1977) componential sub-theory of intelligence. They are significant because they move the discussion of intelligent behaviour away from an emphasis on test scores (IQ), which is a 'product,' that gives no indication of how the score was achieved, toward information processing theory that strives to describe the way in which learning and problem-solving takes place.

A theory of multiple intelligences

In 1983, Gardner published *Frames of Mind*. In that volume, he proposed a view of intelligence, one that was antagonistic to the traditional belief of intelligence as the sum total of one's knowledge, based upon the verbal-spatial orientation of most intelligence tests. Gardner proposed multiple intelligences, with each of these 'human intellectual proclivities' having its own pattern of development and brain activity (Gardner 1983: xvi).

Gardner suggested his theory of intelligence without relying principally on assessment information, but on information drawn from a range of sources including studies of normally functioning and special groups (e.g. as people with brain damage or a severe intellectual disability but exceptional talent in some area called *idiot savants*); autistic children; and prodigies. He also drew evidence from evolution, and information from research on human development, neurology, and cross-cultural studies.

Gardner identified seven areas of potential, which he called intelligences. These included: linguistic; musical; spatial; logical-mathematical; bodily-

Box 3.2

Views of intelligence from the 1920s to the 1960s

Numerous views of intelligence have been proposed since the beginning of the twentieth century. Many theorists followed Spearman's (1904) lead and used sophisticated statistical procedures – such as factor analysis – to describe hierarchies of intellectual skills. Briefly, factor analysis represents a set of variables in terms of a smaller number of hypothetical variables. In other words, specific skills can be grouped into more general abilities in a hierarchical fashion.

Thurstone (1938) – originally an electrical engineer – suggested that more than one general factor (*g*) was necessary to account for the relationship between ability tests, and any one of these *may* be what we should call intelligence. He divided *g* into *primary mental abilities* which are shown in the diagram.

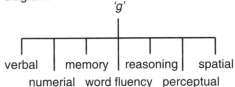

Vernon (1969) extracted two features of *g* which he called *perceptual motor* (*k:m*) and *verbal educational* (*v:ed*) components. Both *k:m* and *v:ed* can be divided further into more specific skills and these, in turn, can be divided into very specific skills.

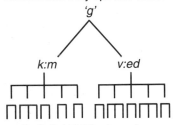

Cattell (1957) viewed *g* as a series of primary factors but he focused attention on two second-order factors (one step down from *g*) which he called 'fluid' ('*gf*'), and 'crystallised' ('*gc*') general abilities. Fluid intelligence is the basic capacity for learning and problem-solving that is independent of education and experience. Crystallised intelligence is the result of the interaction between the individual's fluid intelligence and culture, and consists of learned knowledge and skills. *Gf* can be conveniently described as genotype intelligence (determined by the genetic constitution or heredity) and *gc*, as a phenotype intelligence (determined by the interaction of heredity and the environment).

Guilford's (1959) three-dimensional Structure of Intellect Model (SOI) was a major departure from other theorists (see diagram). He conceived intellectual abilities as an interaction between operations, content, and products. These are shown in the diagram which includes 120 cells (6 products × 5 operations × 4 contents), each of which could represent a single test of a specific product × operations × content interaction.

Box 3.2 cont.

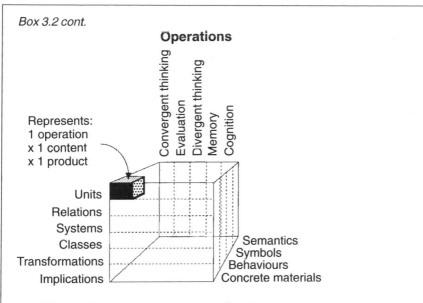

Operations

This model has been criticised as a reduction of Thurstone's work. Eysenck (1967: 83), for example, claimed that Guilford failed to reproduce the essential 'hierarchical nature of the data' and that the model 'cut out the Dane from his production of Hamlet' (p. 83). Eysenck's model, however, bears a strong resemblance to Guilford's cube. Eysenck called operations 'mental processes', and contents 'test materials', but departed from SOI on the third dimension, which he called 'quality', which incorporated mental speed and power.

Finally, Jensen (1969; 1973) viewed intelligence as an attribute with primary abilities that incorporate conceptual learning, abstractions of symbolic reasoning, and complex verbal problem-solving abilities. He described two dimensions, Level I or *associative ability* and Level II or *cognitive ability.* Level I abilities involve simple registration, storage, and recall of sensory inputs and is prominent in short-term memory and rote learning. Level II abilities involve mental manipulation of sensory inputs, and relating these inputs to stored memories, generalisation, and abstraction for transfer, reasoning, conceptualisation and problem-solving. Level II abilities parallel Spearman's *g* in that individual differences might best be demonstrated by scores on standard intelligence tests, or by experimental, conceptual learning.

As can be seen from the brief descriptions above, intelligence has been described in several ways. While the theorising has generated lively debate in the literature, how one translates theory into practical application is not at all clear.

kinaesthetic; and interpersonal (being in touch with one's emotions) and intrapersonal (as in leadership ability) intelligences. They are part of the individual's genetic make-up but are nurtured, or allowed to remain undeveloped, as a result of experiences within the culture and society in which they live. Indeed, the intelligences are modified by changes in the available resources and one's perceptions of ability and potential. In other words, some individuals will develop certain intelligences to a far greater extent than others, but everyone should develop each intelligence to some extent, given the opportunity to do so. A person's profile of intelligences, therefore, is based upon cultural and social experiences. Kornhaber *et al.* (1990) argued that human cognition is best developed and nurtured through tasks within the bounds of 'authentic domains' (p. 184). These are socially valued disciplines where a person can acquire proficiency and knowledge over time, and benefit from feedback from those who are skilled in the discipline.

There is also a relationship between intelligences and domains, but it is crucial not to confound the two realms. A person with musical intelligence, for example, is likely to be attracted to, and be successful in, the domain of music. However, musical performance required intelligences beyond the musical domain (for example, bodily-kinaesthetic and interpersonal intelligences). Furthermore, musical intelligence can also be essential for success in other areas outside of music, such as dance and even advertising. Hence, nearly all domains require proficiency in a set of intelligences, and any intelligence might be necessary in a wide range of domains.

Critics of Gardner's proposition often hesitate at the use of the term, intelligences, preferring to use the term abilities, faculties, or talents. He, in turn, suggests that there is an inherent devaluation of some abilities (such as music or spatial ability) because they are not included in the traditional notion of intelligence which has been reserved – almost exclusively – for logical-mathematical ability.

A componential theory of intelligence

While Gardner's approach to intelligence draws attention to social and cultural determinants, Sternberg's (1977; 1985) componential sub-theory of intelligence focuses on how the individual processes information independent of content or domain. His emphasis is on higher order skills and this distinguishes his theory from many other models of intelligence. These higher order skills include:

- an evaluation of the problem to be solved
- selection of lower order components to help solve the problem
- selecting appropriate strategies to combine components
- decisions about the mental representation upon which the components and strategy should act

- allocation of attention and other resources in accordance with the task
- monitoring the steps toward solution.

Sternberg (1985) proposed that elements of a theory of intelligence should specify the mental mechanisms by which people deliberately adapt, shape, and select real-world environments. His theory was based upon the notion of components of intelligence, in other words, elementary information processes that operate upon internal representation of objects or symbols (Sternberg 1977). Components translate sensory inputs into a conceptional representation (e.g. seeing the Union Jack flag and recognising that it represents Great Britain); transform one conceptual representation into another (e.g. seeing the words 'Golden Labrador' and thinking of a seeing-eye or guide dog as a helper for a blind person); or translate a conceptual representation into a motor output (e.g. seeing a traffic light turn from yellow to red and putting your foot on the brake).

Sternberg (1977) proposed various components which are classified by function and based upon level of generality.

Metacomponents

These are the higher-order control processes – the executive – that are used for planning and decision-making during problem-solving. Sternberg nominated six metacomponents that

- make decisions about the nature of the problem to be solved
- select lower-order components (i.e. performance, acquisition, retention, or transfer) that are needed to complete the task
- select one or more to represent or organise information to facilitate or impede the efficacy with which the components operate
- elect a strategy for combining lower-order components, that may allow the sequencing of components in a way that facilitates performance
- make decisions about the trade off of speed against the need for accuracy, so that time and effort might be devoted to the task in accordance with its demands
- monitor progress so that the individual keeps track of performance and the effectiveness of the problem-solving behaviour.

Performance components

These are processes used in the execution of a problem-solving strategy. There may be many highly task-specific processes although there are others that relate to a wide range of activities such as

- encoding information for later retrieval and use
- making inferences from information given

- mapping aspects of previous situations and drawing parallels to present circumstances
- applying previously learned relationships
- justifying the use of strategies of available options
- responding to task demands.

Acquisition, retention and transfer components

These are processes used in learning new information, retrieving previously stored knowledge, and generalising, or applying knowledge learned in one situation to another.

Some of the variables that influence performance in these three components include

- the recurrence of learning or problem-solving events
- the range of contexts in which information is presented
- the importance of the target information
- the recency of the experience
- the context in which information is presented
- the linkages between presented information and knowledge already stored in memory.

Sternberg (1980) suggested that the metacomponents activate directly – and gain feedback from – the performance, acquisition, retention, and transfer components, and that indirect activation and feedback occur between these four components. Hence, all control passes directly from the metacomponents to the system and all information passes directly from the system to the metacomponents.

SUMMARY

In this chapter we have outlined and described many of the terms commonly found in the cognitive psychology literature. We have emphasised the importance of knowledge, strategies for encoding and decoding information held in memory, and metastrategies that keep track of the success or otherwise of learning and problem-solving activities. This chapter has drawn material from many of the early studies in which researchers worked toward establishing the relationship between an impressive array of cognitive concepts. Toward the end of the chapter we also briefly overviewed the traditional notion of intelligence and two contemporary theories of intelligence that stand in contrast to the notion of intellectual abilities described by Spearman and others. While Gardner's approach to intelligence emphasises abilities, it also stresses adaptability and the importance of cultural knowledge on intellectual development. Sternberg, on the other hand, described the cognitive mechanisms and influences that affect intelligent behaviour. Neither theory has been extensively tested and validated. The theory of multiple intelligences remains just that, a theory. Sternberg's model has been explored through empirical studies but, as yet, there is not a large body of literature to support its conceptual structure.

The general disillusionment with strategy and metastrategy training alone, as ways of improving cognitive competence, led to the exploration of concepts that would help researchers to understand the links between knowledge, emotions, and organisational skills. The literature of neuro-psychology and the work of two Russians (Luria and Vygotsky) provided some direction. Their contributions to research led to an interest in brain mechanisms which, in turn, have focused attention on planning, decision-making and problem-solving. Chapter 4 considers these contributions and the application of this body of knowledge to the study of information processing.

STUDY TASKS

3.1 In note form, list the main points covered in this chapter.

3.2 Early in this chapter we describe a number of mnemonic devices (e.g. rehearsal, clustering). List these devices and for each one, give some practical examples of where they could be useful in your daily life.

3.3 Work out the following arithmetic problem (without using a calculator or a computer!): $(16 \times 24) \div (19 \div 6)$. When you have finished, recall and write down the process you used. Think about what you were doing in terms of the operation of your 'executive'. Also think about your motivation to carry out this study activity.

3.4 Choose either Howard Gardner's or Robert Sternberg's theory of intelligence. Look in your library for either the books or journal articles that your chosen author has published. Spend some time becoming familiar with the work and write a two-page summary of the main ideas.

ADDITIONAL READING

Eysenck, M.W. and Keane, M.T. (1990) *Cognitive Psychology: A Student's Handbook*, Hillsdale, NJ: Erlbaum.

Herrnstein, R.J. and Murray, C. (1994) *The Bell Curve: Intelligence and Class Structure in America*, New York: Free Press.

Neisser, U., Boodoo, G., Bouchard Jr, T.J., Boykin, A.W., Brody, N., Ceci, S.J., Halpern, D.F., Loehlin, J.C., Perloff, R., Sternberg, R.J. and Urbina, S. (1996) 'Intelligence: knowns and unknowns', *American Psychologist* 51: 77–101.

Chapter 4

Brain functions and problem-solving

For almost 150 years, reports have been accumulating about the manner in which the human brain works. Much of this evidence has been collected from reports of damaged brains rather than from those that are intact. The effects of brain damage following head injury or war traumas have contributed to the growing knowledge of brain functions, in addition to more recent accounts of surgery to remove brain tumours or to minimise the effects of severe epilepsy. In the case of tumours, damage to the brain is often diverse as they commonly affect larger areas of the brain tissue in contrast to confined injuries (called focal lesions) caused by bullets or shrapnel which are more specific, and damage is usually confined to a small area.

Perhaps the first 'modern' clinical report of the effects of brain injury came from an American physician, John Harlow (1848; 1868). Harlow recorded the classical 'crowbar case' of Phineas Gage, a gang foreman for the Rutland and Burlington Railroad in Vermont, USA. Gage and his men were clearing a section of track following a landslide and they were in the process of removing a boulder from the railroad when the accident occurred. Gage was tamping gunpowder into a narrow hole drilled in rock when a spark ignited the charge. The rod – one metre long, three centimetres in diameter and weighing over eight kilograms – exploded from the hole, struck Gage beneath his left eye and passed through his head leaving from the skull approximately ten centimetres above the bridge of his nose. In what could only be considered to be a monumental understatement, Harlow reported that 'the patient was thrown upon his back' (1848: 389) but he was conscious and after a few minutes was able to speak. He was placed in the back of an ox cart and taken two kilometres into the village. He walked up a long flight of stairs to his room where he lay waiting for the physician to attend him.

Harlow treated Gage with the most advanced medicines known at the time – vin. colchicum, sulphur of magnesia, calomel, rhubarb, and castor oil. Because of infection in the wound, Gage was bedridden for about three weeks but two months later he appeared to have recovered almost completely. Anecdotal information collected by Harlow and reported after Gage's death in 1868, however, revealed that profound psychological changes had occurred in his emotional state and in his ability to plan and make decisions, although many of his other intellectual faculties remained unaffected.

Since the Harlow accounts, many examinations of brain trauma have contributed to a vast range of symptoms and speculation. Studies of gunshot wounds following the First World War (see Schlesinger 1962) revealed very specific behavioural effects depending upon the location of the injury. For example, damage to the frontal lobe had considerable impact on volition and emotions (collectively called affect) although recent memory, test intelligence, and attention were largely unaffected. Similar findings were reported following surgery. Penfield and Evans (1934), for example, reported that frontal lobe damage led to a loss of initiative and lack of capacity for planned administration, and the destruction of the synthesiser of intellectual operations. However, after all these reports had been accumulated, it did not appear as though there was a single, identifiable effect of brain damage in a specific area of the brain.

Neuropsychology was a developing discipline around the time of the Second World War. A hybrid science, neuropsychology combined the psychological description of human behaviour in areas such as perception, memory, and intellectual activity, with the information obtained from modern clinical neurology, physiology, and biochemistry. Although not distinctly separate, two branches of neuropsychology emerged in the western world. One emphasised a basic experimental approach, while the other had a clinical orientation. Both attempted to understand behaviour through an examination of basic brain mechanisms.

Sherrington (1933) and Lashley (1933) were pioneers of the experimental approach. Sherrington, for example, proposed that behavioural complexity was directly related to the organisation of the junctional connections (i.e. synapses) between neurons. Excitation and inhibition co-operated at nodal point after nodal point in nerve circuits to direct the conduction patterns, and consequently, motor output. Lashley stressed the integrated nature of the brain, and suggested that cortical tissue was mutually dependent, so that the entire cortex or a subordinate part of it was capable of performing the functions of the whole. Later, Gazzaniga (1975) concluded that the cerebral areas which process raw sensory information could be isolated and disconnected by severing the corpus callosum during 'split-brain' surgery (to reduce severe and uncontrollable epileptic seizures). However, processes which involve small cortical cells are more difficult to isolate, as are the channels along which such information passes.

The second approach evolved in response to the practical problems of assessment and rehabilitation of patients with cortical brain dysfunction, and reflects the roots of clinical psychology. Clinical neuropsychology seems to have gained much impetus from attempts to diagnose and rehabilitate brain-damaged soldiers following the First World War. The major thrust in this area was the development and description of test instruments to identify and localise brain damage. Since the mid-1940s, a multitude of measures have been administered to patients who have lesions in various cortical areas, and diagnostic and screening batteries have been published by Halstead (1947), Lezak ([1976] 1993), and Reitan and Davidson (1974) among others. The clinical application of many screening tests was compromised by the number of false decisions that were made when diagnosing brain injury. The situation now is greatly different through cranial axial tomography (CAT scans) and other non-invasive diagnostic techniques.

Knowledge about the functioning of the brain has grown rapidly as a result of developments in medical science and technology, and as a result of clinical case studies (a classic review of the early literature can be found in Klebanoff 1945). Researchers have been interested in brain-function as they related to implicated disturbances of learning and reasoning. However, much of what is known has come from observations of impaired, rather than intact, brains.

ALEXANDER LURIA

The work of the late A.R. Luria arguably has had the greatest impact on our understanding of brain functions (see Luria 1966; 1973). His work focused on the disturbances in complex human behaviour that resulted from brain damage and disease, and allowed for cognitive theorising based upon physical evidence. Luria adopted a syndrome rather than symptom methodology as it provided a more powerful theoretical basis on which human information processing could be examined. Examining the symptoms of isolated local brain trauma (e.g. the loss of a specific aspect of memory, such as word identification) did not appear to lead to a reliable method of locating the cause of a disability within the brain. The reason for the apparent confusion created by the single-symptom approach seemed to lie in the systemic nature of brain functions. In other words, there exists an intimate relationship between cortical zones and subcortical structures, each aspect contributing an important factor to the completion of any activity. Damage to any structure or zone within a system will be manifested by different cognitive deficits according to the focus of the injury.

Luria's (1966) proposition about the study of brain pathology using a syndrome approach (i.e. a pattern of symptoms) would remove the confusion created by the single-symptom approach and yield reliable conclusions about the nature of mental processes. Luria's model of brain activity was developed from the accumulated results of many syndrome analyses. It is based on the notion that mental functions result from the establishment of connections between many cell groups which are often located in distant areas of the brain. These complex networks are called functional systems. Luria proposed that each area of the brain concerned with a functional system introduces its own particular factor which is essential for normal, correct performance. Destruction of a specific part of the brain that mediates some cognitive functions (called a mediating zone), while not necessarily causing a total breakdown in normal performance of the system, may cause the loss of some capabilities while others are left intact.

Luria's functional organisation of the brain

In preparation for considering the pivotal role of information processing within the cognitive approach, it is important to have a basic understanding of the brain as a working cognitive organiser. Luria proposed a model of brain functions that has three units. In general terms, these control the regulation of body tone and wakefulness (a neural system called Block 1); obtaining, processing and storing information (Block 2); and regulation of the complex cognitive activities of the brain (Block 3). Each of these units is organised into hierarchical zones. At the most basic level, the primary zone receives and transmits electrical impulses to the periphery of the brain. It is called the projection zone. The secondary (projection-association) zone represents the areas in which information is processed or plans are prepared, and the tertiary (or overlapping) zones connect a number of areas and are responsible for the most complex forms of mental activity. Let us consider each Block, or functional system.

Block 1: the first functional system

With the mapping of the activities of the reticular formation by Magoun and Moruzzi in the late 1940s (see Magoun 1963), the importance of the subcortex and the brain stem in maintaining and regulating cortical tone at an optimal level was established (Figure 4.1). This discovery supported the principle of vertical organisation of the brain structures and led to the isolation of the first Block of the brain.

The reticular formation assists in maintaining the optimal tonal balance of the brain through three sources of activation. The first source of activation manages the metabolic processes of the organism to maintain the homeostatic balance (e.g. keeping the body at the 'right' temperature). The second activation system is related to the arrival of stimuli from the environment and enables the organism to meet surprises, and is an important basis of investigative activity (e.g. hearing a gun shot). A link is, therefore, made between the environment and the mechanisms of memory and specific cortical areas, via ascending connections from the environment to the brain. The third source of activation is coupled with the organism's intent, that is, with planning and goal-directed activity. It is in maintaining the optimal energy input that the descending fibres of the reticular formation become important. These connections, apparently originating in the frontal regions

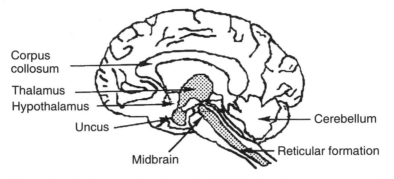

Figure 4.1 A schematic drawing of Luria's first functional system of the brain (the front of the brain is on the left)

of the cortex, transmit the regulatory intentions of the cortex to the subcortical structures. Luria (1973) referred to these descending fibres as the means through which the higher cortical levels of the brain engage the lower systems, thereby modulating their functions and affecting the most complex forms of conscious activity.

Block 2: the second functional system

Located in the lateral regions of the neocortex to the rear of the deep fissure in the folds of the surface of the brain (called the central sulcus), Block 2 includes the occipital (visual), temporal (auditory), and parietal (general sensory) lobes (Figure 4.2). This unit consists of the systems which have adapted to the reception, analysis, and storage of specific sensory information including olfactory and gustatory information, although it is often said that these two are of marginal prominence (tell that to a chef or wine buff!).

The neurons within these lobes or regions respond only to the specialised

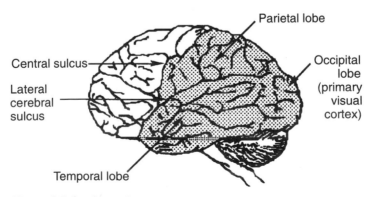

Figure 4.2 A schematic drawing of Luria's second functional system of the brain (the front of the brain is on the left)

stimuli characteristic of the particular sense represented, and they are also hierarchically arranged into one of three levels or zones. The primary zones of each cortical region predominantly contain cells that have high modal specificity. That is, they respond only to stimuli having specialised properties (e.g. to a particular tone, or movement in one direction) depending upon the modality they represent. Superimposed above these primary layers are the secondary or gnostic (i.e. thinking) levels that contain less modal specific (associative) neurons enabling incoming stimuli to be organised into useful patterns. Human thinking activity is polymodal in character, that is, it depends upon a large amount of information and, therefore, relies upon connections between the cortical regions and levels.

The tertiary level of neurons performs the integrative function that transmits information (or thoughts) from one region to others. These zones lie on the boundaries between the occipital, temporal, and postcentral cortex and are concentrated in the lower parietal region. The primary function of these zones is to organise discrete impulses entering the various regions and convert stimuli that have arrived in the brain in serial fashion into simultaneously processed groups of information. In the posterior regions, these zones transform visually or successively represented material into symbolic units. This includes the conversion of concrete information into abstract thinking which permits language operation, the development of grammatical and logical structures, and the comprehension of mathematical relationships. Each area in Block 2 appears to act interdependently to inform the organism of objects and events in the environment.

Block 3: the third functional system

Block 3 comprises the cortical area to the front of the central sulcus and facilitates the organisational aspects of conscious activity (Figure 4.3). Such activities in the main involve the creation of intentional behaviour; the formation of plans and action sequences; the regulation of behaviour according to these plans; and the checking or verification of a plan or action sequence in achieving the desired result. The frontal cortex, similar to Blocks 1 and 2, is divided into three zones: motor projection; secondary premotor; and the prefrontal divisions.

The outlet channel for the prefrontal region is the motor cortex located immediately behind the precentral sulcus in the prefrontal gyrus. This cortical area is projectional in character and contains the giant pyramidal tract of fibres which run to the spinal column, and then to the muscles. Whereas in Block 2, the impulse trajectory is mainly ascending (the excitation passing from the primary to secondary to the tertiary zones), Block 3 is largely a descending system. Plans are formulated in the tertiary (prefrontal) and secondary (premotor) zones and are subsequently passed to the primary (motor) zone which transmits motor impulses to the muscles. The second

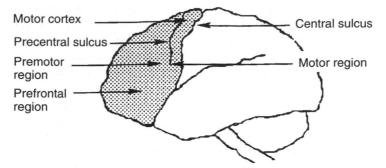

Figure 4.3 A schematic drawing of Luria's third functional system of the brain (the front of the brain is on the left)

characteristic is the absence of a modal-specific zone. Block 3 consists entirely of descending motor systems.

The secondary zone of Block 3 is the premotor area which consists of small pyramidal cells. It plays an organising role (of movements) similar to the secondary zones of the posterior regions of the brain which transform information into functionally organised units. Stimulation of the premotor area – which might occur during brain surgery – causes the firing of groups of systematically organised movements such as grasping or eye, head, or whole body movements.

The tertiary zone of Block 3 is localised in the prefrontal division of the brain, sometimes called the frontal granular cortex because of the lack of pyramidal cells. This cortical area – approximately one-third of the brain's mass – is chiefly responsible for the formation of intentions, plans, regulation and verification of behaviour. The prefrontal region has a vast system of two-way connections with all other parts of the cortex. It is, therefore, capable of receiving input from all over the brain, and initiating descending impulses through the premotor and motor areas. Using the linkages with Block 1, through connections with the reticular formation, the prefrontal cortex is intimately involved in the regulation of the activity state. Through connections with other cortical areas, the frontal lobes may be regarded as the superstructure above all parts of the cortex, performing the more universal function of general behaviour regulation.

COGNITION AND LURIA'S FUNCTIONAL ORGANISATION

Up until the 1970s, modest interest was shown in Luria's functional organisation despite the publication of his fascinating text, *Higher Cortical Functions in Man* (Luria 1966). In 1973, Luria published a popular volume called *The Working Brain* (1973), which outlined his model and provided compelling evidence. By the late 1960s, however, J.P. Das (at the University of Alberta in Edmonton, Canada), took a keen interest in Luria's approach and developed an 'information integration model' (Das *et al.* 1975) that operationalised Luria's functional organisation of the brain in information-processing terms, particularly those activities of the left hemisphere.

The Das *et al.* (1975) model included a sensory register (or input filter), a central processor (representing Luria's functional organisation of the brain), and an output unit. Since the early 1970s, however, Das and several colleagues conducted research that led to a refinement of the original model. Its current version is known as the PASS theory of intelligence – referring to *P*lanning, *A*ttention, *S*imultaneous, and *S*uccessive – and this is shown in Figure 4.4 (see Das *et al.* 1994). Briefly, stimuli (*Input*) are accepted through any receptor (sense or a variety of internal organs) as a complete unit (as in a simple drawing) or as parts of a sequence (as words are in speech). Das *et al.* (1994) referred to these methods of presentation as simultaneous and successive respectively. Stimuli then pass to the central processor which comprises three components: a unit which mediates arousal and attention (Block 1); one that mediates the encoding and decoding processes (i.e. Block 2 or the simultaneous and successive dimensions); and a third component that operates to make and enact plans, and make decisions (Block 3). These processes operate within the medium of the individual's knowledge base. Information then passes from the central processor as thoughts or actions depending upon the cognitive task being attempted in either a simultaneous or successive form.

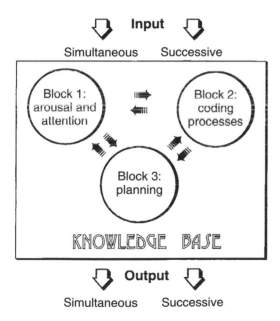

Figure 4.4 A schematic representation of the PASS theory of intelligence

Most of the research directed toward validation of the model, focused attention on Luria's second functional system that processes information in a simultaneous or successive fashion. These were neither new concepts, nor were they limited to the work of Das and his colleagues. A. Kaufman and N. Kaufman (1983) referred to simultaneous and sequential dimensions in their Kaufman Assessment Battery for Children (K-ABC), and also to comparable divisions reported in the work of Nebes (1974) and Neisser (1967). Interest in both the planning (Block 3) and attention (Block 1) components of Luria's model did not begin in earnest until Ashman's (1978) study of the relationship between planning and simultaneous and successive processes. Since then, there have been several studies that have described the nature of planning, and of attention.

One of the notable outcomes of this research has been the development of an assessment battery based upon the PASS model (described in Chapter 6).

Up to the present time, however, there has been no direct connection made between planning, attention, simultaneous and successive processes and electrochemical activities occurring in the brain. In other words, it has not been demonstrated that measures of planning, or other processes based on the Das *et al.* (1994) model are incompetently performed by persons who have damage to the relevant area of their brain. Such evidence would provide substantial validity for the model. Part of the reason for this lack of evidence is the difficulty one now finds in locating individuals who have focal lesions (i.e. damage to only a very specific area of the brain). Most neurology patients have damage to a number of areas in their brain due to major trauma caused through accidents, or tumours, and determining the most common causes of a deficit is difficult, if not impossible.

At this stage it would be useful to describe the four PASS dimensions as this will facilitate discussions about their influence on learning and problem-solving later in the book. In addition, it will obviate the need to redescribe them in the assessment and remediation sections.

Arousal and attention

Arousal refers to activity occurring within our brain that maintains our waking state, or level of alertness. In Luria's organisation of the brain, attention is linked to cortical arousal regulated by the hypothalamus (which keeps our metabolism at some optimum level of performance). There are many factors that might influence our level of arousal. Our physiological state can affect our brain functions. For example, if we have been deprived of sleep for a long period, we may not have sufficient arousal to make us aware of the two trucks approaching side-by-side at break-neck speed, or the sign warning us of a sharp bend in the road ahead. If we are ill, or using drugs, our state of arousal may decline. When we decide it is time for a nap or a sleep, we set up the conditions that suggest to our body that cortical activity can be wound down for the present time. However, arousal is also related to an orienting response that alerts us to new or novel stimuli coming to us from the environment and, hence, it brings into close association the concepts of arousal and attention. Can you recall being woken from a 'dead' sleep by the sound of a noise outside your bedroom?

Attention involves sustaining interest and selectivity. In other words, objects, events, and ideas come in and out of focus. At one point in time, we are clearly aware of certain objects and thoughts, and we 'pay attention' to them while at other times, they fade away to have their place taken in our awareness by some other object or thought. Fluctuations of attention – or shifts in attention – occur as long as we are awake.

Attention, therefore, refers to our awareness and sensitivity to objects, or events that are occurring, external or internal to the person or organism. We might need to maintain our attention to some task we are, or someone else is, performing, or we might attend to some object or event that is new or novel. In the first case, we refer to sustained attention, to a specific source of information over a period of time. On one hand, if the information is of interest (e.g. a fireworks display on a national holiday), we may sustain our attention for a long period of time with little effort. If, on the other hand, the information is of no interest (e.g. a lecture on cognitive processing, perhaps), or if it is boring or monotonous, it may take considerable effort to keep our mind focused, or to remain vigilant. Hence, the importance of the information to which we are attending, the quality and quantity of the target, and the duration over which we are required to remain attentive, will all affect our ability to sustain attention.

Selective attention requires us to make decisions about the information to which we are attending. We may be required to focus on one object or event, or we may need to shift our attention from stimuli to stimuli. Selective attention has been studied for several decades and can be measured physiologically using an electroencephalogram (EEG) as well as behaviourally. The EEG can identify small changes in electrical current that occur in various parts of the brain when electrodes are connected to the scalp. The pattern of electrical activity in the brain changes when the person recognises a target signal and this is recorded as evoked potentials which are clearly evident against the background pattern of wakefulness. The site of evoked potentials across the brain varies according to the task and may predominate in sensory projection areas of the brain. When we were young children, an evoked potential would have shown most activity in these specific areas then, with age, electrical activity would be seen to spread to the frontal lobes indicating their involvement in the processes of attention.

Coding processes

The term 'coding' refers to the input, storage, and retrieval of information. In other words, coding processes allow the individual to make sense of incoming stimuli (encoding), to establish links with knowledge already stored in the brain, and to identify relevant information needed to perform a task (decoding). Luria, and later Das and his colleagues, described two ways in which information is coded: simultaneously and successively.

Simultaneous processing occurs when information is synthesised into quasi-spatial, relational units. In other words, all of the parts of a unit of information are available at the same time. For example, if you were shown a drawing of the Union Jack (or the flag of any country) for only a second or two, you could reproduce the drawing with reasonable accuracy because all the elements of the flag can be seen at a glance. Similarly, trained musicians can tell which notes make up a chord because they know what each note sounds like in a chord structure. All the information is available at one time (see Figure 4.5).

In contrast, successive processing occurs when information is provided one bit (or unit) at a time. The best example of a successive processing task is digit span, to which we have referred earlier. If you are given a telephone number orally, one digit at a time, you do not know the complete number until the end. In this form of processing, the brain must hold each element active until all have been presented and meaning can be derived.

Trying to determine which process is being used at any time is difficult – if not impossible – because of the rich neural pathways that connect all parts of the cortex. Hence, what may seem like a task that depends upon simultaneous processing alone, may involve complex deconstruction and reconstruction within the cortex. Hence, both coding processes may be involved in most complex thinking activities (see Figure 4.6). As a result, most learning events are likely to require students to be competent simultaneous and successive (or serial) processors.

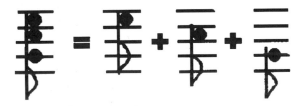

Figure 4.5 Individual notes making a C major chord, second inversion

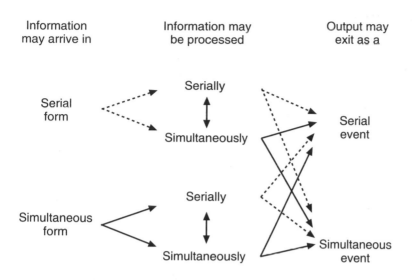

Figure 4.6 The possible involvement of simultaneous and serial processing in problem-solving

Planning

As we noted earlier, the planning processes are mediated by the frontal lobes of the brain. The concept, planning, has appeared in various psychology domains. It has been defined, for example, as the development of a sequence of actions, or the sequence itself (e.g. a plan). Tests of foresight and planning ability were included in the US Military Printed Classification Tests which were used in the 1940s as screening devices for military recruits, especially flight crew. The various planning tests involved preparing a series of manoeuvres or activities, and to foresee and avoid difficulties that could arise in their execution (see Berger *et al.* 1957; Guilford and Lacey 1947).

Plans and strategies entered the field of information processing following the release of *Plans and the Structure of Behavior* (Miller *et al.* 1960). These authors provided a description of an organisational system that included plans (which we would now probably call strategies) and metaplans which were strategies for generating plans. In dealing with new or known situations, the individual draws upon metaplans which are stored in memory and provide the mechanism for generating new plans. While there were a number of criticisms of the Miller *et al.* (1960) approach, the ideas are still quite contemporary (see e.g. Belmont and Mitchell 1987).

There have been many other views of the nature of planning and several approaches have attempted to describe the process in adults and even in children aged 3 to 4 years (see e.g. Hudson and Fivush 1991). Some writers have dealt with planning as an opportunistic activity with five dimensions:

- The first identifies the intended action.
- The second identifies suitable sequences of events or procedures.
- The third deals with observations and data relevant to the planning process.
- The fourth allocates cognitive resources to the plan.
- The fifth identifies decisions about the enactment of the plan.

(Hayes-Roth and Hayes-Roth 1979)

Others have examined the use of plans in the course of our daily lives. For example, Byrne (1979; 1981) studied the strategic activity of expert adults in several everyday situations such as organising dinner parties and interior decorating. In his two studies, Byrne analysed spoken records of subjects 'thinking aloud' while they worked through the problem of deciding upon menus and ingredients for specific recipes, or colours and furnishings used in decorating a house. He argued that planning involved the search of a complex and structured body of information which consisted of several interrelated parts. In his study of mental cookery, he suggested that cooking procedures were imagined during the preparation of the menus. By mentally executing plans in this way, we construct, test, and refine actions when real-world trials might be inappropriate.

More recently, Saariluoma and Hohlfeld (1994) examined long-range planning in chess and found that the time and effort that some players wasted in considering just one alternative solution, effectively limited their finding a solution to the game dilemma. Studies of students with an intellectual disability have connected poor planning to deficits in the person's visual scanning competence (Szepkouski et al. 1994).

In quite a different context, Dixon (1987) developed a framework for understanding how people construct mental plans for carrying out written directions. He proposed that directions are used to construct mental plans within a hierarchical structure. The top level of a plan hierarchy is a general, high-level description of the action to be performed, for example, 'Bake a banana cake' and the lower levels of the hierarchy specify the component actions in detail (see Figure 4.7).

Each element in the hierarchy may be represented by schema that describe a standard way of carrying out a given step.

Plans are constructed in parallel with other complex processes such as reading a recipe book. As soon as the information needed for the plan becomes available, it is incorporated into the emerging plan. Dixon argued that for efficient planning, information relevant to the top level of the plan hierarchy should be given at the beginning of the directions (for example, at the beginning of a sentence, passage or recipe) and that information relevant to the lower levels of planning can be provided as required (as in the example above).

Finally, the motivation and availability of skills necessary for the imple-

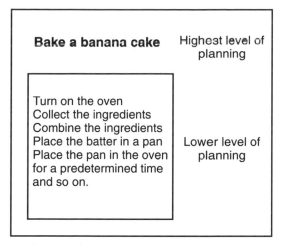

Figure 4.7 Mental plans with a hierarchy structure

mentation of planning has taken the study of planning into the realm of personality theory. One interesting facet of this research has been the identification of planning styles to account for the reasons different individuals may have for selecting alternative steps in the planning process.

Planning style refers not to ways in which plans are constructed, but to the significance of the content to the individual. In the mid 1980s, for example, Kreitler and Kreitler (1986) suggested that some cues may be recognised more readily than others when they have special importance to an individual. People who are disposed toward emotional responses will notice affective cues and solve problems containing emotional information faster, and have a richer network of affective associations than others for whom affect is of less importance.

NEUROPSYCHOLOGY, COGNITIVE THEORY, AND EDUCATIONAL PRACTICE

Education involves not only learning new information but also problem-solving. This is the case at the level of early childhood, primary, secondary, tertiary and career education. It is also relevant in the less formal learning that occurs throughout our lives (e.g. when we plan a vacation, work or hobby, or even a night of entertainment with friends). We could look at the process of education as an exercise in problem-solving involving the acquisition of new information (i.e. learning about the world, society, and the culture in which we live), and dealing with the broad range of situations we encounter that require the integration of information, priority setting, and finding solutions to problems.

Neuropsychology and cognitive theory can assist our understanding of how we go about learning and problem-solving, especially when we consider how we integrate existing knowledge with stimuli that may originate inside or outside of the individual. It is important to realise that cognition is not simply attention, coding, memory, metacognition, or planning, but a fusion of brain activities. While researchers may have focused their attention on individual aspects of cognition in their efforts to understand specific processes, most learning and problem-solving activities are immensely complex neurological events.

Consider, for example, a situation in which you experience trouble with your car driving home. Certainly your senses will bring information about the nature of the problem to you. The engine might splutter, there might be a sickening clunking noise, or there may simply be silence that informs you that something terrible has occurred. After the initial exclamation, 'Oh no!', most adults begin a process of ascertaining what has taken place. Experience plays a role in the success of this problem-solving activity. If a glance at the petrol gauge reveals an empty tank, the solution might be obvious. But if all the engine systems have been working smoothly up to that time, the solution may not be quite so easy. Often we go through a trial-and-error process to determine what has gone wrong and generate a number of specific and general plans for dealing with the situation.

We go through similar processes when we are asked to, for example, write a short essay about our last vacation, or solve the following algebra problem: $(a + b - c) \times (a + d) = ?$ In each case, we draw upon knowledge of prior experiences, formulated into a plan to deal with the task requirements confronting us.

COGNITIVE MECHANISMS INVOLVED IN PROBLEM-SOLVING

As we indicated above, problem-solving is an extremely complex activity that involves intellectual skills (e.g. reading, number), knowledge, and cognitive strategies and metastrategies that modify attention, perception, the input and storage of information, and the retrieval of knowledge from memory. In the context of problem-solving, strategies are tools that enable us to select and operate upon intellectual skills.

In summary, to solve a specific problem, several proficiencies are required. Learners need skills that enable them to comprehend symbol systems and rules governing the relationship between objects and events. They need to demonstrate their knowledge of symbols and rules by expressing them, and they need competence in manipulating and integrating information – being received, or already available – that is relevant to the problem. Problem-solving is, therefore, the embodiment of cognitive theory.

Representing problems

When a problem is encountered, we form a picture in our minds about the nature of the task. This is called the problem representation. There are two dimensions to problem representation. First, we need to know what facts are presented and how they relate to one another within the problem. This is called the task environment. For example, when our car runs out of petrol, we make the connection between the petrol gauge and the status of fuel in the petrol tank, and the link between fuel and ignition that provides power to the engine. Second, we must know where to look in our knowledge base to find information about the task. This is called the problem space. Even for very simple tasks, the problem space we explore is very large. Again, using the petrol example, we ask ourself, 'When did I last get petrol?' 'Does the petrol gauge work?' 'Could there be a more serious problem?' 'Where is the nearest petrol station?' 'How will I get petrol to the car without a petrol can?'

The way we search the problem space leads us to seek solutions that are non-random, that is, we move in more, rather than less promising directions. For example, if we detect the problem, 'Out of petrol', we may consider, 'Noticed a petrol station two miles back. It will take twenty minutes to reach the station. Ring and cancel my appointment. Ask to borrow a can.' And so on. Problems that are poorly presented or ill structured may be very difficult, if not impossible to solve. For example, the following is an ill-structured problem, 'How can we help people who are at war with each other live together in harmony?'

Problem-solving is concerned with finding patterns in the information presented to us. Pattern recognition is one feature that distinguishes novices from experts. A novice is a person who is newly acquainted with a task, or problem situation. For example, someone learning chess will not be familiar with the hundreds of 'standard' moves that chess champions know and use as a matter of course. An expert is considered to be someone who is intimately familiar with the structure of a knowledge base and can use it to advantage. Again, a chess expert is familiar with the standard moves and can recognise the dangers inherent in an opponent's play. Hence, experts recognise patterns more quickly than novices because of their experience and their ability to look at the whole, rather than at individual pieces of information. Expert chess players, for example, see 'typical' patterns in the placement of the pieces, and recognise how to move toward 'Check' or 'Checkmate' from a particular move. This is how chess experts can compete against many players at the same time, and how experienced physicians can diagnose diseases quickly by observing a pattern of symptoms.

Successful problem-solvers are deliberate. They attend to the circumstances confronting them, integrate information quickly, and are able to generate and modify plans to suit the changing circumstances. Thus, problem-solving is not a random activity but involves the use of all our information processing talents.

PROBLEM-SOLVING

Successful problem-solving is a systematic procedure. It involves the examination of all information and the methods available to help solve a problem. The process of problem-solving can be divided into three phases:

1   The *declarative phase* in which the person receives and interprets the instructions, and generates a procedure to deal with the problem.
2   The *knowledge collection phase* in which the learner generates procedures (activities or productions) for a given task.
3   The *procedural learning phase* which occurs after a skill has been established.

(Ashman and Conway 1989)

Whether the goal of problem-solving is the solution of a puzzle or learning how to do mathematical calculations, the process is much the same.

PROBLEM-SOLVING AND COGNITIVE EDUCATION

Cognitive education refers to the application of cognitive theory and methods to education in its broadest sense. Education (as we suggested in Chapter 1) is the process of learning, and learning to learn – which itself is a problem-solving endeavour. Cognitive education, therefore, involves learning how to solve problems. However, as we have stated elsewhere (Ashman *et al.* 1994), students in school – and indeed, in many other educational contexts – are rarely provided with instruction or experiences that allow them to learn about learning, and learn about problem-solving.

On the surface, the process would appear to be quite simple. It should involve focusing attention on how to derive maximum information from the learning or problem-solving situation, how to formulate a suitable strategy for dealing with the task at hand, how to enact the strategy, and monitor performance until the goal is achieved. However, this can be said much more easily than it can be achieved. Let us examine the 'what' and 'how' components of problem-solving.

The skills required

A synthesis of the problem-solving literature provides a list of skills needed to enhance problem-solving abilities. There has been some debate about whether there is a single set (or small number) of problem-solving elements that can be applied to a large number of tasks (domain-general skills), or whether problem-solving simply means having very specific knowledge that is relevant to a particular problem (domain-specific skills). Our view is that both forms of skills are needed.

In some cases, the learner can be given explicit instruction on what must be done to solve a particular problem, while in other cases, only general directions may be required to initiate the process. In the early 1980s, Doyle (1983) distinguished between direct and indirect instruction for problem-solving. The former provides systematic and explicit problem-solving directions with attention being given to the sequence of events and the development of cognitive skills. Direct instruction appears to be more suitable for novice learners and students with intellectual disabilities. Indirect instruction involves the teaching of higher level cognitive processes with students being left to discover appropriate problem-solving procedures and their application to other activities. Doyle suggested that indirect instruction appears more appropriate for older students who have established basic skills and suitable knowledge bases.

How to teach problem-solving skills

There have been several proposals about how problem-solving skills should be developed. Most researchers have concentrated on detailing procedures which relate to a limited range of well-defined problems. For example, Derry et al. (1987) reported a set of procedures for remediating arithmetic skills using a problem solving orientation which included many of the theoretical elements outlined above. However, concern with the need for generalisable problem-solving procedures has led to approaches that may be applied to a range of cognitive activities.

In Fredericksen's (1984) review of cognitive theory and problem-solving, he listed details of how a general class of problems might be addressed. These included several points that prompt the learner to structure the problem-solving activity, including the following:

- Get the complete picture without being concerned about the small details.
- Withhold judgement until all relevant information has been gathered.
- Simplify the problem using words, diagrams, symbols or equations.
- Try changing the way the problem is presented.
- State questions and vary the form of the question.
- Remain flexible in approach and challenge the assumption being made.
- Try working backwards.
- Work toward sub-goals that are part solutions.
- Use analogies and metaphors.
- Verbalise the problem.

A simple problem-solving sequence was suggested by Bransford et al. (1986) in the form of an easily learned mnemonic. IDEAL is the mnemonic for Identify, Define, Explore, Act, Look. Let's deal briefly with each step.

Identify

Identification suggests that the first stage of problem-solving is the recognition that a problem exists. Although this may appear trite, novices and low-ability learners are less likely than others to recognise a problem. For example, novice chess players may not recognise that they are one move away from being in 'Checkmate'. Students with a reading disability may not recognise that a passage of text contains incomplete or inconsistent information, or that irrelevant information has been included. As a consequence, low-ability students fail to deal with the inconsistency and it becomes a hindrance to the process of solving the task (Englert *et al.* 1987).

Define

Once there is recognition that a problem exists, students must have the ability to analyse what the problem is (i.e. to define the source of the problem). Some ineffective problem-solvers do not take the time necessary to consider the root of the problem and, as a consequence, they are unable to identify a suitable strategy.

Explore

Exploration refers to the student's collection of information about the problem and its sources. This is the strategy selection phase of problem-solving when various options might be considered depending upon the type and nature of the task.

Act and look

Once the problem has been identified, defined and explored, the student uses the resources available to act and to maintain a watch on the success of the chosen strategy. A monitoring procedure is used by successful problem-solvers to amend their activity when they encounter stumbling blocks. In contrast, students with an intellectual disability tend not to adapt their activity to suit the new demands of the task. For instance, Byrnes and Spitz (1977) reported that low-ability students tended to repeat their errors when unable to complete the problem. They reported that the youngest children in their study committed many rule violations following wrong initial moves. Instead of profiting from their mistakes, and in spite of the need to obey the rules to succeed, they repeatedly made errors and rule violations. Similar inflexibility has been noted in the strategic and problem-solving behaviour of learning-disabled children (Gerber 1983).

SUMMARY

In this chapter we have established a link between intelligent human behaviour and the complex cognitive processes that take place in the brain. We reviewed Luria's functional organisation of the brain and its adaptation by Das and his colleagues into an information-processing model which involves planning, attention, simultaneous and successive processing.

We also began to establish a link between cognitive theories based in memory and in brain functions, with complex learning and problem-solving activities. What should be clear is that researchers and those who build models on memory, planning and problem-solving are using common features if not necessarily the same terms in their conceptualisation of human thinking.

Here, our discussion of the nature and character of problem-solving has introduced a practical component to cognitive theory, one for which the potential exists for the establishment of close links with educational practice both in terms of the assessment of cognitive functions and the development of effective and efficient teaching-learning programmes. In Chapter 5 we begin with a discussion of assessment procedures based on cognitive theory.

STUDY TASKS

4.1 In note form, list the main points covered in this chapter.

4.2 From memory, sketch Luria's three Blocks of the brain and in each diagram note the main function performed in each.

4.3 We referred to simultaneous and successive processing in the chapter. Make a list of skills or activities that you think depend more on simultaneous than successive processing, more on successive than simultaneous processing, and those you think are impossible to classify. What makes it difficult to classify some tasks or activities?

4.4 Review the section on problem-solving in the chapter. Imagine that you have to teach a child how to tie shoe laces. Think about how you would do this, write it down, and indicate the purpose of each step in terms of the problem-solving process.

ADDITIONAL READING

Brown, S.I. and Walter, M.I. (1990) *The Art of Problem Posing*, 2nd edn, Hillsdale, NJ: Erlbaum.

Gerhard Strube, G. and Wender, K.F. (eds) (1993) *The Cognitive Psychology of Knowledge*, Amsterdam: North-Holland.

Naatanen, Risto (1992) *Attention and Brain Function*, Hillsdale, NJ: Erlbaum.

Temple, C. (1993) *The Brain: An Introduction to the Psychology of the Human Brain and Behaviour*, Harmondsworth: Penguin.

Chapter 5

The tradition of psychoeducational assessment

For as long as human beings have stood upright on the Earth, their performance and skills have been measured. For Neanderthal men and women, assessment would have been in quite a different form than it is in classrooms and other educational settings today, but assessment of human competence and versatility nevertheless is as old as the human race. That Neanderthal families existed was a measure of how successful, creative, and 'intelligent' the family members were. Gathering food, trapping animals and fish, protecting themselves from hostile neighbours, and avoiding being eaten themselves, was an indicator of their mastery over the environment. The Aboriginal peoples of Australia – arguably the oldest civilisation – also attest to the achievements, accomplishments, and intelligence of several nations of people who have settled both desolate, barren land and lush and fertile country, and skilfully survived.

In this chapter we explore the issue of measurement of human intellectual capabilities. We do not trace the measurement of intelligence from our human forebears, but we do consider developments that have taken place during the 1900s. We begin by considering the process of assessment.

THE PROCESS OF ASSESSMENT

What is assessment, and how is it different from testing and evaluation? The three terms are often used interchangeably but they have different meanings.

Assessment is the process of collecting information about someone to identify or confirm a problem, or to make decisions. Assessment may involve information gathered from a test, or collecting other information that might comprise a folio of work, such as examples of a child's writing over a year or more.

Testing has been around almost since the beginning of recorded history. In China over 4,000 years ago, it was common to examine officials every three years to determine their fitness for office. Testing implies the use of an existing measuring device or instrument designed to gather data in a particular way on a specific topic or area of knowledge. In psychoeducational assessment, we have a vast array of measures including intelligence tests, achievement tests (measuring acquired knowledge in a school-related area), or personality tests or related concepts (such as extroversion, and self-concept).

Evaluation is often used to refer to quality. Popham (1993: 7), for example, defined evaluation as follows: 'Systematic educational evaluation consists of a formal appraisal of the quality of educational phenomena'. This definition implies the determination of worth rather than (necessarily) performance. Hence, we might evaluate the effectiveness of a reading programme or a social skills training package.

For the purpose of this book, we have adopted assessment as a generic term, as educators and related professional people are concerned with collecting qualitative and quantitative data that may provide information for a range of purposes. Salvia and Ysseldyke (1995), for example, identified a number of reasons for assessment:

- referral – to identify general areas in which more comprehensive testing might be required, or to clarify to whom an individual might be sent for assistance
- screening – to identify potential problems
- documentation of special learning needs – to determine how the student may be advantaged by special assistance
- eligibility – to qualify a student for a special education programme
- instructional planning – to clarify or specify how a student with a specific learning need might be taught
- placement decisions – to gather data to determine where a student may be placed for the most appropriate programme or services
- student progress – to monitor day-to-day performance or the success of a programme
- programme evaluation – to determine the effectiveness of education programmes at the local, regional, state, or national level (e.g. to assist educational planning or policy-making)
- accountability – to determine the general performance of schools in achieving educational goals for all students.

The most common purpose of psychoeducational assessment appears to be the determination of what individuals have, or have not, learned over a period of instruction (e.g. a school year), or over the course of their lives. This practice is translated into assessment goals that relate to the specification and verification of problems being experienced by students and to decisions about them (Salvia and Ysseldyke 1995). Assessment may not always be aimed at finding problems. For example, assessment might be conducted to determine if a young person would benefit from a programme designed for gifted or talented students. However, assessment also seems to have become the *raison d'être* for educational clinicians and for some teachers. Clinicians, such as psychologists and counsellors, can spend a considerable part of their professional lives administering and scoring standardised psychological and achievement tests with the objective of identifying, screening, and classifying students. Teachers also spend a good portion of their professional lives preparing students for assessment, and administering and scoring tests that provide evidence of mastery over the curriculum (Paris 1995). The commitment to testing, however, varies from country to country, region to region within countries, and even from one school to another.

Several writers have argued that educational testing has moved beyond its functional value. McLaughlin (1991), for example, argued that few tests measure attributes or variables that are directly related to learning, higher order thinking, or problem-solving. Because tests do not explore the complex cognitive processes underlying performance, they do not support classroom practices that are directed toward teaching them. In the United States, in particular, students recognise that certain types of learning are of little value (if any) and teachers complain that students (and parents) focus on test scores alone and dismiss the knowledge that will afford them a deep understanding of the subject area (Paris 1995).

INTELLIGENCE AND INTELLIGENCE TESTING

Until the turn of the nineteenth century, few people concerned themselves with intelligence or achievement tests. Certainly there was interest in the acquisition of knowledge, but this was evaluated in practical ways: the ability to learn and practise a trade or skill, to survive in an unfriendly environment and, for a chosen few, to read, learn, and eventually teach about literature, the arts, philosophy, and religion.

While the forefathers of contemporary psychology measured human cognitive characteristics (such as memory), it was not until Alfred Binet and his colleagues developed the first 'test of intelligence' in the early 1900s that psychoeducational assessment leapt into prominence. In fact, it was not so much Binet's test, or its translation into English by Henry Goddard in 1908, but its adaptation by Terman and Merrill at Stanford University during the years 1910 to 1916, that instilled the now common phenomenon of intelligence testing into western society.

It would be useful at this point to reflect on Binet's intentions when developing his test. In 1904, the French Ministry for Public Education established a commission to develop an assessment procedure to determine which children could or could not benefit from the regular school programme offered at the time. The Commission was given a mandate to determine policy on the appropriate type of educational establishment, the condition of administration, the teaching staff, and pedagogical standards. Binet based his test on his own view of the theory of intelligence and collected a series of short tasks that reflected competence in daily life (e.g.

counting coins) – tasks involving basic reasoning processes which would allow children to respond positively to the education methods and procedures being used at that time.

Binet conceived intelligence as a fundamental human faculty that involved judgement, initiative, and adaptation to a set of circumstances, with emphasis being placed on attention and memory as a means of assessing judgement. His initial test consisted of fifty-four measures and was administered first to children at the Salpêtrière (the old, famous mental hospital), then to normal and 'mentally deficient' primary school aged children in Parisian schools. By 1908, Binet's final product was validated using large groups of children to ensure standardisation at age levels between 3 and 12 years. The intention was not to deny education to children who performed poorly on the test, but to provide them with alternative educational opportunities that would assist them to learn effectively.

Binet also was circumspect about the meaning of the score the child would receive after having completed the test. He wanted to identify intelligence as being separate from instruction and, therefore, none of the test items required reading, writing, or rote memorisation. He also declined to define and speculate upon the meaning of the score he derived for each child after testing. He believed that intelligence was a complex concept that could not be captured by a single number. However, it was not long before the intelligence quotient was defined as the mental age divided by chronological age, and the intelligence quotient (IQ) came into being (Gould 1981).

As we can see from the comments above, assessment of intelligence was originally linked to educational provisions. The test provided an indication of the student's level of functional knowledge, although it gave little insight into an individual's relative strengths or weakness.

Binet died in 1911, but his legacy remained. In the years following the release of the Stanford Binet, there was a dramatic expansion in the use of psychological and educational tests. Without doubt, the entry of the United States into the First World War advanced the cause of intelligence testing. As Cronbach (1975) noted,

> It was in the Spring of 1917 that Lewis Terman filled a briefcase with material of the group intelligence test his student Arthur Otis had just designed, and went East to meet with other leading psychologists of the time. Within weeks they had organized the Army Alpha Examination for use in testing recruits.
>
> (Cronbach 1975: 1)

The Army Alpha, devised for those who were literate, appears to have been based largely on the Binet scale. It included tests of arithmetic, information, practical judgement, synonyms and antonyms, disarranged sentences, number series completion and analysis. The Army Beta was devised for illiterate service personnel and included maze tests, cube analysis, X-O series, digit symbol, number checking, picture completion and geometric construction.

Under the direction of Robert Yerkes, over 1.7 million recruits were tested with a somewhat surprising result. Yerkes (1921) reported that the average mental age of white American servicemen was 13 years. This can be compared with the accepted standard at the time, which was 16 years.

In the late 1930s there were two notable events that established intelligence testing as part of the ongoing fabric of North American life, if not the western world. In 1937, Terman and Merrill produced the first revision of the Stanford Binet which consisted of two equivalent forms, the L and M and, in 1939, David Wechsler introduced the Wechsler Bellevue Intelligence Scale which would later become the Wechsler Adult Intelligence Scale (WAIS). Wechsler claimed that one of the primary objectives in its preparation was the provision of an intelligence test suitable for adults, and that as previous tests were designed for children, the items were of little interest to adults.

Since the early 1940s, there have been adaptations and revisions to both the Binet and Wechsler scales although their form has remained largely the same as it was in the original versions. Testing became a multimillion-dollar industry and the IQ was soon accepted as the most valid indicator of a person's mental capacity. Terman relentlessly emphasised the problem of limited intelligence, the inevitability of the consequences, and that there was an obligation on the part of society to restrain and eliminate those of low intelligence. He stated, 'Not all criminals are feeble-minded, but all feeble-minded persons are at least potential criminals. That every feeble-minded woman is a potential prostitute would hardly be disputed by anyone' (Terman 1916: 11).

INFORMATION FROM PSYCHOEDUCATIONAL TESTS

Psychoeducational testing had its foundations in early experimental psychology and the intelligence testing movement. The latter remains a potent influence on educational practice and the nature of intelligence and its supposed non-modifiability is still debated in the professional literature. A second and more pragmatic influence on the testing movement is found in the use of instruments that were designed to evaluate achievement to classify students for placement in regular or special programmes. These include any one of a hundred tests of academic achievement, aptitude, general ability, specific skill, or self-perception. The overwhelming majority of tests measure the status of the learner at a specific time, using a given test.

Tests that required children or adults to answer questions and solve problems without help we referred to earlier as static tests. They provide a sample of some personal characteristics (e.g. knowledge, and the ability to follow directions) and these samples are assumed to be representative of general concepts such as intelligence or achievement. Tests of intelligence and achievement, in particular, have come under considerable criticism since the mid-1970s because of three characteristics: their bias against minority groups and those with identifiable learning difficulties; their inability to separate out the contributions of motivation, personality, and setting; and their inability to provide information that can be usefully translated into instructional practices.

A third influence on psychoeducational testing is the beliefs held about assessment by those using the tests. In the middle of the twentieth century, there was a pervasive view that one's intellectual capabilities were determined by some combination of heredity and early learning experiences (i.e. the environment) and those capabilities were fixed (i.e. not modifiable – you could not increase or decrease your IQ except in the latter case through brain damage). More recently, Tzuriel and Haywood (1992: 7) argued that changes to testing methods have come about because of the 'democratisation and humanisation of the education system', and by an acceptance that static tests favour some segments of the population over others (and hence, are biased). Despite these comments, the culture of psychoeducational assessment remains entrenched in many educational systems.

Intellectual ability and neurological assessment

Standard intelligence tests are still available and are commonly used instruments by school psychologists, educational psychologists, and counselling and guidance practitioners who have been specially trained in their administration and scoring. They are used primarily to determine exceptionality (children and adults who are well below or well above the average ability of people who are of the same age in the community), and often eligibility for placement in special education programmes.

Revised versions of tests first developed between 1911 and 1939 remain the most commonly used individual, standardised instruments. While it is beyond the scope of this book to describe the many standardised tests that are used by psychologists or other clinicians, we have chosen the most common to outline here, primarily to familiarise the reader with aspects of human behaviour assessed in the domains of intelligence and brain function. It is important to realise, however, that two tests that claim to measure the same constructs (e.g. intelligence, verbal comprehension, short-term memory) may differ significantly in the way in which they sample behaviour and may, therefore, produce different results or – in the case of intelligence – different IQ scores. Most test designers, however, compare performance on their new tests with performance on existing tests in the relevant domain. The concept is called concurrent validity and the evaluation of concurrent validity gives the designer an indication of how well the new and old tests appear to be measuring the same construct.

Wechsler scales

David Wechsler developed his original intelligence test – the Wechsler Bellevue Intelligence Scale – in 1939. In 1949, a children's version of the scale was developed using the same subtests and it became the popular Wechsler Intelligence Scale for Children (WISC). In 1955 the Wechsler Bellevue was revised and called the Wechsler Adult Intelligence Scale (WAIS). An additional version for pre-school and lower primary students – the Wechsler Preschool and Primary Scale of Intelligence (WPPSI) – was released in 1967.

Since then, the WISC, WAIS, and WPPSI have been revised and/or re-normed several times. Subtests of each instrument assess either verbal or non-verbal intelligence, which indicates individuals' capacity to deal with the world in which they live. Short versions of the Wechsler scales are sometimes used when it is not feasible or practical to administer the complete test. Vocabulary (from the Verbal subscale) and Block Design (from the Performance subscale) constitute the briefest short version, although the estimated IQ derived from these two subtests can be taken only as indicative. Other subtests can be added to improve the IQ estimate (see Sattler 1992).

Wechsler scales are arguably the most commonly used English language tests of intelligence. M.S. Wilson and Reschly (1996) showed that they were used three times more frequently by their sample of school psychologists than other cognitive/intelligence measures (see Box 5.1 for a description of subtests in the third edition of the WISC).

Stanford Binet (fourth edition)

The Stanford Binet scale was first developed by Lewis Terman at Stanford University in 1916 from a translation of the original test devised by Alfred Binet in France. Although the Stanford Binet was the first major individual test of intelligence to be used in the United States, it now appears to be the test of second choice for many psychologists. The fourth edition of the Stanford Binet was released in 1985 and is a substantial revision of earlier editions. It is now more like the Wechsler scales, as the fourth edition (developed by R.L. Thorndike *et al.* 1985) includes fifteen subtests that are grouped into four domains: verbal reasoning, quantitative reasoning, abstract/visual reasoning, and short-term memory (see Box 5.2).

British Abilities Test (BAS) and Differential Ability Scales (DAS)

The BAS is an individually administered intelligence test developed in the United Kingdom by Elliott *et al.* (1983) and is suitable for children and adolescents aged 2 years 6 months to 17 years 6 months. It has twenty-three subtests spread across six areas: speed of information processing; reasoning (formal operational thinking skills, matrices, similarities, and social reasoning);

Box 5.1

Wechsler Intelligence Scale for Children (WISC-III)

The WISC-III was released in 1991. Like the adult and pre-school scales, it takes approximately one hour to administer, depending upon the age and ability of the child to whom it is being given. An IQ score is derived with a mean of 100 and standard deviation of 15 (this means that approximately 68 per cent of the population would gain scores between 85 and 115; 100 ± 15). Norms are based on a sample of 2,200 children aged 6.5 to 16.5 years in the United States. Reliability data are provided for the WISC-III and validity data (high correlation between the WISC-III and WISC-R) suggest that the test measures what is thought to be intelligence in a systematic and consistent manner.

The WISC-III (like other Wechsler scales) is divided into two dimensions: Verbal subtests and Performance subtests.

Verbal subtests

*   *Information* – requires answers to factual questions expected to be known by children within the ages of 6.5 and 16.5 years
*   *Comprehension* – requires explanations of customs or cultural values
*   *Similarities* – requires the identification of common features among seemingly unrelated stimuli
*   *Arithmetic* – requires the person to solve mental arithmetic problems
*   *Vocabulary* – requires an explanation of the meaning of words
*   *Digit span* – requires the recall of a series of digits given by the presenter

Performance subtests

*   *Picture completion* requires the person to identify missing parts in a picture
*   *Picture arrangement* requires the sequencing of pictures into a story that makes logical sense
*   *Block design* requires copying two colour patterns using small cubes
*   *Object assembly* requires the construction of objects with jigsaw puzzle type stimuli
*   *Coding* requires copying symbols that represent numbers
*   *Symbol search* (a substitute for Coding) requires searching for a pattern of symbols among a large search group
*   *Mazes* (a substitute for Coding) requires tracing a path through a series of mazes

---

spatial imagery (block design, rotation of letter-like forms, and visualisation of cubes); perceptual matching (copying, matching letter-like forms, and verbal tactile matching); short-term memory (recall of designs and digits, immediate and delayed visual recall, and visual recognition); and retrieval and

Box 5.2

Stanford Binet Intelligence Scale (fourth edition)

This is an individual test which takes approximately one hour for administration, depending upon the age and ability of the person to whom it is being given. An IQ score is derived with a mean of 100 and standard deviation of 16. The extensive set of norms providing validity and reliability data suggest that the test measures what is thought to be intelligence in a systematic and consistent manner, and has been normed in the United States.

Verbal reasoning

- *Vocabulary* – requires an explanation of the meaning of words
- *Comprehension* – requires an explanation of why something is done or should be done
- *Absurdities* – requires an explanation of why the pictures shown in the test make no sense
- *Verbal relations* – requires an explanation of why three elements of a group of items are the same and a fourth is different

Quantitative reasoning

- *Quantitative* – requires mathematical computations
- *Number series* – requires finding the missing number in a series based upon a systematic pattern in the number series
- *Equation building* – requires the ordering of elements to make an equation

Abstract/Visual reasoning

- *Pattern analysis* – requires forming patterns using a form board (for younger children) or set of cubes (for older persons)
- *Copying* – requires copying designs using blocks or with a pencil and paper
- *Matrices* – requires selection of a pattern to fit into a larger pattern
- *Paper folding and cutting* – requires determining what shape would be formed by a drawing depicting a piece of paper cut and folded in a specified way

Short-term memory

- *Bead memory* – requires identification of a bead or a bead string shown for a short period
- *Memory for sentences* – requires the repetition of sentences read to the person
- *Memory for digits* – requires the recall of a series of digits given by the presenter
- *Memory for objects* – requires the recall of a series of objects from a set shown a short time after the presentation of the original items

---

application of knowledge (vocabulary, word reading, verbal comprehension, word definitions, verbal fluency, basic arithmetic, and early number skills).

Scoring of the test produces a general, visual, verbal, and short form IQ. Age-graded scales provide an extensive assessment of the mental abilities of children and adolescents comparable to the Stanford Binet, Wechsler and Kaufman tests. In addition, the test provides school achievement measures of number skills and word reading, and Piagetian variables of formal operational thinking and conservation.

Elliott moved to the United States and constructed the Differential Ability Scales using the same framework as the BAS (Elliott 1990). It is also an individually administered test measuring seventeen cognitive abilities and three achievement levels in children aged 2 years 6 months to 17 years 11 months. Pre-school and school-aged children receive a slightly different set of tests. These include block building, verbal comprehension, picture similarities, naming vocabulary, and general conceptual ability for the younger children. Older children are assessed on verbal ability, number skills, general conceptual ability, non-verbal reasoning (e.g. matrices), spatial ability (design recall, pattern construction), and speed of information processing. Basic number skills, spelling, and word reading are also assessed for children aged from 6 years to 17 years 11 months to evaluate school achievement. This test is reported to have excellent psychometric properties and has been standardised on a US population.

Peabody Picture Vocabulary Test-Revised (PPVT-R)

The PPVT-R was developed by Dunn and Dunn (1981) as a norm-referenced measure of receptive vocabulary. The original test was released in 1959. The test can be administered to persons between the ages of 2 years 6 months and 40 years, and involves a series of line drawings which relate to statements read by the tester. For each set, the person identifies the picture among a set of four drawings to which a statement refers. The PPVT-R is not a test of intelligence, but a test of receptive vocabulary and can serve as a screening test for some learning problems.

Neurological assessments

Neurological assessments are commonly used only when there is the likelihood of brain damage being implicated in a learning difficulty. Most test batteries were developed in the 1940s and 1950s and have been used extensively by clinical psychologists to identify functional losses in patients who have head injuries. The most commonly used were developed by Halstead and Reitan and appear as the Halstead-Reitan Neuropsychological Test Battery for Older Children aged between 9 and 14 years (see Lezak [1976] 1995; Reitan and Wolfson 1993).

Neuropsychological batteries share a number of common measures including a Category Test (measuring concept formation), Tactual Performance (measuring sensorimotor ability), Finger Tapping (measuring fine motor speed) and an Aphasia Screening Test (measuring expressive and receptive language). The batteries assess a wide range of intellectual functions including visual-motor performance, alertness and sustained attention, sensory-perceptual ability, and flexibility and abstraction. Performance on some of the subtests appears to be related to intellectual ability especially in measures of problem-solving, language, and auditory-perceptual analysis (Sattler 1992).

A third collection of subtests that appears to be used less frequently than the Halstead-Reitan battery is called the Luria-Nebraska Neuropsychological Battery (Golden 1987; Golden *et al.* 1985). The tests are intended to diagnose general and specific cognitive deficits, including lateralisation and localisation of focal brain impairments, and to plan and evaluate rehabilitation programmes for children aged 8 to 12 years. Subtests assess motor functions, rhythm, tactile functions, visual functions, receptive speech, writing, reading, arithmetic, memory and intellectual processes.

CHANGES IN PSYCHOEDUCATIONAL ASSESSMENT

In the mid-1970s, the domains of the clinician and the instructor were, for all intents and purposes, mutually exclusive. If a student was perceived to have a learning problem, the classroom teacher would refer the student to the school counsellor or guidance officer (or to a school psychologist) who would administer a battery of tests to determine the nature – if not the cause – of the problem.

Almost invariably, the first test administered would have been an individual intelligence test such as the Stanford Binet, WAIS, WISC or WPPSI depending upon the age of the client. This would be followed, in most cases, by a reading, spelling, mathematics, or general achievement test, with the purpose of identifying the level of the student's academic attainment. The test administrator would then prepare a report on the student and this would work its way through the education or referral system back to the classroom teacher or instructor. It would be read, placed in the person's file, and the business of education would continue in much the same way as before.

Certainly, many school psychologists and counsellors have developed a collection of practical suggestions that might be employed by a teacher to assist a student with an identifiable deficit derived from standardised testing. For example, some counsellors have prepared lists of activities that a teacher might use to improve a student's vocabulary, general knowledge, or basic arithmetic skills. These lists often relate to below-average scores on subtests of the Stanford Binet or Wechsler scales. A difficulty for some counsellors and many psychologists has been their lack of classroom teaching experience and, hence, the difficulty of suggesting valid remediation procedures to classroom teachers whose job is instruction.

Clinicians have been assisted to some extent by manuals that have provided practical remediation activities. For example, in the late 1960s, a manual entitled, *Educational interpretation of the Wechsler Intelligence Scale for Children (WISC)*, was prepared by Ferinden and Jacobson (1969). In their small book there are over thirty pages of remedial activities such as suggestions for overcoming a low score on the Picture Vocabulary subtest (e.g. having the child plot a route from one point to another on a road map while listing the cities en route in order, or having the child choose titles and find the main ideas in a reading activity). While these may be useful, the relationship between the IQ test performance and the child's in-class performance is tenuous at best. In addition, the activities suggested do not often relate to improving student performance on practical class activities.

In some cases, albeit rarely, the school psychologist or the counsellor would consult with the teacher and together they would develop a set of remedial activities or plans designed to address the student's weaknesses. It is not surprising that the classroom teacher was often sceptical of the work carried out by the psychologist, as the outcome of testing generally had no impact on educational practice, and often did little more than confirm the teacher's knowledge of the child. Thankfully, there has been a blurring of the spheres of influence of educational professionals, teachers and clinicians and they now often work collaboratively to develop programmes for students who are experiencing difficulty in school, and for those who are high achievers.

In more recent times, psychological and educational practitioners are likely to collect information about individuals through structured or unstructured observations and interviews. Testing, however, is still common. M.S. Wilson and Reschly (1996) reported a survey of the testing practices of US school psychologists. They sought information on the frequency of use of:

- eleven cognitive/intelligence measures
- sixteen pre-school and family measures
- fifteen rating scales
- ten education measures
- three visual motor tests
- five projective tests
- eight forms of systematic behaviour observations.

The top ten instruments used were as follows: structured observations, Wechsler scales, Bender Visual Motor Gestalt Test (Bender 1951), the Draw-A-Person test (Naglieri 1988), anecdotal observations, Developmental Test of Visual Motor Integration (Beery 1989), Woodcock-Johnson Psycho-Educational Battery (Woodcock and Johnson 1989), and Wide Range Achievement Test (Jastak and Wilkinson 1994).

TOWARD INTERACTIVE ASSESSMENT

Despite the obviously frequent use of standardised tests, test batteries, and various other scales, there has been growing disenchantment with the emphasis on testing, especially in North America, and this has led to a reconsideration of the value of psychoeducational assessment. The long-standing emphasis on IQ testing and serious concerns about the validity of such testing with cultural and ethnic minorities led to a rejection of IQ tests. In the US, a growing number of state legislatures have 'outlawed' intelligence testing and, in other countries, where the dependence on IQ testing was arguably less intense than in the US, interest in traditional IQ testing has also waned.

One developing belief that challenged the traditional view held by early advocates of IQ testing was the modifiability of intelligence. In other words, development of information-processing competence could lead to changes in scores on standardised tests of intelligence. This view of intelligence and cognitive processes was noted by Haywood (1989) and is summarised in Table 5.1.

Such a view concerning the modifiability of intelligence stimulated research on students with severe learning difficulties and also encouraged theorising on the development of cognitive skills. As a result, a pragmatic approach to psychoeducational assessment developed – one that focused not only on the classification of children, but also on the identification of individual needs so that remedial or enrichment programmes could be

Table 5.1 A comparison of intelligence and cognitive processes

Intelligence is
1 largely genetic (i.e. inherited)
2 related to a range of aptitudes (e.g. verbal, spatial, numerical)
3 largely fixed (or modifiable with considerable effort)
4 linked to the ability to learn culturally based knowledge
5 evaluated using measures that assess past learning (e.g. school achievement)

Cognitive processes are
1 taught and learned (i.e. through learning and problem-solving experience)
2 influenced by some fundamental competence, but also by learning and problem-solving habits, motivation, attitudes, and strategies
3 easily modified through effective instruction
4 generalisable across domains of knowledge
5 evaluated using measures that elaborate learning and problem-solving procedures, often in applied settings

designed and provided in a range of teaching-learning settings.

Equally important to the changes in assessment policies and procedures was the growing need for teachers, schools, and education authorities to become more accountable for education outcomes. In other words, if a child was not progressing at school, teachers and administrators could not simply suggest that the student was of low ability and, hence, could not be expected to learn. Parents (and in some cases the students themselves) began to demand demonstrable outcomes for the many years of school attendance – outcomes that were reflected in at least the acquisition of basic literacy, numeracy, and functional life skills.

Attempts to gain a more accurate indication of a child's cognitive potential have been made by counsellors and psychologists informally over many years. There are many practitioners who are intrigued to know how much assistance a child may require to perform more capably on an IQ test, especially when it seems obvious that the child should be performing better than he or she is at the time. While it is contrary to the standardised administration of IQ tests, at least some testers will admit to reviewing items at the end of a testing session 'just to see if the child would have got it right with a few prompts'. In some educational systems, the use of IQ scores has been replaced by sets of comments on what the sub-score result means in terms of performance in specific academic areas such as reading or mathematics. This approach has greater value for the class teacher, as it provides a direct link to understanding applied performance.

Since the late 1950s, there have been a number of reports, presented in the literature, of attempts to demonstrate the modifiability of cognition by introducing a learning component during testing. For example, Haeussermann (1958) assessed how a child determined a given solution and explored the reasons for failure on various items. Schucman (1960) developed an 'educability index' that was derived from a test-teach-test procedure for a child identified as having a severe intellectual disability. The index was considered to be a sensitive detector of cognitive potential.

The view of psychoeducational assessment that has evolved since the early 1980s has been called a transactional view based upon a group of assumptions about intelligence, the nature of cognition, the role of motivation and other affective variables in learning and problem-solving. Haywood et al. (1992b) suggested several assumptions which are summarised as follows:

- Intelligence refers to many aspects of behaviour with individuals' differences in strengths and weaknesses.
- Intelligence is determined by many factors generally considered to fall into two causative roots, genetic or environmental.
- The pattern of cognitive development has a biological basis although 'native ability' is not sufficient to explain individual differences.
- To function successfully in the world, each individual must acquire a

wide range of thinking, perceiving, learning, and problem-solving skills.

- The development of the skills required to function successfully within the world depends upon a person's motivation and attitude to learning and problem-solving.
- Every individual has scope for further intellectual development.
- Intelligence is modifiable to a limited extent although cognitive processes are readily developed and lead to substantial changes in performance.

These assumptions underlie two contemporary developments in assessment. First, there has been work on developing standardised tests of cognitive processes that attempt to identify an individual's strengths and weakness and which might be useful when developing instructional and/or remedial programmes. Two assessment batteries stand out: the Kaufman Assessment Battery for Children (K-ABC), and the Das-Naglieri•Cognitive Assessment System (DN•CAS) based upon the PASS theory of intelligence which was described in Chapter 4. Both of these batteries will be described more fully in Chapter 6.

The second development relates to the need to make assessment more interactive and this derives from the belief that it is important to estimate the potential of the individual, and to discover the circumstances in which learning occurs most effectively. In other words, there is an attempt to discover the instructional conditions under which a person learns or solves problems successfully. Interactive assessment has its foundations in the socio-linguistic tradition of psychology. One of the dominating researchers in this area was Lev Vygotsky.

VYGOTSKY'S CONTRIBUTION TO COGNITIVE EDUCATION

Vygotsky's writings (Vygotsky 1962; 1978) have had a substantial impact upon the theory and practice of cognitive psychology and its application to education. One of his primary contentions was that education should be designed to accelerate children's cognitive development, rather than providing experiences at the individuals' current level of cognitive maturity.

He argued that meaning is socially constructed, hence, learning and cognitive development is affected by the interactions that an individual has with another who is more skilled or knowledgeable. Two concepts have been used to explain the manner in which an individual gains knowledge: mediation and internalisation.

Mediation refers to the need for someone other than the learner to translate knowledge about the society and culture so that it can be internalised by the learner. Internalisation refers to the individual's 'ownership' of concepts or meaning that have been provided through instruction. That is, children must comprehend meaning and integrate the knowledge into their own thinking. In other words, they transform external stimuli to internal 'codes', that are consistent with their own knowledge base by changing and modifying the original ideas, and applying their unique cognitive character to them.

How one learns about the world, therefore, is influenced by one's 'readiness' to learn, and how one is taught. Vygotsky developed the concept of zones of proximal development to express the potential of the individual to learn.

Zones of proximal development

In cognitive education, the term 'zones of proximal development' (ZPD) has become a central concept for understanding the growth of children's cognitive development and ability. In its original Russian, the term is more accurately translated as 'zones of nearest development' (Minick 1987). Vygotsky (1978: 85–6) referred to it as the 'distance between the actual developmental level as determined by independent problem-solving and the level of potential development as determined through problem-solving under adult guidance or in collaboration with more capable peers'. The concept was not well developed by Vygotsky prior to his death and it has been suggested that his ideas have not been transferred accurately into North American literature and research. Minick claimed that Vygotsky was 'proposing a new theoretical framework for analysing the child's current state of development and for predicting the next or the proximal level of development that the child might be expected to attain' (Minick 1987: 118–19).

Nevertheless, the notion of ZPD has become the basis for the development of numerous assessment tools and remediation programmes worldwide. ZPD links assessment and remediation and can be seen in operation in a number of teaching-learning approaches that aim to develop students' independent thinking and problem-solving skills. Another term, 'scaffolding', is linked to Vygotsky's ideas and notion of ZPD.

Scaffolding

Scaffolding is a term that came into use in the early 1980s and refers to the provision of a temporary, adjustable support (like a builder's structure) that is provided by a teacher to assist students develop and extend their skills in the early phases of instruction. The teacher models the desired behaviour, and makes explicit to the children what behaviour is required of them as learners. As questioning and other learning skills develop and begin to facilitate learning, the scaffolding (i.e. the teacher's support) is gradually removed. This withdrawal of direction enables the gradual transfer of responsibility for the instructional input from the teacher to the students (Rogoff and Gardner 1984).

Scaffolding has been described as a way of providing support as an adult assists the learner to move through the ZPD. There are two notions inherent in scaffolding: first, there is a reciprocal relationship between the instructor and the learner – the former provides the content and focus on appropriate processes, and the latter is actively involved in gaining both knowledge and skill; and second, there is a progressive transfer of responsibility for initiating learning from the teacher to the learner. The use of scaffolding in instructional programmes will be discussed in later chapters.

SUMMARY

Significant changes have occurred in the psychoeducational testing field since the mid-1970s. Tests that measure a learner's existing knowledge base or learning outcomes still remain the most commonly used indicators of ability and achievement. Arguably, the most common reason for using assessment devices is the collection of information as a precursor to the development of instructional or remedial programmes. However, it has only been since the mid-1980s that attention has turned away from the static measures of competence to those that explore the learning 'potential' of students, that is, the ease of taking a learner from one level of knowledge or skill to the next.

These new measures draw on the accumulated knowledge of almost a century of research and clinical practice in psychology and education. Importantly, they focus attention of the way in which students process information, learn, and solve problems confronting them. In Chapter 6 we consider a range of these new-generation assessment procedures and evaluate the extent to which they serve the purposes for which they were developed.

STUDY TASKS

5.1 In note form, list the main points covered in this chapter. Think especially about the differences between the assessment methods described.

5.2 List as many factors as you can that might influence the performance of a primary school aged child on a test of intelligence. Do you think these various factors will also affect performance on other forms of assessment (e.g. personality, achievement)?

5.3 List the pros and cons of tests of intelligence.

5.4 We refer to *mediation* and *internalisation* as two key concepts that were raised by Vygotsky and adopted as central features of the interactive assessment movement. Think back over your own childhood and early adolescent years and list some ways in which others mediated your learning. How do you think these experiences were internalised, and were there enduring changes in your life as a result of them?

ADDITIONAL READING

Hodges, J.R. (1994) *Cognitive Assessment for Clinicians*, Oxford: Oxford University Press.

Lidz, C. (1992) 'The extent of incorporation of assessment into cognitive assessment courses: a national survey of school psychology trainers', *Journal of Special Education 26*: 325–31.

Newman, F. and Holzman, L. (1993) *Lev Vygotsky: Revolutionary Scientist*, London: Routledge.

Sattler, J.M. (1992) *Assessment of Children*, 3rd edn, San Diego, CA: Jerome M. Sattler.

Chapter 6

Assessing cognitive skills and processes

As we outlined in Chapter 5, assessment is undertaken for a variety of reasons. Many psychoeducational tests that focus on cognitive ability, skills, and processes have been designed largely for use with special populations, such as children with learning difficulties or developmental disabilities, although they have application to normally achieving children, adolescents, and adults. In this chapter we review a number of tests and testing procedures that focus on cognitive processes and which provide information for instructional design. We begin by examining two test batteries aimed at elaborating the information processing capabilities of individuals.

DIAGNOSTIC SYSTEMS

Many assessment devices deal with behaviour within a single cognitive domain (e.g. intelligence, reading achievement). Since 1970, however, test designers have begun to construct test batteries that measure behaviour across several domains. These batteries are called diagnostic systems.

Diagnostic systems are comprehensive instruments that enable the examiner to link performance in one domain (e.g. intelligence) with performance in others (e.g. reading comprehension, mathematics, spelling). The Woodcock-Johnson Psycho-Educational Battery – Revised (Woodcock and Johnson 1989) is an example of such a diagnostic system designed to assess intellectual ability and academic development. The diagnostic system provides the examiner with an indication of the relative position of the student being assessed in comparison to the sample of children on whom the battery was normed.

The Woodcock-Johnson ability tests are based generally on the traditional approaches to intelligence testing. Other diagnostic systems, however, have their foundation in the more recent views of information processing that relate to, first, the use of strategies to manipulate information received by the organism; second, metastrategies that have a monitoring role in learning, problem-solving, and adaptation; and third, cognitive functions (or processes) that execute mental operations across domains.

The translation of information-processing concepts into a coherent and broadly based theory of intelligence has not been easy. Most writers have been content to build models of cognition and to explore the relationship among the dimensions included therein. Atypical of that approach are two comprehensive test batteries that have been based upon Luria's functional organisation of the brain (described in Chapter 4) – the Kaufman Assessment Battery for Children, and the Das•Naglieri Cognitive Assessment System. The former provides an assessment of both cognitive and academic areas, while the latter focuses on cognitive dimensions alone.

Kaufman Assessment Battery for Children (K-ABC)

The K-ABC (A. Kaufman and N. Kaufman 1983) is an individually administered battery of tests that assess student's performance on the two coding processes identified by Luria (1966) – simultaneous and sequential (successive) processing – and achievement. To refresh your memory, sequential processing deals with stimuli in a serial or temporal fashion (e.g. remembering the correct order of digits in a phone number given by an operator), and simultaneous processing is concerned with information presented as a whole unit, often spatially (e.g. seeing a simple picture containing several elements).

This test consists of sixteen subtests which were normed using North American children between 2 years 6 months and 12 years 6 months, and provides standardised measures of student coding abilities (simultaneous and sequential, which can be combined into a mental processing scale) and academic achievement (see Box 6.1). The body of research literature based on the use of the K-ABC has grown since 1983, demonstrating the reliability and validity of the test, and the use of the battery with a wide range of student populations.

Critique and criticism has also been extensive and a useful early review can be found in the *Journal of Special Education* (1984, vol. 18, no. 3) and in numerous articles published in the *Journal of Psychoeducational Assessment*. However, the K-ABC has not replaced the commonly used intelligence tests (i.e. Stanford Binet and Wechsler scales) and in some countries, such as the United Kingdom, Australia, and New Zealand, the K-ABC has had little impact. This may be due to the continued use of traditional intelligence tests by psychologists, counsellors and guidance officers because of a 'mistrust' of non-traditional measures of intelligence. In addition, some achievement tests have a strong American bias (e.g. Faces and Places in the K-ABC has pictures of US Presidents and North American scenes).

While some clinicians and commentators did not expect the K-ABC to win acceptance in professional school psychology practices, it has taken a share of the testing market, being used by school psychologists almost as frequently as the Stanford Binet-IV, at least in the US (see M.S. Wilson and Reschly 1996).

Box 6.1

Subtests in the Kaufman Assessment Battery for Children (K-ABC)

Here is a list of the complete battery of subtests, with a description of what each one involves. The set of subtests used in the assessment of any child is determined by the child's age.

Sequential processing scale

Hand movements	Involves repeating a series of hand movements in the same sequence as performed by the examiner.
Number recall	Involves repeating a series of digits in the same sequence as given by the examiner.
Word order	Requires touching a series of silhouettes of common objects in the same sequence as presented verbally by the examiner.

Simultaneous processing scale

Face recognition	Requires recall of one or two faces from a group photograph that has been presented previously by the tester for a brief time.
Gestalt closure	Involves naming an object or scene pictured in a partially completed 'inkblot' drawing.
Matrix analogies	Involves selecting the meaningful picture or abstract pattern from a group to match a model.
Magic window	Requires the identification of a picture that is progressively exposed by the tester in a narrow slit which allows only a small part to be seen at any time.
Photo series	Requires placing photographs of an event in chronological order.
Spatial memory	Requires recalling the placement of pictures on a page which is exposed briefly.
Triangles	Requires assembling coloured triangles into an abstract pattern to match a model.

Achievement scale

Expressive vocabulary	Involves naming objects from photographs.
Faces and places	Requires the identification of well-known North American people, characters, or places shown pictorially.
Arithmetic	Involves naming numbers, counting, computing, and understanding mathematical concepts.

Box 6.1 contd.

Riddles	Requires the naming of concrete or abstract concepts when given the characteristics.
Reading/Decoding	Requires the naming of letters and reading orally.
Word order	Requires the child to point to the silhouettes of common objects in the order given by the examiner.

Das-Naglieri•Cognitive Assessment System (DN•CAS)

A second cognitive diagnostic system has been developed by Naglieri and Das (1996). Das was the first to begin information-processing (rather than neuropsychological) research on simultaneous and successive processing in 1972. Since that time, he and his colleagues have carried out trials of many experimental tests of these two coding processes. Das's research (unlike that of Kaufman and Kaufman) has focused upon two additional dimensions of mental ability: attention and planning. Hence, the DN•CAS provides a broad view of children's information processing capabilities by covering four cognitive domains – planning, attention, simultaneous processing, and successive processing (see Box 6.2).

One objective of the DN•CAS is to provide information about the cognitive characteristics of children and adolescents using the dimensions identified by Luria (1966), namely planning, arousal, simultaneous and successive processing. Together with other informal or formal test data, this information could be used to assist teaching practitioners when they are making decisions about diagnosis, eligibility for special education programmes, and instructional programming.

Tests such as the K-ABC and the DN•CAS are important as they take the focus of assessment away from the view that intelligence is somehow fixed, by emphasising that children and adults may deal with the same problem or task in many different ways, each of which might be more, or less, successful for any person. Another assessment procedure has developed from the belief that traditional testing procedures do not provide an opportunity to explore the reasons for children's success or failure. We turn now to a review of several interactive assessment procedures.

INTERACTIVE ASSESSMENT

Interactive assessment (sometimes called dynamic assessment or learning potential assessment) is a general term used to describe a range of procedures that emphasise the processes of thinking, learning, and problem-solving as

Box 6.2

Subtests in the Das•Naglieri Cognitive Assessment System

Planning

Visual search	The person points to a picture, number or letter located in a field around the target which appears in a stimulus box.
Planned connections	The person connects numbers, or letters and numbers in an ascending order, alternating letter/number correctly.
Matching numbers	The person finds and circles two numbers that are the same among others, with the numbers increasing in length as the subtest progresses.

Attention

Selective attention – receptive	The subtest involves rows of picture or letter pairs. The person circles, row by row, all of the pairs that are physically the same (e.g. HH but not HN) or are the same alphabet letter (e.g. Aa not Ba).
Selective attention – expressive	The subtest has three parts. The person reads words (which are the names of colours) as quickly as possible, then labels coloured rectangles, and finally names the colour of the print of words (which are the names of colours).

Simultaneous

Matrices	The person chooses one of six options that best completes an abstract analogy.
Figure memory	The person views, and then locates, a geometric design that is impeded in a more complex pattern.
Design construction	The person constructs a three-dimensional design to match a standard using 2 cm blocks.

Box 6.2 contd.

Successive	
Work recall	Nine single-syllable words are presented in series ranging from two to nine words per set. The person recalls each set of words in the order in which they were presented.
Sentence repetition and questions	The person repeats sentences in which colour words replace nouns and verbs (e.g. The blue is greening) and then answers questions about sentences (e.g. The blue is greening. What is greening?).

well as the outcomes of that assessment. Interactive assessment, therefore, operates more like an open interview than a test session. Feedback on the outcome of the testing process is given to the child who is prompted for clarification or explanation. Lidz (1991) defined interactive assessment as a test-intervene-retest procedure that evaluates the degree and nature of change in the performance of the person being tested, following the intervention (or instruction) phase.

Interactive procedures differ greatly, as will be evident from the several examples described later in this chapter. They stand in contrast to diagnostic procedures that provide a profile of the current status of an individual's skills, knowledge, or ability. For example, the IQ derived from the administration of a Stanford Binet is indicative of a person's general ability at the time of testing and is influenced by the cognitive, affective, and environmental conditions at that time. One assumption of standardised testing of intelligence is that an individual acquires skill and knowledge from the environment in a cumulative way, and at the same rate, as chronological-age peers. Hence, the test compares the individual's performance with peers of the same age.

However, the background of the child and the conditions under which the assessment occurs may contribute to an incorrect estimate of the person's 'true' capabilities. For example, a child may have been tested after a sleepless night, or may be apprehensive about the purpose of testing, or disrupted by the noise of machinery outside the building. If the child comes from a cultural minority or a disadvantaged background in which middle-class western values and knowledge are not prized, the child's performance in the test will almost assuredly be depressed when compared against the norms. Finally, it is clear that individuals with comparable test results on a static test (e.g. a test of intelligence) may have very different ability profiles, and would have achieved similar scores in very different ways.

Interactive assessment, in a general sense, is not new and has been part of teaching and learning from the earliest stages of human evolution. Effective instruction always involves some form of pre-assessment, instruction, and re-assessment to determine the success of the learning process. Furthermore, following the development and extensive use of standardised tests of intelligence during the 1900s, education and psychology practitioners adopted a variety of assessment procedures to augment the information obtained through formal assessment. In the first half of the twentieth century, a number of writers have argued for the use of testing methods that emphasise how learning occurs, and how it might be facilitated, rather than the products of life experience (see Lidz 1987b).

It was not until the mid-1960s that contemporary interactive methods were developed. Three approaches have commonly been described as having a major influence on this area and each has focused on assessing (mainly) children experiencing learning difficulties. These are Budoff's learning potential assessment (Budoff and Friedman 1964; Budoff 1967; Budoff and Corman 1974), the Learning Potential Assessment Device (Feuerstein *et al.* 1979), and assessment via assisted learning and transfer (Campione *et al.* 1985a; Campione *et al.* 1985b). Each of these approaches encourages learners to modify their behaviour during the assessment session.

Modifying behaviour during testing

Interactive assessment is an active procedure. Both examiner and learner engage in a dialogue (or discourse) that aims to explore the degree to which the individual's performance can be modified through intervention. Lidz (1987b) suggested that the examiner actively intervenes to modify the interactions with the learner to induce successful learning, and to monitor the extent to which change is occurring. In turn, the learner is encouraged, directed, and reinforced to become an active seeker and organiser of information.

The key to discovering the degree to which the learner is able to modify behaviour during the testing session is the form of instruction that occurs within it. Some learners will make considerable gains (this is often described by writers in the area as showing great learning potential) while others may make modest or no gains at all even with considerable promoting and encouragement. Some interactive assessment approaches define the type and extent of instruction that can be provided by the examiner (e.g. testing the limits), while others allow the examiner to develop the learning process in an *ad-hoc* way, depending upon the responses given by the learner (e.g. assessing learning potential). The latter may require modification to the format in which an item is given, such as providing additional examples or trials, modelling an appropriate strategy for success, or offering increasingly more direct cues or prompts. The intensity of the interactive intervention varies across approaches, ranging from brief, standardised prompts to complex, individualised probing. A brief report on an interactive assessment study is given in Box 6.3.

An extensive exposition of the various interactive assessments has been given in five substantive volumes (Feuerstein *et al.* 1979; Gupta and Coxhead 1988; Haywood and Tzuriel 1992; Lidz 1987a; 1991). Here we describe only three approaches, those of Budoff, Brown, and Feuerstein and their colleagues.

EARLY INTERACTIVE ASSESSMENT APPROACHES

Learning potential assessment

Budoff and his colleagues viewed intelligence as the ability to profit from experience, and set out to differentiate between children who had an intellectual disability from those who were thought to be educationally disadvantaged. The purpose of learning potential assessment was to estimate general ability derived from reasoning problems which the child could learn to solve, and which allowed a comparison with scores on a Binet or Wechsler scale. Budoff (1987) argued that if the child could demonstrate performance in a learning potential assessment activity at a level approximating a child with an average ability, this was sufficient indication that he or she did not have an intellectual disability. Budoff used existing non-verbal tasks and developed training components to assist the children to improve their performance. These included Koh's Block Design and Raven's Progressive Matrices. Budoff adapted Koh's Blocks by adding cubes with blue and yellow sides to the standard red and white set and the child was asked to make predetermined patterns using the set of cubes. The full set of sixteen designs was attempted by the child first, then training was provided in how to complete the designs by assisting the child to see how the patterns were constructed (e.g. showing the outline of the blocks on the design).

Raven's Matrices determine the ability of the child to see logical relationships between simple and complex geometric designs. The child chooses one of six alternative elements to fill a gap in the design matrix.

The Matrices were used in a similar way to Koh's Blocks. The training component involved using different matrices from those in the test and the child had to decide what element was needed to complete the matrix pattern and explain how the problem was solved.

The Series Learning Potential Test involved a group administered non-verbal reasoning task for children in Grades 1 to 3 (aged 6–8), using pictures that varied according to semantic content, size, colour, and spatial orientation. The test procedure involved a standard pretest and post-test. The intervening training emphasised the identification of the relevant concept pattern detection, the identification of appropriate strategies needed to solve the problem, and the manipulation of patterns.

Box 6.3

Research summary: Rutland and Campbell (1995)

Aims of the study

Dynamic assessment involves measuring the ability of children to undertake tasks when they are both helped and not helped with that task. This study aimed to measure the zone of proximal development, that is, the difference between a child's actual level of development when not assisted with a task, and the potential level when the child is assisted. In addition, the study aimed to determine if the dynamic (assisted) measures used in tests with children who have a learning difficulty and non-disabled children were predictable and valid, and whether the assisted measures related to the child's level of intelligence.

Method

Twenty-six children with learning difficulties and twenty-six non-disabled children participated in the study. The children with learning difficulties were aged between 11 and 14 years, while the non-disabled children were aged between 5 and 6 years. There were fourteen boys and twelve girls, respectively, in each group. The children were administered a short-form IQ test and then asked to search for a present in a box situated inside a collapsible house-like maze. The game was described as a treasure hunt and the children were given a map to help them locate the present. When the children experienced problems, they were given a series of hints (assistance) by the experimenter. Five phases of the experiment included pretests, training, maintenance, transfer and post-tests.

In static pretests, the children were given no hints and provided with a black and white map and allowed a maximum of four attempts to find the treasure. In the dynamic training phase, children who made an error in any of the four trial pretests were helped by the experimenter.

Results

A significant relationship was found between children's IQ level and the number of hints they needed to complete the task. Hence, the assisted measures were found to be related to intellectual ability. In assessing the ability of using the dynamic measures to predict future performance, there was a significant improvement found in the performance of children with and without a learning difficulty between the pretests and post-tests. The results indicate, therefore, that dynamic measures are better predictors of pretest-post-test improvement than either IQ or the initial static test score.

Conclusion

The study suggests that dynamic assessment techniques have something to offer in terms of improving the assessment of children, especially those with learning difficulties. The researchers suggest that assessing the potential of children with learning difficulties using dynamic assessment techniques 'allows one to escape from the negative view that these children will always have a general cognitive deficit as identified by IQ tests' (Rutland and Campbell 1995: 92). However, the authors call for further research to test the validity of dynamic assessment methods for different populations undertaking different tasks.

The Picture Word Game was developed for children from kindergarten to Grade 2 (ages 4–6). It involved the presentation of a series of pictures and required the child to associate a symbol with an underlying concept inherent in the series. For example, the concept 'boy' could be represented by a square since a boy is shown in each picture in the series. No pretest was given but training involved the identification of a suitable strategy to solve the picture problem.

Budoff and his colleagues conducted a number of studies to validate the benefit of the interactive assessment procedure (Budoff and Friedman 1964; Budoff 1967; Budoff and Corman 1974). While the approach appeared to be promising, little research or development of learning potential assessment has been undertaken since the mid-1970s, although Budoff (1987) provided a substantive review of his work in Lidz's comprehensive book on dynamic assessment.

Assessment via assisted learning and transfer

A.L. Brown and her colleagues were also among the early proponents of interactive assessment (Campione et al., 1985a; Campione et al. 1985b). Their approach, referred to as 'assisted assessment' (Campione 1989), and also called the 'graduated prompt procedure', was based on the concept of internalisation of cognitive processes introduced by Vygotsky. Like Budoff, Brown and her colleagues set out to standardise the assessment procedure and develop a data collection approach that aimed at measuring learning and the ability to transfer that learning in an efficient way. Students were asked to learn new rules or principles and the assessor would then determine – through an intervention – how much help the child needed to reach a specified performance criterion of rule use, and how much additional help would be required to have the child transfer the rules to new situations. Campione (1989) argued that the learning and transfer scores provided more information about the individual than standardised tests, such as IQ tests.

In contrast to some other interactive assessment procedures, Brown and her colleagues were concerned with assessment located within content areas. In their early work, they concentrated on matrices and letter completion, in addition to early reading and mathematics skills.

A typical assessment would involve several sessions in which a standardised test would be administered to the child, followed by an assessment of the child's performance level. The child would then be faced with a new task or situation which would require the transfer (generalisation) of skills and strategies implied in the pretest phase. Mediation of these skills and strategies would be provided in the form of hints that would help to solve the problem. Each child would be assigned a score based on the number of hints given during the mediation phase of assessment, indicating the level of independence in problem-solving.

The numerical outcome of assessment is an advantage of the Brown *et al.* procedure but it is also a source of criticism. Lidz (1991), for example, argued that the score suggests a scale of complexity in the need for hints, and equivalence in the quality of hints. She also argued that the context of the assisted learning and transfer procedure has been low-level, initial mastery in an academic domain. When more complex learning is required (e.g. reading comprehension), clinical rather than psychometric procedures are employed. Furthermore, Missiuna and Samuels (1988) suggested that the hints provided to the children during the mediation phase are predetermined and do not allow for modification based upon the child's needs.

Interactive assessment using the early Brown *et al.* approach does not appear to have endured. Research and application on the more clinical teaching approach (called reciprocal teaching) is still used in many classrooms around the world, although it appears more popular in western countries. Campione (1989) claimed that the domain-specific nature of clinical assessment has advantages, particularly as it is possible to select 'target skills' to be taught; to contextualise them within the content area (e.g. reading, mathematics); and to evaluate the effectiveness of the procedure within that context.

The Learning Potential Assessment Device (LPAD)

The third approach, reported extensively in the interactive assessment literature, is the Learning Potential Assessment Device (LPAD), developed by Feuerstein and his colleagues. The concept had its roots in the work of the Swiss psychologist, André Rey (see e.g. Rey 1934; Rey and Dupont 1953) and in the social and cultural issues that arose in the establishment of the State of Israel (1948). At that time, immigration to Israel brought Jews from all over the world, from wealthy and poverty-stricken countries alike. Those from Third World countries were required to make considerable adjustment not only to a new social order, but also to a developing technology.

Feuerstein recognised the need for the development of assessment methods that would accommodate immigrants from diverse cultures and allow for an assessment of their learning potential rather than a measure of their often impoverished prior experiences. The LPAD (Feuerstein *et al.* 1979) was based upon a theory that encompassed two major concepts: Structural Cognitive Modifiability and Mediated Learning Experience.

Structural Cognitive Modifiability (SCM) refers to a belief that human beings have a capacity to modify their cognitive functions and adapt to changing demands in life situations regardless of the cause of their learning problem, age, and severity of an individual's cognitive deficit. SCM is characterised by permanence (i.e. the durability of cognitive change over time), pervasiveness (i.e. expression of change through cognitive processes), and centrality (i.e. change that is self-perpetuating and self-regulating).

Mediated Learning Experiences (MLE) assist in explaining SCM. MLE refers to a process in which an adult assists in the enculturation of a child by mediating between the child and the environment to modify the frequency, order, intensity, and context of stimuli to enable the child to learn about the world in the most effective way possible. Mediation should increase the child's curiosity and sensitivity to the mediated stimuli, and improve the child's understanding of concepts, issues, and knowledge. MLE processes are internalised and become part of the child's learning beliefs and processes. In turn, these allow children to act independently and to modify their learning and cognitive systems.

Tzuriel and Haywood (1992) described six necessary and sufficient characteristics for any interaction to be classified as a mediated interaction:

- *Intentionality and reciprocity* refers to the mediator's intentional effort to produce a state of vigilance in the child to ensure that the information has been registered and that there is a reciprocal belief by the child that personal actions influence other people.
- *Mediation of meaning* refers to interactions in which the presented stimuli pose affective, motivational, and value-oriented significance and that the child attaches this meaning to newly acquired information.
- *Mediation of transcendance* refers to the character and goal of MLE interactions which are beyond the specific situation in which the mediation occurs.
- *Mediation of feelings of competence* refers to the efforts expended by the mediator to communicate to the child that he/she can function independently and successfully.
- *Regulation of behaviour* refers to the mediator's efforts to inhibit impulsive behaviour or enhance reactivity through modelling, encouraging metacognition, and problem-solving behaviour.
- *Mediation of sharing* refers to the sense of interdependency and sharing that exists between the mediator and child.

Culturally based learning and problem-solving

Feuerstein's conceptualisation of culturally based learning and problem-solving behaviour was the foundation on which the LPAD was developed. The model provides the basis for the construction of a number of tests that aim to evaluate:

- the modifiability of the individual when confronted with conditions requiring change
- the extent to which the learner's cognition can be modified
- the amount of teaching necessary to bring about change
- the significance of change
- the strengths and weaknesses in the learner's strategic behaviour.

The problem, task, or situation is first presented to the learner for completion. This may involve mastery of a principle through the application of an appropriate cognitive operation that is dependent upon elementary, prerequisite cognitive processes and proper attitude and motivation. The learner is then given the training necessary to solve the problem. Once mastery is achieved, a series of tasks is presented, each of which is a progressively more complex version of the initial training task. The series of interrelated tasks have varying degrees of novelty, difficulty, and complexity which are achieved by changes in one dimension of the task. This is said to 'simulate the adaptational requirements that often confront the growing individual in real life' (Feuerstein *et al.* 1979: 92). Changes can, for example, be made to the object or situation, the relationship between the object or their specific function, or the cognitive operation required to solve the task.

The tasks can require mental operations such as analogies, logical multiplication, permutations, syllogisms, categorisation, or seriation. The original task, and subsequent variations of it, can be presented in various ways, such as through pictures, concrete objects, words, or numbers. A list of the tasks included in the LPAD Clinical Battery is found in Box 6.4 although only a selection of tasks would be administered (a more complete description can be found in Feuerstein *et al.* 1979).

Each of the LPAD activities bears little resemblance to tasks with which a learner has experience. Indeed, Feuerstein and his colleagues have argued that test instruments should be clearly distinguishable from academic tasks, but should reflect similar cognitive demands.

Lidz (1991) suggested that the LPAD involves three core concepts. First, the learner's behaviour reflects deficiencies in data gathering, the use of data in problem-solving situations, and the inability to communicate solutions and responses to the problem-solving process. Hence, the purpose of interactive assessment is to identify the deficiencies and determine how best they might be overcome. Second, the assessor's behaviour reflects the characteristics of mediated learning which include the six points noted earlier.

In addition, Lidz stated that it is also necessary for the mediator to broaden the learner's knowledge base through MLE and non-mediation interactions. Finally, the task is viewed as a cognitive map which reflects seven dimensions: interesting content; the modality or the way in which the content is presented (e.g. pictorially, verbally); the phase of the mental act (i.e. input, elaboration, output); the cognitive operations involved (e.g. categorisation, identification, seriation); level of complexity; level of abstraction; and level of efficiency (relating to the trade-off between speed and accuracy).

The LPAD is a time-consuming testing procedure because of the need for extensive interactions that will allow the examiner to understand the nature of the difficulties being experienced by the learner. Group testing would seem to be an anathema. However, Feuerstein *et al.* (1979) reported on the development and use of a LPAD with groups of between ten and twenty students.

The LPAD is arguably the most frequently used interactive assessment tool. It requires extensive training to become familiar with the materials and the nature of the intervention (teaching) phase, as the examiner must be sensitive to the need to provide, or not to provide, mediation. Although the LPAD has been used with a wide range of special populations, research dealing with its effectiveness appears to have been limited to a small group of researchers. Critics of the LPAD suggest that it is 'of some limited clinical utility but it is not yet a viable alternative to the proper use of rigorously researched individual IQ tests by well-trained professionals' (Frisby and Braden 1992: 297). There will, of course, be continuing debates over the value of new assessment and remediation approaches until they are eventually accepted, or cease to be used (see also Tzuriel 1992).

It does seem, however, that interactive assessment procedures will continue to be developed for use in a variety of educational and clinical settings. Indeed, there are many groups currently working on the development and refinement of assessment approaches, notably in North America and Europe. One subset of these is called Learning Tests.

LEARNING TESTS

Learning tests evaluate the way in which an individual processes information within problem-solving situations, and the level of assistance offered to the learner in the form of feedback, prompts, or long-term teaching programmes. Several learning tests have been developed and refined in Germany since the mid-1970s (see Guthke and Wingenfeld 1992).

Long- and short-term learning tests

The 'classical' learning test involves a standardised testing procedure that has the same form as the interactive assessment approach in that there is a pretest,

Box 6.4

Tests included in the Learning Potential Assessment Device Clinical Battery

Test	Description
Organization of dots	The test consists of clouds of dots distributed within a frame. The learner is required to organise the dots by linking them to make a number of overlapping geometric figures – similar to a simple version of the child's game called 'Join the dots'.
Raven's Progressive Matrices	This is a set of matrices which involves determining the logical relationship between simple and complex visual forms, usually geometrical in design. Each matrix has a gap which has to be filled by choosing one of the six alternatives printed below the matrix.
LPAD variations of Raven's Matrices	These are adaptations of Raven's Matrices based upon findings of a study of response patterns by Feuerstein *et al.* (1979).
Plateaux tests	The tests consist of plates with nine movable buttons and one fixed button per plate. The learner must lift the buttons to locate the fixed one and then recall its position.
Representational stencil design test	The learner is presented with a series of stencils in a specific order. A model figure is presented and the learner must construct the model design by superimposing the stencils mentally in the correct order, one on top of the other.
Numerical progressions	The test consists of a series of number sequences. The numbers in a sequence are related by rules that govern the progression (e.g. ± 4 in the simple sequence $3 - 7 - 11$).
Positional learning test	This test requires the learner to recall the position of marked cells distributed within a 5×5 grid.
Verbal and figural analogy tests	These tests involve identification of associations in the form 'a is to b, as c is to d'. For example, 'Parent is to child, as horse is to?' (foal).
Complex figure drawing	The learner is required to copy a complex figure.

Human figure drawing	The learner is required to draw a human figure.
Associated recall test	The test requires the learner to use an appropriate memory strategy to recall twenty figures.
Memory of fifteen words	The learner is required to recall fifteen words.

training, and post-test. Guthke and Wingenfeld (1992) described a long-term learning test called *Reasoning* which is appropriate for use with children from Grades 6 to 10. As the name implies, the test is designed to assess reasoning – the core factor of intelligence – in three basic domains, verbal, numerical, and figural. The test consists of verbal analogies, and numerical and figural sequences commonly used in other intelligence tests. However, in contrast to static tests, the students undertake a programme to develop their understanding of thinking skills (metacognition) after completing the pretest and, then are post-tested to determine if there is a change in performance.

Short-term learning tests incorporate the training phase within the test procedure and require only one testing session during which systematic feedback and assistance is given to the learner. There are two types of short-term learning tests, one in which only feedback is given, and the other in which extensive assistance and simple feedback is provided. Guthke and Wingenfeld (1992) described one test of each form: the Sequence of Sets Test and the Raven Short-Term Learning Test.

The Sequence of Sets Test was designed to assess the prerequisite learning skills for mathematics and it is administered to children before entering the primary (elementary) school. Following the presentation of the first three members of a series of sets, for example, 6 – 5 – 4 (symbolised by cards depicting different numbers of little bears), the child makes guesses about how to continue the series, selecting choices from a set of response cards. The test consists of nine items and after each trial, the child is given feedback as to which card selected is correct or incorrect. Incorrect cards are turned, whereas correct cards are put into the sequence. The test is an intensive learning procedure not only because children are able to learn and correct their mistakes as they work on each item, but also because each successfully completed item allowed them to gain experience for solving further items.

The Raven Short-Term Learning Test was designed to assist in the identification of children with an intellectual disability. Children are first given Raven's Coloured Progressive Matrices (Raven 1962) and those who fail are given the same item in a puzzle form as the first intervention. While many children can solve the problem when the matrices are given in concrete form, some cannot but they are allowed to continue trying on their own. Those who learn from their mistakes receive further assistance, while those who do not are given a further intervention with the correct solution and then complete the activity by themselves.

Tests in which children are simply asked to repeat the task can also be called learning tests, as repetition can increase performance. Guthke and Wingenfeld (1992) suggested that patients with brain damage and some neuroses improve their performance greatly by task repetition.

The use of learning tests has expanded since the mid-1980s and there have been numerous applications to the testing of intelligence, memory, social learning ability, psychotherapeutic outcomes, vocational aptitude, and in gerontological research on the cognitive flexibility of older people. The procedures have not been universally accepted (see e.g. Kormann and Sporer 1983) although contemporary criticism suggests the value of pursuing this useful assessment method.

Testing the limits

In the late 1970s, Carlson and Wiedl (1978; 1979; 1992) introduced a testing-the-limits procedure which involved modifying a test in a way that enhanced children's performance. They developed a standardised intervention which provided a sensitive index of intellectual ability using Raven's Progressive Matrices. Their approach involved a standard administration, followed by the child's verbalisation of the solution choice, either before seeing the alternatives, or after making the choice. Alternatively, the child may be given feedback about the correctness of the choice. Verbalisation appeared to increase the children's understanding of the task, and reflected reduced anxiety in the testing situation.

Carlson and his colleagues have also been involved in developing intervention procedures based on Luria's functional organisation of the brain. Using a similar verbalisation procedure during testing and training, they found increased performance on Raven's Matrices was also accompanied by improved visual scanning evident by the eye movement patterns of the children. They also found gains on the reasoning analogies items of the Matrices (Bethge et al. 1982; Cormier et al. 1990).

In a more recent study, Kar et al. (1993) reported the effects of verbalisation on performance using a visual search task that required planning and strategy use (see Box 6.5). The children were asked to say how they would go about searching for the target number presented to them using a series of cards in a step-by-step fashion. As in earlier studies, verbalisation improved performance but especially with children who were identified as being poor planners.

FUNCTIONAL AND STRUCTURAL MEDIATION

The several approaches we have described can be classified according to the form of mediation provided. Feuerstein *et al.* (1987) made a distinction between interventions aimed at changing a person's functioning on a specific task as a result of an interaction between the learner and assessor. The approaches used by Budoff, Campione and Brown, Carlson, Guthke and their colleagues would fall into this classification. Feuerstein *et al.* (1979) claimed that assessment using this form of mediation is limited in terms of the changes that are targeted in the interventions, and are not modified according to the needs of the child.

In contrast, structural mediation is aimed at producing long-term changes in the way students approach tasks and which will determine cognitive functions across a range of mental activities. In effect, the distinction appears to be linked to the context-specific or content-general focus of the mediation that occurs within the testing procedure. Certainly, writers who subscribe to the Feuerstein *et al.* procedures would argue that structural cognitive changes are required if the learner is to gain lasting benefits. Others have suggested that the impact of structural mediation is difficult to judge because it requires evaluating the transfer of learning to tasks remote from the instruction (see Bransford *et al.* 1985; Campione 1989). Mediation is commonly based upon materials that have little obvious link to school tasks, and it is quite possible for students to improve their performance on novel tasks without making gains on academic tasks. Interactive assessment procedures appear to have considerable promise but like some other forms of assessment their effectiveness as reliable indicators of learning or classroom behaviour is yet to be demonstrated.

ESTABLISHING A LINK BETWEEN ASSESSMENT AND INSTRUCTION

Psychological and skill-based assessments are likely to remain an ever-present and concerning aspect of regular and special education as information will continue to be sought to inform or justify a range of decisions made about children. There is little doubt that there are many situations that demand assessment. For example, school psychologists and counsellors need information about students to assist in placing them in appropriate educational settings, and teachers need to evaluate students' progress so that they can judge whether instruction has been successful.

Knowing about students is an important first step toward understanding their educational needs. Information gained from assessment is valuable as long as it leads to decisions about how best to maximise students' learning outcomes, and when it leads to relevant instruction or remediation options. An examination of the assessment literature and observation of testing events

Box 6.5

Research summary: Kar *et al.* (1993)

Aim of the study

The study aimed to determine if children who were good and poor planners benefited from speaking about their strategies when completing a task. Two experiments were conducted. The first was designed to assess if improvement in a planning task could be brought about by speaking about the strategies used when completing the task. In the second, good and poor planners were selected and given a different planning task. Some were asked to speak of their strategies while others were not.

Experiment 1

Twenty-eight Grade 5 children, 10 years of age, were randomly selected from a private school in India. None of the children had a disability. The children were required to undertake a number-finding task. Fifty cards with specific numbers of four digits on the back and a row of five six-digit numbers on the front were presented to the children. The number sought by the children (i.e. the target number) appeared in only twenty-five of the fifty cards, and featured in one of the five numbers on the front of the cards. The target number appeared serially, five times in the twenty-five cards. The children were required to detect the presence of the target number in each of the fifty cards. The time taken to find the target number was the performance score.

The experiment had two parts. In the first part, the children were asked to detect the number without speaking of their strategies. In the second, the children were asked to do the task again but to tell the experimenter how they were going to search for the number, and why they took the steps they did.

The results of the study showed that the children performed better when verbalising their strategies than in the standard instruction condition. Also, the improvement in task performance was found to be higher for those whose initial performance was relatively low.

Experiment 2

The validity of Experiment 1 was tested in Experiment 2 by identifying and classifying children on their ability to plan using a different task, and then assessing their performance in the number finding task. Strategy verbalisation and non-verbalisation were again the experimental conditions.

Fifteen high planners and fifteen low planners were selected from among fifty Grade 5 students in an urban high school. A Visual Search Test was administered to all students and those who ranked the highest and the lowest on that test were chosen for the experiment. The number-finding task, as in Experiment 1, was then administered to those thirty children under two conditions. Under the first condition, both groups (high and low planners) undertook the number finding task without speaking of their strategies. In the second condition, the subjects were asked to verbalise their strategies and explain the reasons for the choice of their particular strategy.

The results indicated that high planners had a significantly faster number finding rate when the target number was both present and absent. The rate of the search improved for both high and low planners when the children were given the opportunity to speak of their strategies, but the high planners did not improve as much as the low planners.

Conclusion

The results of the experiments provide evidence for the positive effects of strategy verbalisation on task performance. In the case of poor planners, verbalising strategies helped them formulate a search plan. The research supports the relative efficiency of minimal dynamic assessment over formal psychometric methods of assessing cognitive competence.

which occur in schools, however, shows that the overwhelming preoccupation of counsellors, psychologists, and many teachers, is screening and classification. In other words, they are concerned with decisions about the status of the individual (Haywood *et al.* 1990). From a perusal of relevant literature, one could easily be forgiven for thinking that there is only limited interest in taking the second step that links assessment to instructional design and programme planning. Indeed, it appears that much of what occurs in the assessment of students with learning difficulties has very little to do with the remediation they receive.

Why is this so, and how can the information derived from formal psychological and educational assessment help teachers to provide effective instruction or remediation?

Let us begin to answer these questions by reflecting upon the history of testing practices. Psychoeducational assessment appears to be concerned mostly with what individuals have, or have not, learned over the course of their lives, or over a period of instruction. This view is translated into assessment goals that relate to the identification of problems experienced by students, and the decisions made about them (see Salvia and Ysseldyke 1995). However, as we claim above, assessment has also become a *raison d'être* for educational clinicians and for many teachers.

Several writers have argued that educational testing has moved far beyond its functional value. McLaughlin (1991), for example, argued that few of the more commonly used tests measure attributes or variables that are directly related to learning, higher order thinking, or problem-solving. Furthermore, because tests do not tap complex cognitive processes, they do not support classroom practices that are directed toward teaching them. In the United States, in particular, students recognise that certain types of learning are of little value (if any), and teachers complain that students tend to focus on test scores alone, and dismiss the knowledge that will afford them a deeper understanding of the subject area.

THE NEED FOR A STRONGER ASSESSMENT–INSTRUCTION LINK

Educational measurement specialists have, for many years, attempted to bridge the gap between psychometrics and the measurement of educational achievement in the classroom. In other words, they have tried to decide what knowledge of children's learning and problem-solving skills (derived from test results) is needed to facilitate the education process.

Diversity and individual differences are intrinsic to information-processing theory which has innervated educational psychology and educational practice since the mid-1980s. A greater emphasis is now being placed on the application of information-processing theory to classrooms, and a greater awareness of the need to focus on individual differences in students' abilities, skills, and learning styles. Despite the proliferation of cognitive education methods and programmes (see e.g. Costa 1991), the incorporation of an assessment-instruction framework has not been employed.

Responsibility for the poor adaptation of assessment information to instruction does not rest solely with test-makers. Without doubt, testing specialists have been reluctant to involve themselves in classroom remediation or instruction, but teachers have also been less than enthusiastic about the ability of psychologists and counsellors to collaborate with them to translate test results and instruction hypotheses into classroom practice. Teachers also have been reluctant to embrace new instructional technologies regardless of their apparent relevance to contemporary mainstream classes or integration settings. Ashman and Conway (1993c) identified a number of pressures that mitigate against the integration of new cognitive methods into classroom practices. These include competition with the introduction of new curriculum policies and guidelines, the challenges associated with teaching classes containing children of mixed abilities and ages, and changes in the level of teacher accountability.

Many teachers believe that strategy training is difficult to reconcile in regular classrooms where teaching to the curriculum takes priority, although it may have some value in special education settings in which a teacher may work with students individually or in pairs to develop thinking strategies.

There have been a number of attempts to link assessment results with remediation and instruction. We review four of those attempts here.

Initiatives from the intelligence testing domain

In much the same way that the teaching and learning process is a collaborative activity between the teacher and student, so testing specialists must work with classroom teachers to ensure that the information gathered by psychologists or counsellors will contribute to the use of more efficient and relevant instructional strategies within the classroom. At the informal programming level, many consultants have developed a collection of remediation suggestions that teachers might employ to deal with students' learning deficits, based upon performance profiles established through standardised testing. The extent to which these assist regular or specialist teachers to provide practical classroom activities for students with special needs is questionable.

Information derived from standardised tests such as the Stanford Binet or WISC may reflect a student's knowledge or reasoning deficiencies, but it is difficult for a teacher to implement specific programmes that might address these problem areas in, for example, Vocabulary or Similarities, Coding or Block Design that has relevance to the curriculum. Similarly, data drawn from achievement tests may indicate a student's problem with reading comprehension, verbal analogies or the arithmetic operation of division.

Knowledge of a student's deficit skills might prompt specific remediation from a special education teacher away from the student's regular classroom, but again, many standardised tests contain items that bear little resemblance to the curricula and quickly become out of date (and somewhat irrelevant) when there are changes to curriculum policies and classroom teaching practices. For example, many achievement tests contain items dealing with the addition, subtraction and multiplication of fractions. Since the introduction of the decimal system in countries such as Australia, this aspect of the curriculum is no longer a major topic in mathematics or science.

Initiatives from the information processing domain

Following shortly after the development of their battery of information-processing tests in the mid-1970s, Das and his colleagues began developing remedial programmes to overcome simultaneous and successive processing deficits in children who had been identified as having a learning or intellectual disability. A distinctive feature of the various training studies with students with learning disabilities was the use of novel and simple laboratory tasks. This was based upon the argument that a cause of poor academic performance is the failure of students to apply coding strategies appropriately to a nominated academic task. Moreover, it was thought that strategic behaviour would be integrated more effectively by the learner when training was isolated from, rather than integrated into, academic activities. The desired outcome of training was improvement on coding tasks drawn from the simultaneous-successive battery and the generalisation of one or a number of processing skills to academic tasks presented after training.

Three studies using primary school-aged students with learning difficulties demonstrated some improvement in coding performance, and on related academic measures of reading (Brailsford 1981; D. Kaufman 1978; Krywaniuk 1974). Training studies involving students with mild intellectual disabilities have not produced generalised learning outcomes. Parmenter (1984) and Conway (1985), for example, both failed to obtain generalisation from training in coding strategies using late adolescents and primary school-aged students with an intellectual disability. Conway suggested that these individuals were unable to perceive the importance of applying the newly acquired strategies to tasks outside of the training programme.

The results of the Parmenter and Conway studies prompted Das (1985) to suggest that the failure of students with an intellectual disability to transfer their learning to academic tasks was a specific limiting characteristic of this population, and which was not found in other groups of students with special needs, such as those with learning difficulties or a cultural disadvantage. However, an alternative explanation may implicate instructional procedures that did not reinforce strategic behaviour in a manner appropriate for the students involved in the studies.

Like Das and his colleagues, A.S. Kaufman *et al.* (1983) recognised the need for instructional programming applications based upon the K-ABC. The K-SOS (Kaufman-Simultaneous or Successive) was designed as a remediation programme that would flow directly from the assessment process using the K-ABC. However, in a review of the evidence for the K-ABC/K-SOS assessment-instruction link, Salvia and Hritcko (1984) found little to suggest that instruction should be linked to K-ABC profiles, and no evidence of generality of processing strategies over time and tasks. Hence, it appears that while the K-ABC/K-SOS offers a logical link between assessment and remediation, there is little evidence of its adoption by teachers.

There have been literally hundreds of intervention studies based upon information-processing theory conducted since the mid-1970s. Many of these have addressed the specific processing deficits of students drawn from a range of at-risk groups. Few, however, have attempted to link data drawn from a comprehensive cognitive assessment to specific remedial programme components. Hence, it is difficult, if not impossible, to draw conclusions about the efficacy of the assessment-intervention nexus in the information processing domain. This is an area, however, on which we shall devote more attention in later chapters.

Initiative from the interactive assessment domain

Interactive assessment provides information on the student's ability to transfer what has been learned. This is not easily discerned from static assessment such as the K-ABC or the Das-Naglieri•Cognitive Assessment System, as the nature of the data collected relates to the specific task at the time of testing only. While there have been many versions of interactive assessment, the Learning Potential Assessment Device (LPAD) remains the most widely known.

As we indicated earlier, two important considerations for the tester in interactive assessment sessions are determining, first, how much aid, or direction must be given before the student can deal with the task independently; and second, how effective the student is in retaining, applying, and generalising what has been taught during the assessment session. Feuerstein *et al.* (1980) developed a training programme designed to improve the reasoning skills of culturally deprived and educationally disadvantaged adolescents – although in practice, most remediation efforts have been directed toward adolescents with intellectual disabilities. In the same way that the LPAD encouraged students to be active learners, Feuerstein argued strongly that instruction must also encourage students away from being passive acceptance learners who wait for teachers to tell them what to do next, to them becoming active modifiers of their environment so that they could move toward increasingly higher levels of intellectual functioning.

The Instrumental Enrichment (IE) programme is based upon a set of goals that relate directly to the proposition that students can increase their capacity to benefit from experiences in formal and informal learning settings. Some of the goals include the acquisition of vocabulary, concepts, operations and relationships relevant to problem-solving; the development of insight and understanding of one's own thought processes (i.e. metacognition); the formation of proper study habits so that they become spontaneous and automatic; the development of motivation based upon the intrinsic interest generated by the task; and the transition of the student from a passive recipient, to an active generator of information. We shall not elaborate on IE further at this point as it is described more fully in Chapter 8.

From the clinician's point of view, however, interactive assessment techniques have yet to be substantiated as methods that will provide psychologists and others with a better understanding of children's learning difficulties than static measures alone. Das and Naglieri (1992), for example, stated that interactive assessment would be tolerated only by clinicians who conduct ability testing if: (a) the improvised procedures were a small part of the assessment process; (b) the interactive assessment did not invalidate the use of standard procedures; and (c) the process would be of benefit to the child. They stated that interactive assessment could be a precursor to remediation or instruction, although it is difficult to accommodate both within the usual assessment activities that are carried out in schools.

On the one hand, these views argue for maintaining existing static testing procedures because of tester resistance, and the separation of assessment for classification purposes and assessment for programme development. In an ideal world in which the clinician had unlimited time for testing and programme development, such a two-phase testing approach may have merit. The dichotomy of assessment for classification, and assessment for programme development, however, is unlikely to satisfy the pragmatic needs of school and clinical staff who are under time pressures and who deal with diverse learning problems. In addition, it maintains the separation of clinician and teacher, which is indefensible in contemporary schools where professionals must interact in a common arena. We are not arguing that the professional responsibilities of clinician or teacher be subsumed into one, but rather that there is an inherent inefficiency in testing for classification, and testing again to establish goals for instruction or remediation.

APPLYING COGNITIVE ASSESSMENT TO CLASSROOM INSTRUCTION

Much of the discussion about instruction focuses only on what the student is or is not doing to learn or solve problems. When attention is given only to the learner, many other significant features of the learning environment – those that directly affect learning outcomes – are neglected. We have suggested four groups of factors that interact to affect successful and unsuccessful learning outcomes. These include those components which relate to learner competencies and skills, to the content being taught, the physical setting in which learning occurs and, finally, those which relate to the instructor. In our view, it is unrealistic to make instructional decisions that are unrelated to, or removed from, the context in which learning occurs. It is for this reason we believe that information derived from assessment processes must be linked to classroom instruction practices.

There can be little dispute that the overwhelming majority of programme planning decisions that occur within the classroom are made on the basis of teacher judgements of student ability and class progress. Some attention, therefore, must be given to the place of informal evaluations. Informal evaluations include teacher-made tests or checklists, as well as the more general considerations of the total learning environment such as informal observation of students' learning activities and ability (see Sattler 1992).

We believe that the teaching approaches used by regular classroom and specialist teachers must be conducive to instruction that meets individual student needs. In other words, the way in which instruction is provided must enable students to learn in the most effective manner and, ideally, in their preferred way.

A general classroom-based assessment procedure

In a study undertaken at the University of Queensland, Ashman and a number of colleagues developed a model of support for students with learning difficulties (described in Ashman and Conway 1993a). That model was based on the assumption that the school and its personnel, in particular the classroom teacher, must take responsibility and action for both the identification of students' learning problems and their remediation. The model emphasises the close link between assessment and instruction (Figure 6.1). It must be emphasised that this prototype would need modification to meet the needs of specific learning situations, and the availability of personnel and resources. However, the very close link in this model between assessment and instruction is of importance to us here.

It is most unlikely that all students in any class would be subject to an individual assessment by a psychologist or counsellor. For this reason teachers must have a general assessment procedure available for monitoring student progress which involves formal and informal assessment, consultation and team decision-making. At this point, we briefly overview the model.

Phase 1: screening

All teachers monitor students' performance in the course of regular classroom lessons and these observations are the first phase of assessment and remediation. In some schools, additional assessment procedures may be available, such as screening programmes for children in their first or second year of school that identify those who may require some 'early intervention'. Having identified a number of students at-risk, then the teacher may, for example, amend classroom practices to take into account the needs of these children, either through individual tutoring or the introduction of a parallel support programme outside the home class. The outcome of these initiatives is judged as successful or otherwise by the teacher, the child's parent, or other specialist teachers who may be involved.

Phase 2: consultation

If the teacher judges that a student has made little progress on the basis of classroom performance or informal assessment or is still experiencing some continuing problem, the class teacher may bring the child's problem, the assessment, intervention, and outcome information to a teacher support team (TST) meeting. The team could be comprised of several class teachers and may include the principal, specialist teachers, librarian, speech therapist, and the counsellor. The team would review the case, prepare an individualised education plan for the student, and assist the teacher to decide on the steps to be taken and the outcomes to be measured or evaluated. These may include prolonging or modifying the original intervention, or beginning a new one. The teacher would then act on the advice of the team and monitor progress.

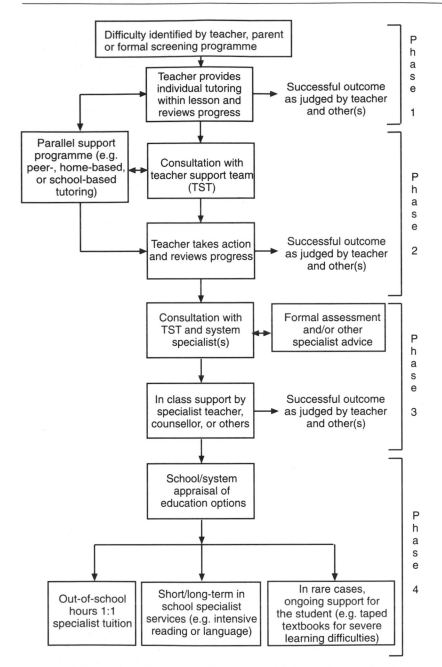

Figure 6.1 Flow chart of the cyclical assessment, intervention, and review process
Source: A.F. Ashman and R.N.F. Conway (1993) 'Examining the links between psycho-educational assessment, instruction and remediation', *International Journal of Disability, Development and Education 40*: 23–44. Reproduced with permission.

Phase 3: the role of testing

If the student's progress remains unsatisfactory, the teacher would consult once again with the support team and other specialists. At this stage, formal assessment by a psychologist or counsellor may be sought.

Such a procedure might include interactive assessment and/or standardised test batteries (such as the DN•CAS). While the teacher may observe that a student takes a long time to commence or finish a task, often they may not have the time available to explore the student's thinking processes, and may overlook certain characteristics or processing deficits that might inhibit successful learning and problem-solving. A processing profile generated from a more extensive assessment may provide valuable information.

We cannot emphasise too much that even the most psychometrically sound testing battery will serve no purpose unless the assessor, specialists, and classroom teachers work together to identify how and where the student's strengths and weaknesses are reflected in classroom activities. These collaborative efforts must form the basis of Phase 3 of the assessment-intervention procedure.

Phase 4: school system options

If the collaboration is successful, an effective intervention should result. In some situations, however, it may not be possible to provide the degree of support or individual tutoring needed by a student in the regular classroom. In such a case, other support options need to be considered. It may be necessary, therefore, to take action for which the school system (rather than the school) assumes responsibility. Any special intervention, however, should combine the planning, processing, and curriculum content needs of the students.

In either case, a review of the student's individualised education plan should ensure that assessment information has been translated into school-based action, and material and/or personnel can be provided to the school so that the intervention can be implemented. School system personnel would then be responsible for evaluating the intervention regardless of where it took place.

SUMMARY

As education policy and practice have moved toward greater inclusion of children with special needs in mainstream classes, teachers have come under greater pressure to provide an appropriate education for all children in their care. Perhaps more than ever before, there is now a need for all information relevant to the teaching and remediation of students to be accessible to, and usable by, teachers. Up to the present time, much data collected by testing specialists have not been of assistance in programme planning or instructional design.

However, with the developing emphasis on cognitive processes there has been a keen interest to develop assessment devices and procedures that reflect the way in which students learn and solve problems. A review of test categories in various editions of the *Mental Measurement Yearbooks* (e.g. Conoley and Impara 1992) will show that there have been few new tests of intelligence or achievement published over the past decades. Most of those currently available are revisions of instruments that have been on the market for many years, and apart from the K-ABC and DN•CAS the emphasis is on ability testing rather than the student's information processing competence.

Some well-known assessment instruments have a clear link to information processing. Raven's Progressive Matrices (of intelligence) for example, has been used as a measure of logical relationship or simultaneous processing in the original or adapted form. The Digit Span subtest of the WISC has similarly been used as a measure of serial processing in digit, or word forms.

Some subtests of the Halstead-Reitan Battery (e.g. Visual Search) and also the Porteus Maze Test (Porteus 1965) also have a direct connection with the information-processing domain through their foci on rudimentary planning skills.

Apart from this relatively small collection of tests, there are few published, commonly available instruments that specifically address a person's strategic or metastrategic behaviour. Hence, establishing a learner's information-processing profile has not been an easy task and, for most researchers and clinicians, there has been a need to rely on a large aggregation of experimental tests or interactive methods from which we can judge a learner's processing strengths or deficiencies. The time is right to work toward the establishment of clear and unambiguous links between assessment and instruction.

STUDY TASKS

6.1 In note form, list the main points covered in this chapter.

6.2 Write down the main points that discriminate between traditional tests of intelligence (e.g. Stanford Binet), tests that focus on information processing (e.g. DN•CAS), and interactive assessment procedures.

6.3 Undertake a search of library resources manually or using CD-ROM systems and locate material that relates to the influence of culture on test performance. How might the influence of culture be minimised?

6.4 Toward the end of the chapter, we described an assessment-instruction model. Look carefully at the model and evaluate its usefulness in terms of accommodating the four agents that affect students' learning, and the instructional cycle to which we referred in Chapter 1.

ADDITIONAL READING

Hamers, J., Pennings, A. and Guthke, J. (1994) 'Training-based assessment of school achievement', *Learning and Instruction 1*: 347–360.

Haywood, H.C. and Tzuriel, D. (eds) (1992) *Interactive Assessment*, New York: Springer-Verlag.

Journal of Cognitive Education.

Lidz, C.S. (1991) *Practitioner's Guide to Dynamic Assessment*, New York: Guilford.

Chapter 7

Instruction and remediation

One of the important principles discussed in Chapter 1 was the need for a continuous teaching-learning process that involved assessment, preparation, instruction, and evaluation. In this chapter, and later, we focus on the instruction, and evaluation aspects of the cycle. We discuss a number of issues related to teaching and remediation, and describe instructional techniques that bring into focus strategic behaviour, problem-solving, and related concepts.

Before beginning, we shall review the terms cognition and metacognition as many training models and programmes are not clearly identified as being either cognitive or metacognitive. Cognitive approaches teach students to follow a sequence of steps or procedures that have typically been pre-determined by the teacher to ensure that students incorporate the strategy (or strategies) for a specified use. Cognitive strategies taught in this way remain as the teacher's strategy and, hence, may not be employed by students when the teacher is not there to remind them to use it.

Metacognitive strategies go further, requiring students to plan and monitor their own performance and decide whether it is appropriate to use the strategy at a particular time or not. Many metacognitive training programmes teach self-interrogation or self-checking strategies that assist in monitoring performance. Metacognitive strategy training encourages students to think about their learning in a variety of learning situations. While most teachers concentrate on cognitive training, it is 'a necessary but insufficient procedure in itself to ensure independence in learning' (Westwood 1993: 30).

CATEGORIES OF COGNITIVE INSTRUCTION

Three categories of cognitive instructional techniques have been suggested: situated cognition; cognitive strategy instruction; and a dual approach (Kulieke and Jones 1993). In situated cognition, the teaching of cognitive strategies is part of the general learning process in which the student acquires competence through exposure to a wide range of learning situations. Skills and strategies are not directly taught but emerge from the experiences of each learner, the reinforcement they receive from teachers, and from the content to which they are exposed. As teaching materials become more complex, the student adapts cognitive skills across a range of applications which, in turn, increases the depth of understanding of those skills in much the same way as a spider's web is built from constant links between individual points.

Cognitive strategy instruction refers to the direct teaching of a range (or repertoire) of specific and general cognitive skills that apply to particular content areas and to a number of learning tasks. Many specific cognitive strategy training studies fall into this category, particularly as there is a clear body of research that indicates that students at all levels of development can benefit from training on specific tasks such as essay writing and research skills. There is a danger that teaching within a cognitive strategy training framework may mirror the fragmented approach to teaching found in early behavioural studies and instructional methods. Cognitive strategy training must not produce a series of discrete strategies for content-specific tasks. Instead, students must be taught to apply the strategies across tasks.

The dual approach has a recursive element involving a before, during, and after sequence of activities. Before undertaking the task, the student prepares by activating prior cognitive knowledge by asking questions and speculating about what may happen. The during stage allows the student to compare the strategies required with those predicted, and make any required amendments. The after phase allows the integration of the newly acquired strategies within the existing cognitive skills repertoire.

While each has its own form, most cognitive education approaches share common features. Kulieke and Jones (1993) argued that all three move away from the traditional approach to learning in which others (e.g. teachers) determine the sequence of skills to be taught, to recipients of knowledge (students). All three approaches emphasise the importance of internalising declarative and procedural knowledge through activities such as defining problems, self-questioning, linking new information with existing knowledge, monitoring learning, and connecting learning to practical activities and issues. In this way, the three approaches avoid the teaching of isolated facts and skills, and enable the integration of thinking and understanding with content knowledge. Another commonality between the three approaches is the emphasis on self-regulated learning, including the need for the student to take responsibility for learning and problem-solving. This also includes being aware of strategies and knowing when to use them, how to monitor progress, and when to make changes as a result of feedback.

PREPARING INSTRUCTION BASED ON ASSESSMENT OUTCOMES

An important principle of the instructional cycle is the requirement that assessment underpins any instructional activity to ensure that the programme is appropriate to the needs and capabilities of the students. It is important that both strengths and weaknesses in student performance are taken into account, and that process and content are adequately assessed. For this reason, assessment, which allows the teacher to understand the way a student attempts a task, is more beneficial than having a score representing correct and error responses. For example, knowing how a student attempted a mathematical task, and what errors were made in obtaining the incorrect response is more valuable that simply knowing that the answer was incorrect. By knowing the processing errors, the teacher is better able to plan an instructional programme that addresses not only the mathematical content, but also the student's processing or cognitive abilities at the same time.

Some programmes focus on developing the cognitive strengths found during assessment, while others emphasise the importance of developing the weaker skills to enhance the students' repertoire of learning and problem-solving 'tools'.

Assessment and preparation, however, must take both content and process into consideration. Rohwer and Thomas (1989) reflect this belief in arguing three classes of instructional conditions necessary for students to acquire both domain-specific (content) knowledge and metacognitive (process) knowledge in classrooms. First, there is a need to design instruction that places demands on student knowledge of content and process, and both should be evaluated. Second, the instructional setting should support and encourage the use and application of content and process skills. Third, the classroom environment must be free of methods or teacher assistance that reduce, or even eliminate, the need to use both content and process skills.

These three conditions are not often demonstrated in the classroom as there is often an emphasis on the acquisition of facts through the use of a prescribed textbook and an assessment approach that concentrates on content. The importance of content is given further emphasis through teaching methods that include note-taking, listening to teachers summarise the main points, writing essays and, in senior years, coaching students on the key facts to assist in external examinations.

None of these approaches place any major reliance on students to take responsibility for learning, to encourage them to work individually or collectively, or help them understand the processes involved in learning. The dilemma for the teacher is deciding whether some content should be covered in detail, giving students an in-depth understanding of the content and processes involved in fewer topics, or a superficial coverage given to many topics. Most teachers seem compelled to choose the latter option.

The following questions may help redirect teachers' attention to the importance of gathering as much information as possible to guide the preparation phase of instruction:

- What content strengths and weaknesses are shown in the assessment?
- What processing strengths and weaknesses are shown in the assessment?
- Does the student show a preference for any particular learning strategies?
- What affective responses (e.g. motivation, effort) did the student show while attempting the task?
- Were the tasks within the student's ability range?

INTEGRATING LEARNING STRATEGIES AND LEARNING COMPONENTS

There has been an increasing emphasis in recent years on the importance of teaching for understanding and meaning, as well as for content knowledge. This is especially true in the field of cognitive education. Indeed, Mayer (1992: 411) suggested that 'cognitive theory offers a new vision of what to teach, how to teach and where to teach'. It is relevant here to consider each of these points briefly.

What to teach

If we accept that content and process are both important, we need to teach the problem-solving and thinking skills that underlie the domain-specific content being taught. We then have to consider whether we teach the process skills separately, in the same way that mathematics, reading, and art are taught as discrete bodies of knowledge, or integrated into the domain content.

Some cognitive educators argue that cognitive and metacognitive strategies should be taught as discrete skills that can be applied across content areas, while others believe in embedding strategy training within the content to ensure that students can clearly see the relationship between strategic and content knowledge.

How to teach

If we choose to integrate processing skills into teaching practice, a change would be required in teaching practice. This would involve moving away from teacher-centred, domain-specific instruction toward student involvement in the teaching-learning process. This has often been called the discovery approach to learning in which students are guided in exploring a topic, rather than relying on the teacher to provide the knowledge the students must learn. An approach that involved students exploring a curriculum topic would require the teacher to think of the academic content from the students' perspective, and provide learning experiences that allowed content knowledge to be 'discovered'.

Where to teach

If both the content and the practice of teaching were to change, then the location of instruction may also need to change. The most obvious change might be that students would no longer need to sit at desks watching the teacher's presentation. Instead, there would be increased use of classroom practices that encouraged co-operative learning activities that stimulated discussion and exploration.

If Mayer's (1992) approach was adopted, content would be taught within a problem-solving and thinking skills framework, and the teaching of skills in isolation through drill and practice would play a minor role in classroom activities.

STUDENTS' LEARNING STYLE AND INSTRUCTION

In preparing a teaching programme, consideration needs to be given to the characteristics of the learner. The behaviourist approach to instruction (outlined in Chapter 2) focuses attention on the learning situation. The cognitive approach emphasises student learning characteristics as they directly affect learning outcomes. Schmeck (1988), for example, suggested that there is a close relationship between personality, motivation and stages of development; learning styles, strategies and tactics; and learning outcomes.

Learning style operates at three levels – deep, elaborative, shallow – and affects the extent to which students benefit from instruction. Students with a deep learning style focus on concepts, organise ideas into networks, and analyse and synthesise material to ensure full understanding. Students at the elaborative level are also productive thinkers who individualise their understanding through personal language, and by relating the information they are learning to personal experiences. Students who have a shallow learning style focus on repetition and rehearsal, and work at a literal level when reproducing information.

The effect of learning style on instruction also depends on the learning outcomes sought by teachers. If the desired result is rote memorisation of content, the student using a shallow learning style will be most effective. However, if the desired outcome is for students to understand the processes involved, and apply those processes to other learning tasks, the student who used a deep or elaborative learning style would be most successful. Schmeck (1989) concluded that we need not only to be aware of students' learning style, but also to include strategies that develop deep and elaborative learning styles in our instruction.

TEACHING THINKING SKILLS

There has been concern since the mid-1980s that students are unable to develop or employ effective learning and problem-solving skills (Resnick 1987). The response to this assertion has been the development of a range of thinking skills programmes that have been taught either in isolation, or as part of an integrated teaching-learning approach. However, it appears that there is no clear understanding of what is meant by a 'thinking programme' or what should be included in the syllabus. Often there is confusion between thinking programmes, metacognitive programmes, and cognitive training programmes.

Thinking skill programmes typically include six dimensions:

- metacognition
- cognitive processes (including problem-solving, decision-making, comprehending)
- core thinking skills (including representation, summarising and elaboration)
- critical thinking
- creative thinking
- understanding the role of content knowledge.

These are not discrete or hierarchical. In other words, it is possible to engage a number of dimensions at the one time (Marzano *et al.* 1988).

ACQUIRING COGNITIVE AND METACOGNITIVE SKILLS

Metacognition is a higher order skill that relates to one's awareness of the thinking process and it can operate at a number of levels that are more or less evaluative. Metacognition can be, for example,

- tacit – implied without being openly expressed, as in problem-solving in which no particular strategy has been used
- aware – conscious use and awareness of a particular strategy
- strategic – organised thinking through deliberate use of a particular process
- reflective – deliberate and considered planning, monitoring and the evaluation of a particular process.

A number of approaches have been used in teaching metacognitive awareness. Fogarty and Bellanca (1993), for example, prepared a training manual to teach students each level of metacognition mentioned above. Their programme involved fifty lessons but, up to the present time, there has been no empirical evidence reported of the effectiveness of the programme. Other training approaches are based on the belief that students may be at different levels of metacognitive functioning in different activities, and employ a variety of techniques to enhance metacognition including direct explanation, scaffolded instruction, cognitive coaching, and co-operative learning (Paris and Winograd 1990). These approaches can be used independently or concurrently. In the following sections we discuss each approach, using examples of their application drawn from the literature.

Direct explanation

Direct explanation involves teaching a student about the nature and application of a specific strategy. Verbal self-instruction (described in Chapter 2) is a good example of students being taught a procedure to assist them to internalise a strategy. The original approach involved cognitive modelling, overt external guidance, overt self-guidance, faded overt self-guidance, and covert self-guidance. The direct explanation approach extends the original procedure to explain the sequence of teaching steps.

The common features of a direct explanation approach were summarised by Paris and Winograd (1990) and are shown in Table 7.1.

In early studies, the final step was not included, although, more recently, researchers have found that by adding the monitoring step the sense of student ownership of the strategy is enhanced.

Paris and Winograd (1990) reported three advantages of the direct explanation approach to metacognition training. First, they provided a clear link between the academic task and the strategy, and assisted in breaking a difficult task into manageable components. Second, the development of the

Table 7.1 Common features of a direct explanation approach

What the strategy is	The teacher describes the critical features or provides a definition or description of the strategy
Why the strategy should be learned	The teacher explains the purpose and potential benefits of the strategy
How to use the strategy	The teacher explains each step in the strategy including how to use specific techniques in each step
When and where the strategy is to be used	The teacher explains when it is appropriate to use the strategy
How to evaluate the use of the strategy	The teacher explains how to assess whether the strategy was useful and what to do if it was not

strategy forced the teacher to consider the cognitive components of the task and structure them in a way that the student could follow. Third, direct explanation could be used in whole classes or small groups to make the task of managing students' learning and behaviour easier.

The advantages also create their own disadvantages. Having a student follow a strategy developed by a teacher may not match the cognitive or metacognitive learning style of the student, particularly if the whole class is to use the same strategy. Unless the teacher allows students to re-word the strategy (in their own language), it is likely to remain the teacher's strategy and will be applied only to that specific task, or not at all. A teacher may, for example, make the assumption that all students can learn effectively using the same generic strategy and require students to memorise a teacher-generated strategy that has been prepared for another group of students. The assumption that direct explanation is more economical because it can be applied to whole classes cannot be demonstrated until there is a research base of studies conducted at the whole-class level. To date studies have been reported with few students (three in the study by Danoff *et al.* 1993, summarised in Box 7.1), often with learning difficulties, and instruction takes place either in individual or small-group situations away from the regular classroom.

Scaffolded instruction

One of the most common features of cognitive and metacognitive programmes is the use of scaffolded instruction that provides support to learners to enable them to achieve objectives they would not have accomplished without that support (Palincsar 1991). The support is both temporary and adjustable, as the ultimate goal is for the student to gain independence. By its nature, scaffolded instruction cannot be a formal set of procedures, as it relies on the skill of the individual mediator/teacher to use the components to meet the needs of the student. Scaffolding includes modelling, questioning, and feedback depending on the task, the needs of the particular student, and their level of ability.

While there are many types of scaffolding used in instruction, Langer and Applebee (1986) listed a number of common components (Table 7.2).

The basis of scaffolded instruction derives from the work of Vygotsky (see Chapter 4) which emphasised the role of social interaction in which learning is mediated by an expert guiding a novice through a task to ensure that the learner acquires the expert's skills. Hence, the teacher's role becomes one of facilitating the students' cognitive and metacognitive skills through questioning, modelling, and supporting students' use of appropriate strategies.

Box 7.1

An application of the Self-Regulated Strategy Development model

The application of the Self-Regulated Strategy Development (SRSD) model, in a study based on writing in elementary schools, provides a good example of the direct instruction of a cognitive strategy (Danoff *et al.* 1993). Based on a series of earlier studies using the SRSD, Danoff *et al.* taught students a specific strategy, incorporating the mnemonic given below.

The writing strategy
1   Think of a story you would like to share with others.
2   Let the mind be free.
3   Write down the story part reminder (mnemonic):

W – W – W What = 2 How = 2	⇨	**Wh**o is the main character; who else is in the story? **Wh**en does the story take place? **Wh**ere does the story take place? **What** does the main character want to do? **What** happens when the main character tries to do it? **How** does the story end? **How** does the main character feel?

4   Write down the ideas for each part.
5   Write your story – use good ideas and make sense.

Students memorised the strategy, including the mnemonic, and then applied it to their writing. Following the use of the strategy, the teacher and the students discussed how the strategy helped to correct errors. The results of the study indicated that the students' story writing improved and was maintained. The researchers argued that there is a place for direct explanation of writing strategies because 'important cognitive processes are more visible and concrete ... [and] ... although most of the students were familiar with the parts of a story, strategy instruction helped them to understand and use what it was they knew' (Danoff *et al.* 1993: 317).

Mediated learning experiences

The term 'mediated learning experiences' is derived from Feuerstein's Theory of Structural Cognitive Modifiability (Feuerstein *et al.* 1980) where mediated experiences are considered an essential part of both assessment and remediation. In an instructional sense, MLE is the application of the principles of adult–child interactions to assist cognitive development in a teaching environment. Mediation ensures that students acquire relevant cognitive skills when they may have been unable to gain those skills through previous learning experiences.

Table 7.2 Common components in scaffolding

1 Recruitment	The tutor enlists the student's interest
2 Reduction in the degrees of freedom	The tutor reduces the size and complexity of the task to the level at which the student can recognise a fit with the task requirements
3 Direction maintenance	The tutor keeps the student focused on the task
4 Marking critical features	The tutor highlights the features of the task that the student can use to compare personal performance with desired performance
5 Frustration level	The tutor assists in reducing stress
6 Demonstration	The tutor demonstrates the appropriate method for completing the task so that the student can imitate it back in a more appropriate form

The activities that can occur in mediated learning include

- assisting the student to focus on the task by reducing the number and complexity of stimuli
- providing opportunities for students to have repeated exposure to important stimuli
- providing opportunities for students to perceive and understand relationships between previous and current experiences
- providing opportunities for students to generalise their experiences

(Arbitman-Smith *et al.* 1984)

In addition, mediators

- supply information needed to learn relationships
- ask questions rather than give answers
- arrange events so that student learning is guided
- guide student deductions
- build student confidence
- maintain a metacognitive focus

(Haywood 1993)

The following five mechanisms of mediated teaching provide a focus for the many models that have incorporated the concept of mediation or MLE.

Process questioning

Process questioning provides a metacognitive challenge by redirecting thinking back to the students. Teachers ask 'how' questions rather than supply answers. This focuses attention on students asking questions of themselves, rather than relying on the teacher's answers.

Bridging

Bridging provides a cognitive link to other situations so that students' learning is not fixed to one task. The role of the teacher is not to provide examples of bridging, but to have students draw examples from their own experiences or situations in which the same processes could work. In this way the students see the broader application of the process in their own terms and in relation to their own experiences, rather than being limited to teacher-contrived situations with which they may be unfamiliar (Haywood 1988).

Challenging or requiring justification

Challenging or requiring justification should occur for both correct and incorrect answers. The aim of the strategy is to encourage students to reflect on their responses – whether they are correct or not – and consider alternative solutions.

Teaching about rules

Teaching about rules addresses the issue of generalisation. When a rule applies to one situation, students are encouraged to consider whether the rule would apply to other situations. Again, the role of the teacher is not to prescribe a rule but to mediate on students' deliberations.

Emphasising order, predictability, system sequence and strategies

Emphasising order, predictability, system, sequence, and strategies are not taught as specific components in any lesson but are drawn together throughout the day's lessons. Aspects of each of these can be included as the opportunities arise.

RECIPROCAL TEACHING

Reciprocal teaching exemplifies the concept of scaffolding. It was developed by Palincsar and Brown (1984; 1986) to assist students with reading comprehension, and involves the application of scaffolded instruction to an academic area. Since its development, reciprocal teaching has been used widely across many academic areas (see Bruer 1993; Hartman 1994).

Reciprocal teaching is based on four principles (Palincsar *et al.* 1988):

- increasing students' reading comprehension by equipping them with strategies needed to monitor comprehension and construct meaning
- having teachers and students share the responsibility for acquiring

strategies, with a gradual transfer of responsibility from the teacher to the students
- having students participate in discussions with an encouraging teacher
- ensuring that students learn to control the dialogue.

Four strategies are emphasised in reciprocal teaching: summarising, questioning, clarifying, and predicting. Summarising requires recall, an understanding of what has been read, and an activation of background knowledge to integrate information in the text. Questioning based on text information requires the student to monitor the content to identify important points. Clarifying requires a critical evaluation of the content. Finally, predicting requires the drawing and testing of inferences, using existing knowledge. All four skills are required for efficient reading comprehension (Palincsar and Brown 1984; 1986).

The five-step procedure used in reciprocal teaching is shown in Table 7.3.

Not all teachers will use all aspects of the reciprocal teaching model. As Hartman (1994) pointed out in his review of the model, some researchers have adapted the model by eliminating or modifying some steps.

The development of the reciprocal teaching model has been thoroughly documented in the literature, particularly by Palincsar and Brown (1984; 1986) and Palincsar (1991). An independent study by Kelly et al. (1994) in New Zealand demonstrated the effect of the model for students within regular primary school classes. Reciprocal teaching was incorporated within the daily reading schedule of two classes for twenty minutes a day, for a school term. While the experimental group in the study was engaged in reciprocal teaching, the remaining students in the room followed the standard reading programme. The reciprocal teaching groups were deliberately heterogeneous to ensure a range of peer models.

Kelly et al. (1994) found that reciprocal teaching enabled students to make significant gains in their performance on comprehension tests in contrast to the group who worked on the standard programme. These gains for reciprocal teaching students persisted over an eight-week post-intervention period and these students also generalised their newly acquired comprehension skills to other writing genre. Importantly, the gains were achieved using content drawn from the standard reading programme in regular classes, and with no additional resources needed for either the students or teachers.

While the Kelly et al. (1994) study illustrates the successful application of a scaffolded instruction model, there are a number of limitations and unanswered questions about reciprocal teaching (Paris and Winograd 1990). First, teachers must be empathetic in their teaching and knowledgeable about the processes involved. Teachers who are unwilling to allow students to lead instruction, or who do not understand the concept of sequencing in cognitive strategy development, may have limited success in implementing reciprocal teaching. In addition, there is the possibility of students passing on incorrect

Table 7.3 The five steps in reciprocal teaching

Stage 1 Teacher demonstration	The importance of the step lies in the modelling of a strategy that students will later adapt in the dialogue sessions in Stages 3 and 4. At this stage, the 'expert' (teacher) has the knowledge and skills, while the 'novices' (students) are unable to apply the cognitive skills.
Stage 2 Student learning and practice	The role of the teacher continues to be that of the expert, although student involvement increases through teacher prompts and guided practice.
Stage 3 Teacher-student groups	In this stage the focus moves to a small-group setting in which the teacher initiates the dialogue about the four comprehension strategies. Students are encouraged to take a more active role than before and, over time, students take turns leading the group. At this point there is a change in the instructional language from teacher language to student language, as students accept responsibility for generating questions, providing feedback to other students, and reviewing the use of the four strategies. The teacher's role then becomes one of supporting the student-teacher.
Stage 4 Student groups	The teacher now moves out of the group and students manage the group alone. The teacher provides support across groups rather than at the individual group level. Students continue to use the same strategies as in Stage 3, providing the scaffolding for other students in the group.
Stage 5 Student self-regulation	By Stage 5, students have acquired the four comprehension strategies and have internalised their operation. The scaffold is no longer required.

information in stages 3 and 4, although as Paris and Winograd observed, this difficulty is not restricted to this approach.

COGNITIVE COACHING

Cognitive coaching includes strategies such as direct explanations, modelling, mutual dialogues and encouragement, and may include components of other approaches such as scaffolding. In the application of cognitive coaching to reading comprehension, Paris and Winograd (1990) used posters, metaphors, and analogies in teaching metacognitive strategies to primary school students.

Cognitive coaching makes three contributions to metacognitive instruction.

First, when teachers and students have a common goal, there is an opportunity for co-operation. Second, coaching involves ongoing assessment, hence, feedback can result in changes to task difficulty and expectations with the result that students continue to be challenged. Third, as cognitive coaching involves mutual regulation, students share their views about the thinking process.

STUDENT COLLABORATION

Student collaboration refers to a collection of teaching-learning approaches that use the skills and knowledge of students to enhance strategic and metastrategic behaviour in the classroom. Sharan (1990) suggested that collaborative and co-operative learning approaches:

- enable teachers to manage large numbers of students in a single group ensuring that their time is spent productively
- encourage students to be active members of small work groups
- encourage each student to assist and support others to develop their knowledge and skills
- encourage a high degree of engagement in group activities
- appear to have a positive effect on students' in-class behaviour.

They derive their conceptual foundation from the interactional perspective described by Vygotsky (1978). He argued that children gain relevant information, new patterns of thought, and problem-solving strategies from the interactions they have with their peers. Through collaborative exchanges, students internalise new strategies and metacognitive concepts that are implicit in their communications.

The contemporary notions of peer collaboration and co-operation have connections with instructional methods that have been used down the centuries. Collaborative learning approaches now include a range of peer tutoring and buddy systems at the individual or small group level, to whole-class activities. Here we describe two of the most popular models, co-operative learning and peer tutoring.

We now turn our attention to four approaches characterised by learner collaboration: co-operative learning, peer tutoring, cognitive apprenticeship, and self-regulation.

Co-operative learning

The term 'co-operative learning' is most frequently applied to situations in which students work in small groups in the classroom using a set of teaching-learning strategies that encourage co-operation between the group members (Goor and Schwenn 1993). The aim is to ensure that students work together to maximise their own and other group members' learning. As a result, group support and group motivation is important, particularly as the tangible rewards are provided to the group, not the individual.

Goor and Schwenn (1993) have identified six elements in co-operative learning:

1   The use of heterogeneous groups that are able to be changed.
2   The goals and rewards are shared by the group to promote interdepend-ence within the group.
3   The classroom management system is designed to maximise group learning.
4   The classroom is organised to allow group work.
5   The students are taught how to work co-operatively and teach one another.
6   The specific co-operative strategy used in the lesson is selected to match the goal of the lesson.

There are several co-operative learning models (Goor and Schwenn 1993; Olson and Platt 1993; Valletutti and Dummett 1992). The most commonly reported include Team Accelerated Instruction (TAI), Student Teams Achievement Divisions (STAD), Jigsaw, Teams-Games-Tournaments (TGT), and group projects. In the TAI approach, there is a combination of individual and group work as each student is assigned a different activity within the group, based on ability, and each student then contributes certain skills to accomplish the group goal. In the STAD approach, students study a task as a group, and then compete in quizzes and competitions as a group. In the Jigsaw approach, each student is taught one piece of the information that is required by the whole group to solve the task. By adding this one piece of information, each student contributes to the group solution. Cooperative Academic Games (CAGs) involve card games that define different roles for the students to enable them to achieve a group goal. The games emphasise group co-operation, and social and cognitive skills and are designed to be played four or five times, as students strive to complete the task in the shortest time.

Group projects would be the most familiar co-operative activities under-taken in primary classrooms. Members of a work group contribute to the preparation and presentation of some predetermined product such as a poster on a specific topic.

In all co-operative group activities attention must be given to the interactions that occur between group members as those actions directly influence the outcomes (Gillies 1994). It is important, for example, to develop the students' skill in providing information, which includes explanations, as this allows for clarification, and organisation of information. Group dynam-ics and outcomes are influenced by a number of factors such as the ability levels of the participants, gender mix, and even personal characteristics such as extroversion or introversion (Ashman and Gillies in press; Gillies 1994).

One of the most important factors influencing the success of the group activity is the way in which the class is organised, and the appropriateness of the task for independent student participation.

In a study using secondary school students in Israel, Shachar and Sharan (1994) found that co-operative learning was more successful than whole class teaching over a trial period of six months. In whole-class instruction activities, western students dominated discussion, while in the co-operative learning condition, there was almost equal turn-taking between western and Middle-Eastern students. There were also more interactions between students in the co-operative groups than occurred during whole-class lessons. Shachar and Sharan found that academic achievement was higher as a result of the co-operative learning experience than for whole class lessons, and that the quality of student interaction within the groups was a significant contributor to the achievement of the goals set for the work groups.

There have been numerous studies undertaken on co-operative learning that clearly demonstrate the advantages that accrue to students who work together to achieve a goal. Not only do students gain academically but also co-operative learning prepares them for out-of-school activities in which co-operative problem-solving is required for success.

Notwithstanding this, co-operative learning is often considered by teachers to be too difficult to set up in a classroom, as it requires both teacher and student preparation to work successfully. In addition, it requires a commitment by the teacher to allow students the freedom to explore the task, rather than relying on a teacher's presentation. To be effective, co-operative learners need to

- develop the self-confidence necessary to provide assistance, advice, or instruction to others
- identify when a classmate, someone in their family, a friend, or co-worker is requesting or in need of assistance, advice, or instruction
- analyse the nature, scope, and sequence of an instructional task
- synthesise and execute a learning plan in a training or tutoring situation
- stimulate interest and involvement within the work group
- create or prepare creative activities for instruction
- evaluate the outcomes of the assistance or instruction.

(Valletutti and Dummett 1992: 187–8)

The benefits to be gained from co-operative learning do, however, seem to outweigh the modest preparation that it requires.

Peer tutoring

Peer tutoring has been used extensively in both cognitive and behavioural teaching-learning situations. Students with special education needs have often been involved in peer tutoring projects, particularly those exhibiting learning or behavioural difficulties. Four forms of peer learning have been identified:

- parallel/co-ordinate – students exchange information while working on the same assignment
- didactic – one student acts as the instructor to others
- collaboration – students take the instructor role in rotation
- onlook – one student observes the work of another.

Of these, the didactic and collaborative methods have become known as peer tutoring (Valletutti and Dummett 1992). Variations of peer tutoring include cross-age tutoring, where students in a higher grade tutor younger students; tutoring of students within the same class; regular students tutoring students with special needs and vice versa; and adult tutoring of students. Reviews of peer tutoring research, particularly for students with learning difficulties (see Byrd 1990; Scruggs and Ritcher 1988), have demonstrated the effectiveness of peer tutoring in increasing: academic performance; the self-esteem of both tutor and learner; motivation to learn; and cognitive processing skills.

Byrd (1990), for example, outlined the structure and research evidence for two classroom tutoring systems, Classwide Peer Tutoring (CWPT) and a later development, Classwide Student Tutoring Teams (CSTT). In CWPT, the academic skills to be addressed are chosen by the teacher. The class is divided into two teams, and then subdivided into tutoring dyads, with each student taking on the role of tutor and learner alternatively. Following ten to fifteen minutes' practice, students attempt a test and the scores and bonus points are displayed for the class to see. At the end of each week the 'team of the week' is determined by the number of points earned by the individuals in the group. Researchers using this approach have demonstrated significant gains in academic skills such as essay writing and improved classroom behaviour.

In contrast, the CSTT approach employs both CWPT and the Teams-Game-Tournaments (TGT) strategy discussed earlier. Rather than having two large groups with *ad-hoc* dyads as occurs in CWPT, CSTT uses selected dyads based on academic performance, and teams remain the same for four to eight weeks. Although a smaller research base exists for this approach, studies have shown a significant improvement in mathematics performance for students using the approach.

Peer tutoring requires teacher preparation for it to succeed (Valletutti and Dummett 1992). Teacher tasks include identifying appropriate content areas, matching tutors and learners depending on the goals of the activity, training tutors, allocating work space, preparing materials, evaluating progress, and communicating results. One distinct advantage of peer tutors is the translation of content and processes into student language by the students themselves. This is important because students communicate in a format they understand which is often free of the middle-class, adult language structures that teachers commonly use in their oral presentations.

Peer tutoring can be used in schools as well as in many other teaching-learning contexts. Rich and Gentle (1995), for example, used peer tutoring to gain insights into ways in which the needs of college students with learning difficulties could be met. They employed an Individual College Plan (ICP) which the special education adviser developed collaboratively with the students. In tutoring sessions with the special education tutor, students were guided in the development of strategies such as predicting, self-questioning, summarising from texts, and time management. In addition, tutoring on academic content could also take place using a college peer. The special education tutor worked alongside the college peer tutor to provide encouragement and to help with the application of cognitive and metacognitive strategies that had been learned in earlier sessions.

The approach reinforced the importance of integrating strategic and content tutoring while also acknowledging that some peer tutors may not have sufficient awareness of cognitive and metacognitive strategies to incorporate them successfully into a tutoring session. As the peer tutor in the Rich and Gentle (1995) study also had a learning difficulty, the strategy gains were shared by both tutor and learner. While the approach worked for the students in the case study, Rich and Gentle pointed out that no single model will work for all students, and that any strategic instructional approach should be tailored to the student's learning style and needs.

Cognitive apprenticeship

The cognitive apprenticeship model (Collins *et al.* 1989; Collins *et al.* 1991) is based on traditional adult craft apprenticeships adapted to the teaching of reading, writing, and arithmetic. The concept of apprenticeship is seen in both adult and child learning activities through the use of techniques such as coaching, modelling, and observation. Unlike adult apprenticeship for vocational training, cognitive apprenticeship combines strategy training with skills such as social interaction, observation, practice, and reflection (Rojewski and Schell 1994). The approach also incorporates scaffolding procedures as it involves observing a model of the targeted process and then developing a conceptual framework before attempting the process under guidance.

The approach has four interdependent elements: content, methods, sequence, and sociology (Rojewski and Schell 1994). *Content* refers to the areas of knowledge and skills that experts use to solve complex problems, namely knowledge from the specific content area (domain knowledge), understanding from knowledge of previous experiences (heuristics), monitoring and organisational skills (control or metacognitive strategies), and techniques that have been used previously in learning new tasks (learning strategies).

Methods include strategies which are common to other instructional approaches such as guided practices (e.g. modelling, coaching) and exploration (e.g. verbalising the problem-solving process, reflection).

The teacher uses these methods to mediate learning to ensure the students' active participation. Rojewski and Schell (1994) provide examples of how students can be involved by exploring methods at the beginning of a topic to generate interest, then visiting locations outside of school to allow students to learn the experts' 'tricks of the trade' (heuristics), followed by discussions that allow further development of both knowledge and learning skills. The outcome, they argued, was a rich conceptual network of real life content applications to a specific context.

Sequence refers to the three sequencing approaches identified by J.S. Brown *et al.* (1989): increasing capacity, diversity, and developing global strategies before specific skills. Teachers choose from the three, or combine approaches for different topics to provide variety or to meet individual learning needs. The approach allows for students of differing ability to participate in a programme, using the same sets of experiences, but with different individual outcomes.

Sociology refers to beliefs, values, culture, and social settings in the real world that form the context in which learning occurs. Hence, in the cognitive apprenticeship model, sociology refers to context-based learning, developing motivation through real, rather than contrived problem situations, using co-operative learning, and developing a language of learning.

C.D. Lee (1995) provided an example of the cognitive apprenticeship model when teaching literacy interpretation skills to African American high school students by setting up two learning environments. One involved small work groups, scaffolded learning experiences based on the students' own social discourse, African American literature, and the use of student's social knowledge. The other had a traditional white middle-class orientation typical of high school teaching methods.

The students in the first setting made significant improvements in their independent mastery of problem-solving strategies while those in the traditional setting did not. Consistent with many other strategy training approaches, the greatest gains were made by students with lower ability at the pretest stage. Lee argued that cognitive apprenticeship focuses on 'how to make public and visible to novice learners those powerful problem-solving strategies and heuristics that more expert readers practice flexibly and use strategically' (C.D. Lee 1995: 627).

The cognitive apprenticeship model requires that teachers facilitate learning through modelling and supporting student's learning, not through providing answers. In line with many other approaches discussed in this chapter, cognitive apprenticeship challenges the common views on what should be taught, how teachers should teach, and how students should learn. As a method of cognitive strategy training, the approach remains relatively untested in a research sense, but holds promise as a technique that may be useful, particularly in settings where instruction has a strong social-cultural base. Ideally, every co-operative learning procedure should be designed to develop student independence in learning and problem-solving and encourage the acquisition of skills that allow for initiative and self-management.

SELF-REGULATION

There has been a strong and consistent emphasis in the cognitive and metacognitive strategy literature on the use of self-regulation procedures, particularly for students with learning and intellectual disabilities. Interventions have included self-management, self-explanation, self-instruction and self-understanding. Self-regulation is one aspect of metacognition (the other being an individual's awareness of their cognitive strengths and weaknesses). It involves students selecting task-appropriate strategies from their repertoire and monitoring and evaluating the effectiveness of the strategy. Students can be considered self-regulated 'to the degree that they are metacognitively, motivationally, and behaviorally active participants in their own learning process' (Zimmerman 1989: 4). The expected outcome from self-regulation is the maintenance and transfer of strategies (Kamann and Wong 1993).

Five components of self-regulation have been identified: metacognition, learning strategies, motivation/self-efficacy, contextual sensitivity, and environmental utilisation/control (Lindner and Harris 1992). Typically, students who are good self-regulators perform well on academic tasks. As Paris and Newman (1990: 99) noted: 'self-regulated learning is a hallmark of academic expertise'.

Three instructional conditions assist in the promotion and development of self-regulated learning in the classroom. These are: effective instruction that provokes students to change their theories; effective instruction that makes thinking public; and effective instruction that promotes active participation and collaboration. While other factors are also important (e.g. the classroom environment, students' physical state), Paris and Newman (1990) focused on those factors under teacher control that either assist or hinder the development of self-regulated learning. In all three approaches, there is a need for teachers to have a commitment to the use of self-regulation to encourage student learning, and to talk-through strategies in an open classroom environment where discussion and self-regulation is encouraged.

There are two crucial aspects of self-regulation that are implicit in the construct of metacognition: private speech and self-instruction. Private speech is usually seen as an aspect of self-verbalisation, although its definition varies from researcher to researcher. Private speech has been used to assist recall of text content using a method called self-initiated post-reading strategy (Simpson 1995). Students rehearse the important content area concepts in a chosen book as if presenting the information to an audience.

Three study processes are used that promote successful independent learning: selective allocation (encoding key concepts); generation (using one's own words to transform and reorganise information including images, examples, and applications); and cognitive monitoring (evaluating understanding, strategy selection, and corrective action use). When applied more generally than to only one book, the approach becomes part of the students' repertoire of strategies and can be generalised to other learning situations. The approach has the potential to be effective in senior high school and university, where critical thinking is required rather than the simple recall of facts.

EFFECTIVE INSTRUCTION

For students to incorporate a new strategy into their repertoire, they must make a commitment to do so. In other words, they must 'own' the strategy. Simply practising a strategy does not increase the likelihood of its use. By making the value of a strategy clear to students, by demonstrating and modelling its value on practical examples and providing opportunities to apply the strategy, students are more likely to recognise its value and take ownership (Ashman and Conway 1993b). Taking ownership leads to amended beliefs about learning.

We have already indicated that students must be active participants in the teaching-learning process, and classroom discussions provide valuable opportunities for students to listen to the way in which others have dealt with problem-solving experiences. Open discussions are important as they allow students to evaluate strategies, consider difficulties, and explore alternative strategies that might be used in future learning activities. At the same time, teachers can listen to the way in which students talk about their learning and problem-solving, and they can facilitate the use of more effective approaches if necessary.

COGNITION, METACOGNITION, AND MOTIVATION

In Chapter 3, we emphasised the interrelationship between the strategies needed to complete a task and the learner's affective reactions to the activity. Short and Weissberg-Benchell (1989) noted that good cognitive processors are able to balance their cognitive and metacognitive skills, and their motivational styles. Some students, like those with learning difficulties for example, are unlikely to be able to do so. Short and Weissberg-Benchell suggested that skilled learners are more aware of their learning styles, task demands, appropriate strategies needed to complete the task, and the relevance of using their background knowledge to facilitate learning. The contrast between skilled and unskilled learners is often easily seen in their motivation, and the way in which they attribute success and failure.

Research on attributions has shown that students with learning difficulties often attribute success to luck, and failure to their lack of ability (Cole and Chan 1990). While this may suggest that all students experiencing difficulties have common motivational and attributional characteristics, each student will have a specific motivation and attribution profile.

How can motivation and attributions be incorporated in strategy training? Short and Weissberg-Benchell (1989) argued that many strategy training approaches focused indirectly on motivation and attributional skills through teacher and student modelling, discussion, thinking aloud, and self-monitoring. The additional important ingredient was the use of a deliberate and systematic approach to providing the scaffolding needed for students with difficulties to acquire skills and accept that they are responsible for their achievements. In studies where success has been reported in developing students' domain-specific skills *and* improving motivation, training has emphasised realistic goal-setting, self-monitoring of behaviour, and self-reinforcement. Programmes that concentrate on these areas have been the most successful in producing long-term gains for students.

An example of the effects of motivation on strategy use can be seen in a strategy training study by Dole *et al.* (1996), who initially taught Grade 5 and 6 students strategies that were implemented within a reading comprehension programme. While the experimental group achieved significantly better results than the alternate reading and control reading groups, the results were not consistent across the experimental group. Two students were selected from the experimental group, one who had poor pretest performance and one who had a high pretest performance level. The weaker student showed greater gains because she was motivated to use the strategy. Success on the strategy encouraged her to continue using it, and consequently her comprehension scores increased. The more capable student found that the strategy was unhelpful and preferred her prior strategies and, consequently, her performance decreased.

This study highlights the importance of ensuring that the target strategy meets the student's needs. If the strategy works against the student, motivation will decrease and, as in the case above, student performance may decline. We shall consider other aspects of affect in Chapter 9.

SUMMARY

The discussion we have provided in this chapter emphasises the importance of actively involving the student in the learning or problem-solving task, and we have described a number of approaches designed to achieve this. Those approaches that focus only on strategic and metastrategic behaviour may not encourage students to change their thinking because they fail to recognise the value of strategies and metastrategies; fail to engage the learner's attention; or communicate with the student in a way that transmits the declarative and procedural knowledge needed to perform effectively. Procedures such as co-operative learning and peer tutoring have been successful because they *involve* the student in the learning context. Paris (1988) provided a useful conclusion for the chapter when he identified the characteristics of successful strategy training methods, as follows:

1   The strategies should be functional and meaningful.
2   Instruction should demonstrate what strategies can be used, how they can be applied, and when they are helpful.
3   Students should believe that strategies are useful and necessary.
4.   There must be a match between the instructed strategy and the learner's perceptions of the task ecology.
5   Successful instruction must instil confidence and feelings of self-efficacy.
6   Instruction should be direct, informed, and explanatory.
7   The responsibility for generating, applying, and monitoring effective strategies must be transferred from the instructor to student.
8   Instructional materials must be lucid, considerate, and enjoyable.

Adoption of these eight criteria should predict the success of current and future training programmes. In Chapter 8, we examine a number of cognitive and metacognitive strategy training programmes. Some satisfy all eight criteria, some do not.

STUDY TASKS

7.1 In note form, list the main points covered in this chapter. Pay particular attention to the link between assessment and instruction.
7.2 Think about how you might teach a student the spelling of words that include 'silent' letters (e.g. psychology). What cognitive and meta-cognitive processes would you emphasise in your instruction?
7.3 Choose one of the teaching procedures described in the chapter (e.g. reciprocal teaching) and conduct a search of the literature in your library. What are some of the main applications for the procedure and how successful have they been?
7.4 Consider a number of learning situations (e.g. classroom, vocation, with peers). What part does motivation play in each context and how can motivation be improved?

ADDITIONAL READING

Dole, J.A., Brown, K.J. and Trathen, W. (1996) 'The effects of strategy instruction on the comprehension performance of at-risk students', *Reading Research Quarterly* *31*(1): 62–88.
Foot, H., Morgan, M.J. and Shute, R. (1990) *Children Helping Children*, Chichester: John Wiley.

Lee, C.D. (1995) 'A culturally based cognitive apprenticeship: teaching African American high school students skills in literary interpretation', *Reading Research Quarterly* 30(4): 608–30.

Strain, P. (ed.) (1990) *The Utilization of Classroom Peers as Behavior Change Agents*, New York: Plenum.

Chapter 8

Cognitive methods for teaching and learning

In Chapter 7 we outlined a number of issues that are fundamental to cognitive education and drew attention to several training procedures that have focused on teaching students to act strategically. In addition, we summarised several general models that facilitate students' awareness of their cognitive activities (e.g. reciprocal teaching, peer tutoring).

These cognitive education models appear to work effectively but their use in classrooms and other instructional contexts is far from widespread. Many have been advocated by researchers to improve or change classroom teaching practices but teachers have been reluctant to embrace innovations that appear to increase their workload, or seem difficult to integrate into typical classroom activities. Even those approaches that have clear classroom applications (such as collaborative learning) have not been widely used because of the need for teachers to be familiar with the approach before it can be introduced.

The move toward a cognitive approach to education has seen the development of a considerable number of general strategy training models that seek to teach cognitive strategies either within the context of specific academic content, or without alignment to any specific teaching area. The majority of these models – although not all – satisfy a number of underlying principles, similar to those outlined by Houck (1993). The principles are as follows:

- Learning that occurs within a curriculum context is preferable to learning in isolation.
- Instruction and learning experiences should be integrated and balanced.
- Instruction occurs as a continually recurring (recursive) process where learning on new tasks builds upon previously acquired skills.
- Mediation by teachers and others assisted the learner to focus on the task.
- Instructional routines and thinking aloud methods are included to provide good models of strategic thought.
- New knowledge is always related to existing knowledge.

- Scaffolding allows the learner to take control of content and process.
- Peer-mediated learning is supported to motivate and assist students to gain insight into other students' problem solving behaviour.
- Immediate feedback is provided on the success of problem-solving behaviour so that the student can make adjustments as needed.

In this chapter we outline several cognitive education models. We describe the common features and the differences that set them apart.

STRATEGY TRAINING

Cognitive strategy training has been the subject of literally thousands of journal articles, book chapters, and books since the mid-1970s. In a special issue of the *Journal of Learning Disabilities* (1993, vol. 26, no. 6) a prototype model was outlined which was intended to develop the strategic behaviour of secondary students with learning difficulties (Ellis 1993). While no empirical evidence had been gathered in support of the new approach, a series of critiques were included that compared it to others that had already been in use for some years.

To some extent, the development of a new model of strategy training is a little like rearranging familiar sun lounges around a very popular swimming pool. The elements that contribute to successful learning and problem-solving are quite familiar (i.e. the strategies and techniques), and the context in which they are brought together is often predetermined (i.e. the teaching-learning environment). The only difference seems to be the configuration. In other words, while there are very clear differences between some approaches, the ultimate goal remains the same – to ensure that students and teachers are aware of the students' cognitive and metacognitive abilities and that these abilities are incorporated into the teaching-learning process. Ellis's (1993) model provides us with a starting-point from which we can explore the various configurations of cognitive education.

Integrated strategy instruction

Ellis's (1993) model sought to change classroom teaching practices so that instruction and learning was strategic. Four teaching processes were defined: orienting, framing, applying, and extending. Within each, Ellis provided both general and specific strategies so that the teacher could act as a mediator of learning (rather than as an instructor of strategies), by selecting content, method of presentation, and procedures that would aid in strategy acquisition. As a result of using the model, it was expected that students would come to understand the demands of the curriculum, determine how best to approach a task, and how to monitor their effectiveness when attempting that task.

While criticism can be levelled at any approach, Ellis's model emphasises the importance of changing the focus of teaching if students are to develop strategic behaviour and content knowledge. Similar integrated content-strategy training models (not described here) have been advocated by Deshler and Schumaker (1986: Strategies Intervention Model), Ellis *et al.* (1991: Working Model for Teaching Learning Strategies), and Lenz *et al.* (1990: the Content Enhancement Model).

COGNITIVE TEACHING/TRAINING MODELS AFTER VYGOTSKY

In Chapter 5, we drew attention to the influence of Vygotsky in the development of assessment procedures that targeted students' cognitive characteristics. The same influence has been felt in the field of instructional technology. Here we review three prominent cognitive education pro-grammes currently used by teachers in a number of countries. Each focuses on the explicit training of cognitive strategies based on a theoretical model and assessment strategies (see Chapters 5 and 6). What sets these apart from some other programmes is the continuing professional support available to the practitioners who use them.

Instrumental Enrichment

Instrumental Enrichment (IE) was developed by Feuerstein and his col-leagues in Israel (Feuerstein *et al.* 1980) and has been adopted in a number of countries, arguably most widely in its country of origin, Israel, but it also has advocates in the USA, South Africa and in parts of Europe. The approach clearly fits within the assessment, preparation, instruction and evaluation model (Chapter 1), through the use of the Learning Potential Assessment Device (described in Chapter 6), followed by an instructional programme, Instrumental Enrichment.

In his earlier work, Feuerstein (1970) identified two types of learners: passive-acceptance learners and active-modifier learners. The first group are those who receive information with little, if any, attempt to become actively involved in their learning. Teachers acknowledge the cognitive limitation of these students and teach to those limitations but provide no challenge to the students' cognitive functioning. Active-modifiers challenge existing limita-tions and seek to develop their cognitive skills. Teaching this group involves developing the weak cognitive skills of the students so that they begin to apply strategies to the tasks presented to them. The clear goal of IE is to ensure that all students, including those with special needs, become active modifiers of their learning environment.

IE has been described by Haywood (1992a: 207) as 'a conceptually rich, imaginatively operationalized program' which is designed to stimulate the acquisition of cognitive processes so that students' perceptions, learning, thinking, and problem-solving are enhanced across a wide range of cognitive activities. One notable characteristic of IE studies is the need to implement the model for sustained periods. For example, teachers are expected to include IE lessons in their teaching programmes two or three times per week for several years to ensure that the student acquires the general cognitive skills that can be applied across learning domains.

IE was designed for classroom use with students over the age of 10 years and it has a remedial emphasis. It is based on a series of fifteen instructional units (or instruments) of increasing complexity, each designed to develop thinking processes using paper and pencil exercises (see Box 8.1). Each instrument focuses on a group of deficit cognitive functions and is designed to correct them. Twenty-eight cognitive dysfunctions were identified including unplanned, impulsive and unsystematic exploratory behaviour, and an inability to select relevant, as opposed to irrelevant, cues when defining a problem. Correction of these is also included in the training tasks.

One of the instruments used early in the programme is called Organization of Dots (a very simple example – not included in IE materials – is shown in Figure 8.1). The student joins dots on a page to reproduce a predetermined pattern. The focus of the task is the reduction of impulsivity and encouragement of the student to identify the relevant cues (dots) in reproducing the shape from the cloud of dots on the page. A higher order instrument, Transitive Relations and Syllogisms, requires the student to analyse premises and propositions. Some IE tasks have been adapted for students with a vision impairment and some examples are given in Box 8.2.

Instrumental Enrichment is based on the Vygotskian concept of mediated learning which refers to the role of the teacher or parent in providing a structured learning environment and feedback to the student. It has been suggested that mediated learning experiences are fundamental for cognitive development and may overcome some socio-cultural deficits that can affect intellectual development such as poverty, emotional disturbances, and poor educational opportunities (Haywood 1993). Feuerstein et al. (1980) acknowledged that the amount of mediated learning that each student requires will vary according to the degree of socio-cultural deprivation. The issue is not whether the student can acquire thinking processes, but the quantity and frequency of mediated learning experiences that is required for the student to achieve those skills.

Evaluations of IE have been conducted using participants drawn from a wide range of ages and ability levels. Independent evaluators of IE have generally been more critical than supportive of the approach (see Blagg 1991). Others have suggested that the evidence in favour of IE has been 'inconclusive or equivocal' (Haywood 1992b: 10). Notwithstanding this, there are several points that can be drawn from the literature:

Box 8.1

Instrumental Enrichment exercises

The fifteen instruments described below comprise all those available to an Instrumental Trainer. Only a selection of these would be used in any programme, with the teacher choosing those thought to be most appropriate for the student.

Organisation of dots Identification and outlining of dots from a 'cloud' to show a set of overlapping geometric shapes (e.g. squares, triangles, diamonds, stars). At upper levels, the shapes become more intermingled and require progressively higher levels of discrimination, precision, and segregation.

Orientation in space I, II, and III This series of three tasks deals with spatial orientation relative to one's own body. It involves developing concepts of right, left, front, back, beneath, and beside. The task is to represent the relationship between fixed objects and a human figure which changes its orientation.

Comparisons Exercises involve the forced comparison of two objects on dimensions such as size, form, number, spatial components, temporal components, as well as abstract components not immediately perceived (e.g. function, composition, power).

Categorisation The child learns to label, compare, discriminate and combine objects according to specific classification, but then these same objects may be regrouped according to a different set of criteria. The presentation may be verbal, pictorial, schematic, and figural.

Analytic perception Involves looking at an object in terms of its component parts to identify the relationships between parts. Figures have to be completed, specific shapes identified and coloured, and patterns matched with their component parts.

Family relations Exercises teach kinship and family relations through the drawing of family trees and genealogical maps so that the child learns to recognise relationships and, the multiple roles (and their attributes) of each person, (e.g. grandfather, father, brother). This task uses verbal, symbolic, and graphic modalities of presentation.

Temporal relations These exercises train the child to register, process, and order temporal relationships by isolating each of the factors of time, distance and velocity and then determining their interrelationship. They are problem-solving activities requiring the collection of relevant information such as starting points, routes, time, and average speed, and combining those so that multiple factors are dealt with simultaneously.

Numerical progressions The child learns to develop a sequence (usually numerical) which establishes a relationship between two events, the pattern by which the relationship repeats itself, and the discovery and formulation of the rule which generates the pattern.

Instructions This instrument requires the child to read an instruction and act on it using a systematic and ordered approach. The child is required to gather data, order the object in the desired relationship, and carry out the instruction (e.g. draw a large, red triangle in the bottom left-hand corner of the page).

Illustrations A series of pictures show a progression of events where the child must perceive a problem, recognise what is happening in the situation, and search for a solution by generating comparisons and relationships.

Representational stencil design These tasks require the mental construction of a design. The child copies coloured, solid, and cut-out stencils printed on a sheet by specifying which stencils must be used, and in which order they must be mentally superimposed on each other to recreate the desired pattern.

Transitive relations In these exercises the child makes inferences about new relationships from those existing between objects and/or events by using the terms greater than, equal to or less than. The child must learn rules and apply them by translating verbal problems into signs, decoding the relationships in the signs, and applying them to an abstract problem.

Syllogisms These deal with formal propositional logic by expanding the concept of sets. The child learns about the laws governing sets and their members, the implication of these laws and the construction of new sets by various operations such as logical multiplication.

Find:

In:

Like this:

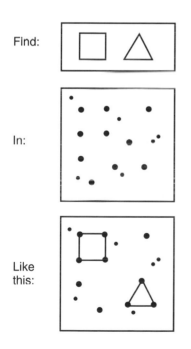

Figure 8.1 A graphic showing the requirements of the Organization of Dots exercise

Box 8.2

An adaptation of Instrumental Enrichment activities for students with a vision impairment

This material is reproduced from *Journal of Cognitive Education* (1995) 4(2–3): 115–17.

a) A blind pupil is making a figure by rubber bands

b) A blind pupil is looking for the spatial relationship between each arrow and the rectangle by means of small pin banners with abbreviated writings in Braille

---

1 Intensive training is needed for the teacher to understand the background and processes of the approach and to learn how to implement it.
2 Students require at least seventy-five hours of instruction to show
   enduring changes in their cognitive abilities.
3 Gains can be made on measures of intelligence, some school subjects,
   formal reasoning, and in motivation and enthusiasm for learning.
4 Successful outcomes have been obtained with students who are immigrants, culturally different, culturally deprived, or who have learning
   difficulties.

Bright Start

Bright Start was designed as a cognitive curriculum for children aged 3 to 6
years who were 'educationally handicapped' in some of the basic processes
of systematic thought (Haywood *et al.* 1986; 1992a). While there is a strong
influence of Feuerstein's Instrumental Enrichment in Bright Start, mostly on
the development of cognitive functions and mediated learning experiences,
the approach also includes aspects of Piaget's stages of cognitive development
(Piaget 1952; 1960). These influences combine to form the five components
of the model's conceptual structure (Haywood *et al.* 1986):

- mediational teaching style
- small-group cognitive units
- a cognitive-mediational method of behaviour management
- parent-education
- ancillary services.

The use of a mediational style implies that the teacher acts as a catalyst in
developing the students' understanding and thought processes. The important outcome is students' ability to generalise experiences from the lesson
rather than a recall of the specific content. Hence, students learn a series of
cognitive strategies that can be applied across a variety of tasks and situations.
Haywood *et al.* described the anticipated outcomes as:

> The goal is to extract from every encounter the children have with content
> materials the maximum learning of generalizable principles and strategies
> of perceiving the world, of thinking systematically, clearly, and effectively,
> of learning, and of problem solving.
>
> (Haywood *et al.* 1986: 137)

Students work on the cognitive units in small groups for a short period each
day. The original eight cognitive units were designed to be taught in
sequence. These include

1 Self-regulation or self-control.
2 Thinking about behaviour and the consequences of behaviour.

3   Quantitative relations through basic number concepts.
4   Systematic comparisons across dimensions.
5   Changing perspective through role play.
6   Classification across dimensions.
7   Patterns.
8   Distinctive features as a method of classifying objects and events.

In a revision of the model, some changes were made to the grouping of activities within tasks, notably collapsing of the behaviour steps into one initial step, and the development of a bridging task to Grade 1 activities (Haywood 1995).

The cognitive units focus first on the social behaviours of the students, and then on academic tasks. The programme establishes a set of behavioural expectations that can be maintained during the teaching of other units. All units place importance on students' taking responsibility for their social behaviours in the same way as they take responsibility for thinking through cognitive activities.

A description of the teaching procedure to be used in each unit is set out in the training manual developed by Haywood *et al.* (1992a) with fifteen to thirty lessons being provided for each unit. There are one hundred and fifty lessons in the curriculum, each including a rationale, a main activity, variations that can be carried out on the main activity, a generalisation activity, bridging activities and cognitive mastery criteria. Box 8.3 gives an example of a Bright Start teaching lesson for self-regulation.

Another important feature of the model is the involvement of parents throughout the training process. Parents help by undertaking classroom observations, providing in-class assistance for students, working with students on cognitive tasks at home, and attending parent training sessions. In other words, parents play an important role in the children's development. Staff of ancillary services – such as speech therapist – are kept informed of the methods used in Bright Start in the hope that these may contribute to the students' cognitive development during the staff's own interactions with the children. There is an expectation that the ancillary service providers will not use methods that are contrary to those in the Bright Start programme.

Evaluation studies of the Bright Start curriculum have been conducted both by the authors and independent researchers. Haywood (1995) provided a summary of the research that has been conducted with students with an intellectual disability, low socio-economic background students (Haywood *et al.* 1986), and students with learning difficulties or an emotional disturbance. He reported a significant improvement in students undertaking the Bright Start programme when compared to others participating in a non-cognitively oriented curriculum based on the McCarthy Scales (McCarthy 1972). In addition, Bright Start students had greater confidence in their ability and were less likely to ask the examiners whether their answers were

Box 8.3

A Bright Start lesson

Self-regulation is one of the first units taught within the Bright Start programme. Lesson 18 emphasises four cognitive functions:

- gathering clear and complete information
- self-regulating
- using spatial references
- comparisons.

The rationale for the lesson is the strengthening of the children's ability to regulate their bodies by holding them in specific positions, to see the connection between representation (pictures) and reality, and to gather information by looking carefully.

The main activity is based on a series of six drawings (see examples below) of a child and a chair. The children are asked to play 'Can You Do What I Do?' by adopting the action in the pictures and discussing the position of the child in relation to the chair (e.g. beside, in front of).

Variations are suggested and a generalisation activity is given such as having a child model a pose – pretending to eat – and having other children copy it.

The bridging discussion is designed to focus on looking carefully at the pictures to gain all the information needed for the activity.

Finally, the cognitive mastery criterion requires each child to explain the need to look carefully at the model before initiating the pose.

Box 8.3 contd.

correct than children in the alternative programme.

In European studies, similar outcomes have been reported to those of Haywood *et al.* (1986). Students in speech and language rehabilitation settings, for example, showed gains in language test performance even when the training programme was abbreviated in terms of content covered and duration (van den Wijngaert 1991; Warnez 1991). In France, Paour *et al.* (1993) involved students from disadvantaged immigrant families, as well as more affluent French families. While the Bright Start immigrant students received only two of the cognitive tasks, they outperformed the advantaged students in nine of the ten comparison tests, including Raven's Progressive Matrices. Importantly, a follow-up study conducted when the students had been in regular schools for two years, found that the Bright Start students continued to demonstrate superior performance, this time on standardised French Ministry of Education tests.

Studies in Israel with socio-economically disadvantaged families of recent immigrant status (Tzuriel and Kaniel 1992) have also demonstrated the effectiveness of providing children of such families with a structured cognitive programme. Following a ten-month programme using five cognitive tasks, students in kindergarten outperformed control students who were given a basic remediation teaching programme. The Bright Start children also maintained their gains over a two-year period especially in reading and mathematics.

Evaluating the performance of children in Bright Start, as for Instrumental Enrichment, is problematic. Many researchers have used only one or two of the cognitive units and/or provide the programme for a limited time. In other words, the children may not have had the opportunity to gain maximum benefit from the programme. It is likely that students who complete the entire programme over an extended period of time would make substantial gains. These data, however, are not yet available to us.

Cognitive Enrichment Network Education Model (COGNET)

COGNET was designed to develop students' thinking skills using a whole-school approach (Greenberg 1990). The programme is based on a set of beliefs about best practice for meeting students' needs: first, students must learn how to learn in a social context, within which an adult acts as a mediator of the learning experiences; second, schools must provide a setting in which to practise the knowledge and skills required in the world beyond the classroom; and third, schools must provide the environment in which students can actively explore new ideas with the help of mentors.

COGNET has three key components:

1   A classroom model which employs a specific approach to the way students learn.
2   A parent involvement programme.
3   A networking component for teachers and schools.

The model is used predominantly in the primary/elementary school and, more specifically with low-achieving students or students at-risk of educational failure in kindergarten to Grade 6. It has been implemented in culturally and socio-economically disadvantaged areas, predominantly in the United States.

COGNET has some aspects in common with Instrumental Enrichment and Bright Start. It emphasises the importance of a mediated approach to learning, with teachers providing the opportunities for students to explore new ideas with the help of a mentor (teacher). The classroom is viewed as a laboratory in which thinking processes are considered to be as important as the curriculum content. The school community contributes to the development of children's cognitive development in its unique way and the model can be adapted to meet the specific characteristics of each school using the skills of staff who become COGNET consultants once trained. Parents are also involved in the teaching-learning process and are included in classroom activities as volunteers who contribute to specific aspects of the programme.

COGNET was designed to operate across the school for at least a two-year period of professional development. The projected outcomes from such an involvement were expected to meet a number of criteria including

*   the development of teachers' knowledge and skills about the mediation of children's learning experiences
*   the development of the student's knowledge of basic cognitive processing

concepts and affective/ motivational factors that influence successful learning

- the selection and adaptation of the school curriculum to allow the classroom to become a learning laboratory in which the students are expected to learn.

COGNET is not an addition to regular classroom activities or a replacement for the curriculum (Greenberg 1990). It is an instructional approach developed through a series of staff training sessions in which teachers learn about ten cognitive processing concepts (Building Blocks of Thinking) and eight affective/motivational factors (Tools of Independent Learning) to teach students how to construct their own learning strategies (see Table 8.1 and Box 8.4). The teaching materials are contained in a teachers' handbook developed by Greenberg and her associates (see COGNET 1995) which provides coverage of the Building Blocks of Thinking and the Tools for Independent Learning. Each tool and block is highlighted in a mini-lesson which provides the teacher with introductory activities; group practice and review; instructions for independent work; and a functional living skills discussion in which the concepts are shown to have application to broader school and community settings. The application of these aspects within a lesson has been described by D. Wilson (1996).

D. Wilson (1996) taught a group of second graders the Approach to Task block using two cartoon pictures each of a teacher saying 'Listen carefully'. In the first picture, a student sits still at the desk, focused on the teacher, and ready to listen. In the second, the student is waving her hands wildly and kicking papers. The aim was to demonstrate the behaviours needed to commence a lesson.

Table 8.1 The cognitive process (Building Blocks of Thinking) and affective factors (Tools for Independent Learning) emphasised in the COGNET programme

Building blocks of thinking These assist students to develop the prerequisites for learning and assist them to understand the way in which they learn	Tools for independent learning These increase the level of student motivation and the desire to learn
Approach to task	Inner meaning
Precision and accuracy	Self-regulation
Space and time concepts	Feeling of competence
Thought integration	Goal of directed behaviour
Selective attention	Self-development
Making comparisons	Sharing behaviour
Connecting events	Feeling of challenge
Working memory	Awareness of self-change
Getting the main idea	
Problem identification	

Box 8.4

Wilson also used the Feelings of Competence Tools which were designed to reduce egocentricity and increase the child's awareness of others. The teacher used the learning of a recent new task and asked the students to reflect on the process they used when developing the knowledge or skill and asked them to consider how that knowledge could be applied to other situations. The anticipated outcomes were the development of independent thinking and self-confidence.

Four evaluations of COGNET have been undertaken between 1988 and 1994. All studies included students who attended regular classes in elementary schools and who were not designated as special education students. Comparison groups were established, although the students were not randomly assigned to the experimental or comparison conditions.

The gains made by COGNET students on standardised academic tests indicated an advantage over the students in the comparison group in each study (Greenberg 1995). However, it is difficult to compare the results across studies as the method of assessing gains was different in each study. Non-academic gains have also favoured COGNET students when compared to peers who have been involved in regular early childhood programmes. Assessment of intrinsic motivation, attention, classroom behaviour and parent involvement all demonstrated greater gains for COGNET groups in comparison to their non-COGNET peers.

Four outcomes of COGNET evaluations can be identified (Greenberg 1995): COGNET can assist children to learn how to learn; academic performance can be improved; the gains for academically at-risk students can be as great, or even greater, than those of average or above-average ability; and teachers can learn how to change the way in which they interact with students to develop their thinking and learning skills. While results from the four evaluation studies of COGNET give a clear indication of the potential of the programme, additional studies using larger samples and a consistent methodology will provide important additional information to augment the growing research base.

TRAINING OF PROCESSING AND PLANNING SKILLS

The approaches discussed above reflect the importance of teaching students basic thinking and motivation/management in preparation for later academic learning. In contrast, the following training model emphasises the importance of teaching planning and coding as specific rather than general thinking skills.

The PASS Remedial Program

The model has its roots in the information processing assessment and training studies of Das and his colleagues (Das et al. 1979; Das et al. 1994).

The earliest studies focused on teaching information processing skills isolated from curriculum content, with the expectation that these skills would transfer to other processing skills (near transfer) and to academic tasks that required the application of the processing skills (far transfer). As the model was based on a research paradigm rather than on a teaching model, the measurement of transfer was considered a more critical feature than learning of cognitive strategies in a classroom context. In the earliest studies, students were pretested and post-tested using information processing and reading tests and the experimental group was trained in simultaneous or successive processing (Brailsford *et al.* 1984; D. Kaufman and P. Kaufman 1979; Krywaniuk and Das 1976). An example of a simultaneous and a successive processing task from these earlier studies is shown in Figures 8.2a and 8.2b. Note that the tasks are designed to be free of academic content, although no task can be considered to be truly content-free. Results of the studies showed that students trained to use a specific process improved their performance on that process and some transfer to specific reading tasks also occurred (see Das *et al.* 1990).

In the current approach, the PASS Remedial Program (PREP: Das *et al.* 1997) focuses on providing an obvious link between strategies and academic

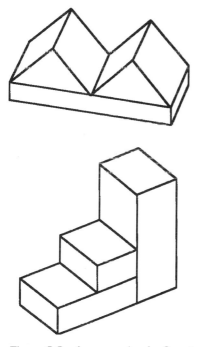

Figure 8.2a An example of a Construction task used in training simultaneous processing

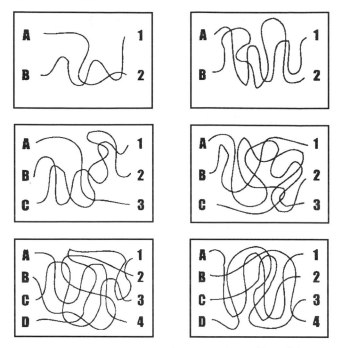

Figure 8.2b An example of a Strings task used in training successive processing

content. However, the initial instruction is still provided on processing tasks that are unrelated to current academic content due to the belief that students acquire processing strategies more easily if they are not confronted with the academic content on which they are failing. The training programme includes ten training tasks, with six focusing primarily on successive processing and four on simultaneous processing (see Das *et al.* 1994). Within each task there are both global training tasks and bridging tasks, with three levels of difficulty provided for each task. Although planning and attention are not taught specifically, the programme addresses these areas incidentally. Figures 8.3a and 8.3b show a a content-free processing task, and a bridging task to reading similar to those. Notice that the processing task in Figure 8.3a involves shapes which are free of academic content (spades and diamonds). In this exercise the child joins the shapes moving from left to right always passing through the starburst. In the bridging exercise shown in Figure 8.3b, the child joins letters to construct words.

Up to the present time, the training programme has been used in small groups of students with learning or reading disabilities. Consequently, it is a remedial rather than a preventive programme. Two studies have been conducted by the authors of the model (Carlson and Das 1992; Das *et al.* 1995). In both studies, students were taught to develop cognitive skills (e.g.

Join: S to D, D to S, S to D, D to D, D to D   S= ♠

       D to S, S to S, S to D, D to S   D= ♦

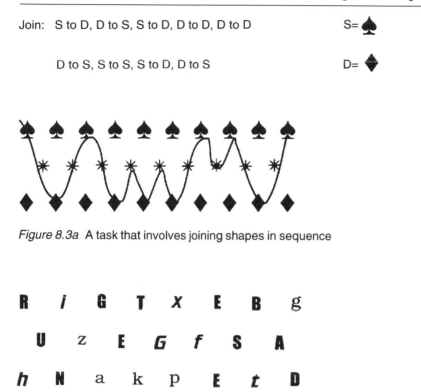

Figure 8.3a A task that involves joining shapes in sequence

R *i* G T X E B *g*

U z E *G* *f* S A

h N a k p E *t* D

Figure 8.3b A bridging task that involves joining letters in sequence to make words

categorisation, prediction, monitoring performance, sound blending) related to reading and to develop an awareness of rules underlying the cognitive skills. In the Carlson and Das (1992) study, experimental and comparison groups were used in which the experimental group received two fifty-minute lessons per week for three months, while the comparison group continued in a traditional learning difficulties programme for students in the United States, who were labelled as Chapter 1 students or students with a learning disability. The results showed significant improvement in the performance of the experimental group in both processing skills and word decoding. In the Das *et al.* (1995) study, the experimental students were given fifteen sessions of PREP, taught in small groups, and they showed significant gains over a non-intervention group in reading decoding. While the results of these two studies suggest that process training can assist in specific aspects of beginning reading, they do not indicate any change in the students' general cognitive competence or the students' ability to apply their processing skills to other content domains.

While PREP is clearly different from general cognitive programmes such as Bright Start and COGNET, it has some common features. There is a clear link to Vygotsky (Das and Conway 1992), although the focus on a mediated learning approach is not emphasised in PREP. In addition, PREP has a direct link to an assessment protocol, the Planning, Attention, Simultaneous and Successive model (PASS: Das *et al.* 1994) and its later formal structure in the DN•CAS (Das and Naglieri 1996).

Planning instruction programmes

Several studies following the PASS model have sought to improve students' ability to plan. Training was provided to students who performed poorly on planning measures, although planning skills were not taught directly. Teachers used a combination of discovery learning and inductive inference to encourage the student to analyse problems carefully, and to self-monitor and self-correct. The teacher's role was to encourage and facilitate verbalisation through prompts, and to assist students to analyse the strategy they used, and consider how they could improve their performance on later tasks.

Two studies have focused on planning skills in non-academic tasks (Cormier *et al.* 1990; Kar *et al.* 1992), and another two have emphasised planning in mathematics (Naglieri and Gottling 1995; 1996). In the first studies (Cormier *et al.* 1990; Kar *et al.* 1992), students who were previously poor planners made significantly higher gains than those with good initial planning scores. An important feature of these studies was the use of participants who were regular education students, rather than students with special needs or from disadvantaged backgrounds.

In the second set of studies, instruction in the use of planning skills in mathematics was given to students who had a learning difficulty. Naglieri and Gottling (1995) demonstrated that teaching planning skills to students with low planning ability had a greater impact than for those who already had good planning skills. The second study (Naglieri and Gottling 1996) involved students in twenty-one intervention sessions over two months. Each session contained three ten-minute phases of mathematics/discussion/mathematics. The discussion period focused on how the student performed on the mathematics task and what changes they could make when completing a similar task next time. In addition, the researchers provided weekly feedback to the teachers on how they could facilitate discussion in regular classroom sessions. Their results again indicated that students who were initially poor in planning made the greatest gains (80 per cent overall). Students who were initially high in planning made less improvement (42 per cent overall), and the level of gain varied from student to student.

These studies draw attention to the potential benefits of training students in a specific metacognitive weakness (in this case planning). Up to the present time, the results have come only from short-term studies using specific curricular activities. Additional research that tracks the long-term effects of training students to become more systematic in their planning may show far-reaching consequences.

Process-Based Instruction

Process-Based Instruction (PBI) was developed from the premise that students must be taught to become independent learners and problem-solvers rather than acquire these skills in a haphazard way through trial-and-error over the course of their education (Ashman and Conway 1993c). Many students (even in the higher grades) wait to be told what to do, or they do not have the necessary skills to complete the task set by the teacher. Part of the reason for the inactivity of students in the classroom is due to a lack of instruction in how to accept responsibility for their involvement in the teaching-learning process. Rarely are students explicitly taught how to plan and to make educational decisions that facilitate learning.

PBI evolved from two lines of research and from educational 'best practice'. The emphasis on thinking skills came from research on metacognition, planning, and problem-solving, while the classroom environment aspect evolved from research on classroom climate and instructional techniques such as co-operative learning. The model explicitly aims to integrate the four agents responsible for effective learning (the student, teacher, setting, and curriculum) to which we referred in Chapter 1.

The classroom practices and the teaching strategies employed in PBI are the same as those already established and in common use by teachers throughout the world. Indeed, care is taken to ensure that teachers who are learning about PBI realise that they are not being asked to abandon their established, successful teaching methods. PBI was developed to

- integrate learning processes and curriculum content
- increase student participation in the teaching-learning process
- link the four factors that affect successful learning outcomes (the learner, the teacher, the setting, the curriculum)
- teach learning strategies that are applicable across content areas
- establish – or re-establish – a history of student learning success.

PBI is not a teaching method as such, but a framework, or model, for classroom teaching and learning which enables teachers to present information to students in an effective manner.

There are two key concepts in PBI: plans and planning. A plan is a sequence of activities and thoughts that leads to success on a specific task, while planning is the process of developing plans for known or unknown, real or speculative, tasks or problems. The rudiments of planning are established during the first few years of a child's life, but conscious awareness of the nature of the planning process does not emerge until the early grades of school (Scholnick and Friedman 1990). While many pre-school, primary or secondary school teachers may allude to plans and planning during classroom activities, few formalise the principles of planning with their students with the intent of making the process a conscious and deliberate activity. The goal of PBI is to teach students how to be effective planners in curriculum and extra-curricular activities.

The mechanism for change in PBI is the plan (see Box 8.5). The word 'plan' is used in the everyday sense to mean a scheme of actions or ways of working toward a goal. In PBI, plans are thoughts and actions that lead to the successful completion of the task. A PBI plan must have a starting-point, so that students know where and how to begin; a sequence of steps, with each step in the plan leading effectively toward the next; and thinking, or metacognitive, steps that require observations, judgements or decisions about what is taking place. It is the inclusion of metacognitive steps that makes a PBI plan different from other action-only sequences. Furthermore, as PBI plans are designed for student use without direct teacher assistance, they must also lead to the successful completion of the task (defined in many ways, depending upon the purpose of the activity).

So, PBI plans must contain four components:

- cueing – where and how to start
- acting – the necessary sequence of actions needed
- monitoring – an evaluation of the effectiveness of the plan
- verifying – an assessment of whether the task has been completed successfully.

While there are four essential components, PBI plans may have more than four steps. There may be loops within plans that provide a number of acting and monitoring steps or a number of monitoring and verifying steps.

Making and using plans, however, is not all that Process-Based Instruction entails. Certainly, plan use is important but it is really the 'when, where and how' of plan use that enables students to learn systematically about the planning and problem-solving processes.

PBI involves plan use through four teaching-learning phases:

1   Introduction – when the students are introduced to plans for specific curriculum tasks.
2   Establishment – when plans are applied to curriculum tasks that have similar teaching-learning demands.
3   Consolidation – when plans are applied to tasks within a specific curriculum area having similar forms, or to different curricula.
4   Incorporation – when plans can be developed and amended for a wide range of learning areas.

Each of these phases is important in the student's learning. In the course of our daily lives we operate within all phases depending upon our experience and the specificity or generality of the tasks we attempt. In other words, for

Box 8.5

About plans

Ashman and Conway (1993c) provide many examples of Process-Based Instruction (PBI) plans suitable for pre-school to senior secondary school classes. Here is an example of a plan for constructing a bar graph which was made by a Grade 6 (age 12) teacher together with her students as an integral part of a mathematics lesson. You can see that the plan has cueing (Steps 1 and 2), acting (Steps 3, 5, and 6), monitoring (Step 4) and verifying (Steps 7 and 8) components and that these are represented by more than one step.

Constructing a bar graph that shows tabulated information

1 What should a bar graph look like?
2 What information/equipment do I need?
3 Draw axes and decide scale.
4 Check scale/spacing against information.
5 Label graph (axes, bars).
6 Draw bars.
7 Check all information.
8 Verify with a friend.

Note also that Steps 2, 3, 5, and 6 may also include some monitoring procedures.

There are a number of points to make about plans. First, plans can be made by teachers, students, or by the teacher and student(s) co-operatively. Second, one teacher's – or one student's – plan may not be the same as another person's plan for the same task. Third, an untried plan must always be considered to be a prototype. Plans must be open to change so that they suit the needs of individual students. Fourth, a prototype can be adapted for the use of most (if not all) students in regular classrooms regardless of their ability and skills. Students' plans become personalised when they record their individual plans in their own words. A plan in the student's own words ensures ownership and increases the likelihood that it will be used when the student is attempting a relevant activity.

---

one activity, young students may need to develop and apply a plan with a very specific purpose (e.g. for adding 14 and 23). After the mathematics lesson, the students may need to apply a general plan for packing up material in readiness for a period spent outside the classroom. It is essential, therefore, that students learn about the process of planning from both general and specific perspectives so that they can develop and consolidate their knowledge and experience about plans and the planning process.

There are many ways of making and using plans but the initial action involves introducing students to plans and planning – this is part of the Introduction phase. Many teachers use class discussion as a forum about plans and planning and relate these plans to the students' own experiences.

With young children, the teacher may discuss household routines that help family members get to work or to school on time. For older children, the tactics used by a football team for breaking the opposing team's defence can be a useful example, while for most secondary school students, plans and planning are familiar concepts but they may never have related those concepts to school activities.

Teachers integrate plans into their teaching activities in many ways during the Establishment phase. Some, for example, use plan-development activities as a regular whole-class teaching strategy, while others encourage students to prepare and adapt plans to suit their personal needs. The familiarity of students with plans and the planning process, their level of academic achievement, and the teacher's desired level of control over classroom routines, will influence the way in which the teacher uses plans within the four instructional phases.

For students to appreciate the nature of the planning process, they need a clear understanding of how to develop, use, and adapt plans to suit a variety of situations. This is the purpose of the Consolidation and Incorporation phases. As students become adept at making judgements about what actions or decisions are needed to deal with new situations, they draw on their past planning experiences and knowledge of planning outcomes to guide their behaviour. The Incorporation phase, therefore, reflects knowledge of how to develop, use and adapt or translate plans in different situations in which general plans are necessary; an understanding of the constellation of learning and problem events that are appropriate at the students' particular developmental levels; and an ability to anticipate when planning success or failure may occur.

So students must have the opportunity to amend plans made by the teacher as a prototype for the whole class, to suit their own learning style and skills. They must also be encouraged to develop their own plans. It is the transfer of responsibility for the planning process to the student which is the key to success in PBI. Students no longer need to wait for teacher direction to begin a task, and they know how to overcome blockages to learning when they are encountered. Ultimately, this independence leads to an increase in student participation in the teaching-learning process and in motivation.

Keeping the planning process active also means being mindful of problems which can limit the effectiveness of PBI. When students are learning to make and use PBI plans in the classroom, many incorrectly begin by making sets of directions which lack metacognitive aspects. This may occur because many tend to be concrete, activity-based thinkers and place emphasis on the actions involved in completing a task rather than on the decisions that are needed to maintain progress. It is crucial that both the teacher's and the students' plans clearly identify the metacognitive processes that are involved in completing the task.

Gaining experience with PBI

Teachers and other educational professionals generally learn about PBI through a training workshop or inservice programme. Occasionally during the early stages of training, a teacher may say: 'I already do this in my class'. Certainly, many teachers use classroom strategies that resemble some PBI techniques. For example, they may provide their students with a sequence of activities which specifies how a task is to be done, or they may use discussion sessions in which the ways of achieving a curriculum goal are discussed. What is often missing, however, is the systematic application of plans across instructional phases which teach students how to plan independently, and the opportunity for students to adapt teaching strategies to suit their personal needs and skills.

Only three empirical studies on the effectiveness of Process-Based Instruction have been reported (see Box 8.6). Of some importance, however, has been the result of the application of the model in regular classrooms because it was introduced, implemented, and maintained by the teachers themselves rather than by the researchers. As with many other cognitive education programmes, further evidence of the efficacy of the model is needed before it can receive unqualified endorsement.

COGNITIVE METHODS IN CURRICULUM AREAS

The importance of integrating cognitive teaching and learning approaches within curriculum areas has been demonstrated consistently since the mid-1970s (see a review by Pressley et al. 1989c). While many studies have focused on specific skills (e.g. reading, comprehension, mathematics), there has been increasing attention to the application of cognitive methods in vocational education and in the physical and social sciences. In the following sections, we summarise a number of studies to show the diversity of approaches employed by researchers and education practitioners.

Reading

Perhaps the greatest impact of cognitive instruction has been in the area of reading and, in particular, reading comprehension, because of the importance of reading in all academic areas. Mayer (1992) highlighted this importance even at the literal level of comprehension where the student must separate relevant from irrelevant information to find the main idea of a passage, or in piecing together information in a text to confirm or disprove ideas that have been generated. The development of reading comprehension using a cognitive framework can best be described as one of establishing comprehension strategies and expertise for increasingly difficult texts, rather than as the mastery of a sequence of reading skills that can be taught individually (Dole et al. 1991).

Box 8.6

Three PBI studies

Ashman and Conway have collected data from students who have been taught using PBI over several years. In one study (Ashman and Conway 1993b), we compared the academic achievement and planning performance of 147 10 to 13-year-old boys and girls over a seven-month period. Approximately half were attending regular primary classes in which PBI was used, while the remaining students were in comparable non-PBI classes.

PBI was implemented in accordance with the model, and consistency in its application was monitored on a weekly basis by either the investigators or a trained consultant. In all cases, the consultation focused upon ensuring that teachers were familiar with the development and introduction of plans and that there was consistency in the use of the PBI approach. These consultations involved observing lessons in which the teachers used plans; assisting teachers to prepare more effective PBI plans; or discussing plan use and adaptation. Teachers typically applied plans to reading and mathematics activities, although some extended plan use to social studies and science lessons.

The PBI students were more successful than their peers on measures of reading, mathematics and planning ability. Teachers' ratings of the perceived effectiveness of PBI were also collected from those involved in the study. Overall, teachers reported that PBI led to positive changes in their teaching approaches and positive learning outcomes for their students.

Judith Wright from Edge Hill College of Higher Education in Lancashire conducted a study in which PBI was applied within the context of a reading intervention programme in two primary schools. Her study, concerned with the development of phonological awareness and metalinguistic concepts, involved sixteen students aged 7–10 years who were experiencing reading problems. Children were withdrawn from their regular classroom to a special education setting and each child was involved in approximately one hour of instruction per week (across two sessions) over two and a half school terms. PBI plans were used as the vehicle for instruction. Participants were tested before and at the conclusion of the study, and again after a period of five months. Wright reported significant improvements in the students' phonological skills, metalinguistic awareness and ability to plan to solve reading and spelling tasks strategically. Qualitative changes in the children's attributional beliefs in relation to reading also occurred.

In a third study, Conway and Hopton (1997) implemented a PBI staff training programme within a primary school. Following a staff inservice programme, Hopton acted as a resource person, visiting the school on a weekly basis to provide support to individual teachers and to monitor the implementation of PBI within the various classrooms. Data analysis showed that students in the PBI school had significantly improved their performance on reading when compared to students in a comparable school where the training programme was not introduced. Students also improved their performance on specific planning measures.

Students experience a number of difficulties when attempting to comprehend written material. For example, the material itself may be in a form that does not allow the student to gain ready access to the information needed. This may result from the haphazard way in which it was compiled or because the content presupposes background knowledge which the student does not have. A study based on history textbooks by Beck *et al.* (1991) exemplifies this issue. They used both the original and an adapted version of the text in instructing primary-aged students. The aim of the study was to ensure that students understood the relationships between content sections, understood the importance of background knowledge, and could interpret the content in terms of the comprehension questions being asked. Their results demonstrated that students who used the revised presentation format (in contrast with those who used the original text) increased their comprehension and recall of idea units, and provided elaborated answers which went beyond the simple restatement of facts.

As an indicator of the importance of teaching content for understanding rather than recall only, Beck *et al.* (1991) found that above-average, average, and below-average students showed improved scores using the revised material. However, the gains for the below-average group were comparatively greater than for the above-average group. This highlights the importance of incorporating cognitive strategies within academic training to assist these students of below-average ability develop skills that they do not use spontaneously, and the value of strategic behaviour to students (as shown by Cormier *et al.*, 1990; Naglieri and Gottling 1995).

Reading strategy and students with special needs

We mentioned earlier that studies based on the Das model of information processing introduced metacognitive strategies independent of curriculum content, then measured transfer to reading tasks (Brailsford 1981; D. Kaufman and P. Kaufman 1979; Krywaniuk and Das 1976). More recently, the value of strategy training taught within reading for students with learning difficulties and intellectual disability has been reported extensively in the literature. Many interventions have been aligned to particular cognitive education approaches such as improving information-processing skills, promoting comprehension monitoring, and increasing metacognitive awareness.

Another approach to teaching cognitive skills within a curriculum area involves the identification of the student's information-processing strengths and then the use of that strength to improve reading performance. This approach was used in the Kaufman K-SOS training manual (A.S. Kaufman *et al.* 1983). Hence, if the student is strong in sequential processing but weak in simultaneous processing, the teacher would concentrate on using sequential processing skills in reading activities. The difficulty with this approach comes with the student's failure to develop the weak processing strategy and thus they may rely on a less efficient strategy to attempt the task. For example, a comprehension task that requires a student to identify the main idea in a passage requires a simultaneous processing strategy. While a sequential processing strategy may achieve the correct answer, it is clearly less efficient.

Approaches to basic word attack skills

The debate on the relative merits of whole language (i.e. teaching reading within the context of stories and other reading material) and the direct instruction of reading skills to reading (i.e. teaching specific reading skills such as decoding or sight words) has dominated the literature for many years (see *Remedial and Special Education* 1993, vol. 14, no. 4). Some commentators have suggested that the issue has been blown out of proportion. For example, Bruer (1993) stated: 'Although the debate was great, the issue isn't.' Bruer argued that despite the controversy, most students acquire basic low-level word recognition skills and that the real issue is the acquisition of higher-level comprehension skills. In terms of cognitive education, the debate is of little importance as cognitive strategies can be applied to both approaches or a blend of the two. While cognitive strategy training has been employed in teaching all aspects of reading, the greatest emphasis has been given to reading comprehension.

Comprehension training

An examination of comprehension studies will show a transition from direct instruction of comprehension (see Gersten and Carnine 1986) to the concept of explicit instruction of strategies (Pearson and Dole 1988), to cognitive apprenticeships, and reciprocal teaching, to an integrated comprehension-thinking approach (Pearson and Raphael 1990).

Pearson and Raphael (1990) claimed that previous approaches have taught us valuable lessons in how to teach thinking and comprehension skills. First, decontextualising the skill from the context will not succeed and may result in misrepresentation of the skill and students' inability to apply the skill in classroom reading or problem-solving activities.

Second, there is a need to develop teacher-reliant, not teacher-proof, materials. For example, teaching materials need to encourage students to think and explore strategies that might be used, rather than rely on helping them retrieve facts. In other words, we use the teaching materials to emphasise the interdependence of teacher and students as the key players in the instructional process, and we rely on naturally occurring events and exploit them to guide instruction. Teachers who rely on textbooks or worksheets to provide both the teaching content and the practice, fail to use students' combined attributes of knowledge, problem-solving, and affect, that can contribute to small-group and whole-class learning.

Third, Pearson and Raphael (1990) recommended that decomposition of skills into smaller components does not always lead to mastery of the larger skill. The stepping-stones become ends in themselves, rather than enabling skills for the larger skill. For example, the teaching of discrete pieces of knowledge on how each part of an engine works has limited value if the student does not know how the whole engine works. In the same way, teaching how to complete each skill required to make a model boat (e.g. cutting, joining, gluing) is of limited value if the student cannot then apply those skills to complete the project.

A study aimed at increasing the comprehension skills of army personnel (Wittrock 1988) reflects the importance of Pearson and Raphael's warnings. Poor self-concepts, an acceptance that they could not and would not read, and a failure to understand what comprehension involved, provided Wittrock with a challenge, not only to teach reading skills but also to change the personal learning characteristics of the soldiers. Wittrock found that he needed to combine attention, motivation, and comprehension strategies to improve reading comprehension. For example, rather than teach comprehension skills in isolation, he sought to look at the learner's characteristics and their understanding of the comprehension process. In particular, he found that the soldiers did not understand why they were learning specific comprehension skills, and that it was essential to choose the content carefully and to present the material in a way that stimulated their interest and increased their motivation. These changes combined to produce improvement in comprehension skills.

One study has demonstrated the application of many of the principles that are considered important in the current approach to integrated thinking and comprehension training. Englert et al. (1994) developed a training procedure called POSSE (Predict, Organise, Search, Summarise, Evaluate) which incorporated comprehension skills training with an awareness of the social and cultural factors that affect classroom learning. The model accounts for an individual student's experiences with text, and the need for collaboration and interaction between students during comprehension lessons. The model draws upon the Vygotskian concept of supported learning, together with features of thinking skills curricula such as mind maps (i.e. the spatial representation of ideas on paper). Englert et al. (1994) found that students with a learning difficulty acquired a deeper understanding of comprehension processes taught in the programme.

Reasons for this success were attributed in part to the following features of POSSE. First, there was an emphasis on discourse or language in which students were encouraged to develop a language for thinking, talking, and learning from texts. Second, the reciprocal teaching process used in the study emphasised student language. Third, there was an emphasis on student ownership of strategies, with students themselves developing strategies rather than relying on teacher direction. Fourth, students were involved in classroom interactions that challenged their understanding and encouraged them to speak out. Finally, the programme focused on the relationship between ideas rather than on the recall of discrete facts. Englert *et al.* (1994) acknowledged the considerable amount of time taken to implement the programme, particularly as it required a major change in the way both teachers and students approached learning. The approach, however, reflected many of the teaching strategies that would have encouraged students' strategic behaviour.

Writing

Writing is arguably the least researched of the basic skills and many students leave school with only a rudimentary understanding of how to write competently in the various genre (e.g. narrative, argument). Following various studies in which the importance of cognitive strategies (including planning, translating and reviewing) were demonstrated in successful writers, there has been some attention given to teaching cognitive strategies in writing. The poor performance of students both with, and without, learning difficulties, on tasks such as essay writing, projects, and examination papers, demonstrates the need to teach both specific and general cognitive strategies.

The Self-Regulated Strategy Development model (Harris and Graham 1992) for writing follows a seven-stage procedure which includes strategy discussion, modelling, mnemonics, and collaborative practice. Success relies on the students remembering a teacher-generated strategy taught through a mnemonic. However, teaching a specific teacher-generated method may not be appropriate for all learners, particularly at the secondary level when students may have already consolidated a number of personal strategies. Notwithstanding this, the students in the Harris and Graham study improved their writing performance. In a later study (MacArthur *et al.* 1995) strategy instruction (i.e. the self-regulated strategy development model used earlier) and process training (i.e. a writing strategy based on the sequence of planning, drafting, revising and editing) were combined in a computer writing study for elementary-aged students, with positive outcomes in narrative and informative writing.

Spelling

Educational policy and practice are never static and fad and preferred teaching methods come and go in all areas of the curriculum. For example, during the 1950s and 1960s, teaching spelling through drills and rote learning was popular. In the 1980s spelling was considered to be almost an unimportant literacy skill. It was thought that students *kood be kreatif n ther splng* provided the message was received by the reader. It seems that the pendulum is swinging back toward the need to teach spelling once again. Alternatively, students are being actively encouraged to use word-processing packages on home computers where both spelling and grammar checking facilities can be used before submitting assignments.

The inability to spell correctly influences performance across subject areas and is a common problem for students with learning difficulties (Vaughn *et al.* 1993). Metacognitive skills are important in the spelling process because of the need to draw upon a repertoire of strategies when trying to spell an unknown word. Good spellers usually have a better understanding of the metacognitive requirements of spelling tasks and use a greater variety of spelling strategies than those who are poor spellers. The latter children neither develop, nor consistently use, metacognitive strategies when confronted by a spelling task (see Snow 1989).

Self-monitoring of performance (SMP) and self-monitoring of attention (SMA) are two strategies that have been used to help students with learning difficulties to spell in elementary schools. R. Reid and Harris (1993), for example, initially taught students a five-step spelling study procedure for a period of one week, followed by one week of SMP and one of SMA. They were taught to graph their performance each lesson and to verbalise how they went about the process of spelling (an SMP strategy). The SMA strategy taught students to assess their on-task behaviour in response to a taped tone. Reid and Harris found that students made the most progress when they employed SMP and SMA, although the students retained their knowledge about spelling longer following SMP than SMA training. Students reported that having to stop their spelling activity to record on-task behaviour in SMA was distracting and it broke their concentration. This study is useful for alerting us to the fact that what might appear to be a good method for learning (in this case self-monitoring) may not be the most effective when put into practice.

Mathematics

Mathematics instruction has focused on domain specific knowledge with only modest attention being given to cognitive and metacognitive strategies (Schunk 1990; Sweller 1990). Bruer (1993) argued that students entered school with a series of informal mathematical experiences which are not based on a knowledge of specific mathematical procedures. During the school years, mathematics education focuses on mathematical procedures, rather than the experiences and background knowledge of the students. As a result, many students often leave school with the computational skills to solve standard problems but lack the understanding that will allow them to apply those skills to novel problems.

Specific factors which have contributed to student difficulty in mathematics include knowledge of their own capabilities (e.g. self-efficacy), impulsive behaviour, and the students' perceptions of the task and their ability to problem solve generally (Montague and Applegate 1993). In addition, many students do not analyse problems, monitor their progress, or review their performance on completion of the mathematical task, all of which are important cognitive skills that lead to successful learning and problem-solving.

Early studies of mathematical cognition pointed to the distinction between the cognitive requirements of completing basic operations and those required in completing oral and written problems (Kirby and Ashman 1984). While both tasks require the application of processing and planning, the format places different demands on the student. While basic numeration tasks demand both declarative knowledge (operational signs) and procedural knowledge (sequence of completing the algorithm), oral and written problems draw upon a different set of skills because of the way in which they are represented (i.e. orthography). Hence, students need a range of mathematical skills, processing and planning skills that are accessible to meet the demands of specific tasks.

Problem-solving in mathematics relates closely to general problem-solving processes considered important in cognitive education (Mayer 1992). In reading a mathematical problem, the student must combine both strategic problem-solving and comprehension of the mathematics and reading requirements. For example, take the following word problem:

Sue has 110 cm of tape and Mary has 40 cm. If I join them together, how many metres long will the piece of tape be?

To complete the problem the student must have comprehension knowledge (reading and understanding the task); certain factual knowledge (the number of centimetres in a metre); and mathematical computational knowledge (110 cm + 40 cm = ? cm = ? m).

Where students are trained on computational skills alone, there is no opportunity to develop the problem-solving skills that are also essential. Knowing how to solve a mathematical problem is different to understanding how to solve it. In a study of students aged 6 and 7, Bryant (1985) demonstrated that students employ different strategies when confronted with verbal problems and concrete materials or written problems requiring mental calculation. Bryant concluded that instructing students in specific strategies has little point unless the students are instructed in recognising when to use that strategy and how it can be applied across situations.

One way of assisting students to make the bridge between mathematics and problem-solving is to represent the mathematical problem diagrammatically so that the student is able to represent the relationships in a non-word format (Lewis 1989). Another is to teach students to use self-questioning strategies and to develop a set of general techniques or knowledge structures (called schemata) that can be applied across problems rather than teaching specific strategies for specific problems (Hutchinson 1987).

Braselton and Decker (1994) used a graphic organiser approach to help elementary-aged students to read and complete mathematics tasks. They based the method on the premise that reading in mathematics was particularly difficult because of the combination of words, letters, symbols, numerals, and graphics that occur infrequently in other reading situations. Their graphic problem-solving organiser incorporated both cognitive and metacognitive strategies. Within the graphic organiser, the students were taught to complete the following steps:

1 Restate the question – using the student's own words to demonstrate understanding of the demands of the question.
2 Find the needed data – identifying only the information needed and excluding unnecessary information.
3 Plan what to do – preparing the sequence of steps to complete the task.
4 Find the answer – using the plan to complete the task.
5 Check – a metacognitive step in which the student reviews the steps and checks whether the answer is reasonable, rather than correct.

The use of a diamond shape for the organiser was explained by the authors as reflecting the fact that the beginning and end of the problem is a specific point, while between the two there is a need for lateral thinking. Braselton and Decker's (1994) approach followed a typical strategy training approach in which the teacher focused the student's attention on problem-solving strategies, modelled the use of the organiser, provided guided practice, and then encouraged independent practice.

While most research on the development of cognitive strategies in mathematics education has focused on early level mathematics, a different set of difficulties arise while teaching more abstract, higher levels of mathematics, including algebra and calculus. Miles and Forcht (1995) developed a procedure called the Cognitive Assault Strategy. They noted that many students with learning difficulties had trouble with language and, hence, had difficulty in formulating and expressing the steps involved in solving a mathematical problem. They relied on teachers to adopt a mentoring role and guide the student rather than provide direction. The student wrote a title for the algebra example and then wrote the problem out below it. The student then verbalised each step as it was recorded, and the teacher/mentor assisted by questioning the steps and thought processes. Following the completion of the steps, the student recorded the verbal explanation for each working step so that each working step had a matched verbal step.

SUMMARY

A major concern for teachers who wish to include cognitive and metacognitive teaching in their classrooms is the reality that, with few exceptions, most models have been applied only in small group settings. While many early strategy training studies were undertaken away from the classroom, and were subject to criticism for this reason, this pattern of cognitive research has been slow to change. Some recent approaches have begun to focus on applications to whole-classes, although these studies have frequently been applied in specific subjects, such as reading or mathematics. In addition, most applications have been designed specifically for students with learning difficulties, mild intellectual disabilities or those who are socio-economically or culturally disadvantaged.

Conducting cognitive and metacognitive training in small group situations, and away from the classroom almost guarantees that skills learned will not transfer to that class. Mainstream teaching practices will not change unless the teacher is directly involved in the programme. We shall discuss this issue further in Chapter 10.

There is not only a need to demonstrate that cognitive strategy training procedures work, there is also a need to obtain evidence of their operation in regular classrooms where the overwhelming majority of instruction takes place. Pressley *et al.* (1983: 39) posed the question, 'Can memory strategies be trained in the classroom?'. Their answer drew attention to the need for improved academic performance, gained through laboratory training to be observed in the classroom because students are 'not as persevering or compliant as they would be when they are instructed and tested individually in a laboratory setting' (p. 39). The answer does not lie in understanding the differences between laboratory and classroom performance, but in finding ways to alter curriculum presentations and instruction to ensure that strategic behaviour is a conscious, conspicuous part of all teaching and learning.

STUDY TASKS

8.1 In note form, list the main points covered in this chapter. Pay particular attention to the inclusion or exclusion of cognitive concepts (see Chapters 2, 3, and 4) in the various cognitive instruction models described.

8.2 Review the body of literature related to any of the major models to which we have referred in this chapter (e.g. Instrumental Enrichment, Process-Based Instruction). Consider how effective your chosen model would be operating in a regular classroom, or in a special education setting.

8.3 Review the literature in an academic skill area (e.g. reading, spelling, mathematics). What intervention techniques appear to work effectively?

8.4 Many of the cognitive education models were developed with special populations in mind (e.g. students with a learning or developmental disability). Consider how appropriate one or two of these models would be for application to tertiary education or on-the-job training in industry.

ADDITIONAL READING

Brooks, P.H. (1992) 'Cognitive education: the case for a preschool curriculum', *Journal of School Education 3*: 143–52.

Journal of Cognitive Education

McGilly, K. (ed.) (1994) *Classroom Lessons: Integrating Cognitive Theory and Classroom Practice*, Cambridge, MA: MIT Press.

Pressley, M., Ed-Dinary, P.B., Gaskins, I., Schuder, Bergman, J.L., Almasi, J. and Brown, R. (1992) 'Beyond direct explanation: transactional instruction of reading comprehension strategies', *Elementary School Journal 92*: 513–55.

Schwebel, M. (ed.) (1990) *Promoting Cognitive Growth over the Lifespan*, Hillsdale, NJ: Erlbaum.

Chapter 9

Cognitive skills and social behaviours

In the previous chapters, we focused on the influence of cognitive and metacognitive training programmes in academic areas (such as reading and mathematics). In this chapter, we turn our attention to social behaviours that occur in classrooms and also to specific behaviours such as aggression and depression. While a considerable research base has been established in the academic domain, comparatively little has been written about the cognitive aspects of social skills. In part, this is due to the continuing influence of behaviourism which has dominated the field. The one exception is in the area of social skills training in which the use of alternate approaches, including socio-cognitive approaches, has begun to emerge as an alternative to teaching behaviour skills in isolation from the situation in which they occur. This chapter begins with a review of the influence of behavioural approaches.

BEHAVIOURAL APPROACHES TO SOCIAL SKILLS TRAINING

Let us recap the behavioural approach to teaching and learning.

Behavioural principles have guided teaching in the management of student behaviour since the 1940s. Teachers have reinforced positive behaviours to shape a desired behaviour, or ignored or punished unacceptable behaviours to reduce their occurrence. Such has been the dominating theme in behaviour management texts and research. Behaviourism has been an attractive approach for a number of reasons.

First, the behavioural model suggests that if a behaviour is learned, then it can be *un*learned, and a new behaviour can be learned in its place. This suggests that biological, social, intellectual, and affective influences do not exist. The fact is that these and other variables *do* play a major role in the students' social behaviours and with specific behaviour disorders such as Attention Deficit Hyperactive Disorder, aggression, and depression.

Second, the behavioural model is based on the assumption that all behaviours can be modified if the reinforcers or punishers are sufficiently powerful. This suggests that student behaviours should be managed from outside the individual, and that teachers can establish and maintain in each student, social behaviours that are acceptable to teachers, rather than those behaviours that may meet the needs of the student concerned – even if they seem inappropriate to others.

Third, the behavioural model is based on the assumption that all behaviour must be definable, observable, and measurable. While this is a useful concept when observing behaviours, it denies the existence of internal factors (e.g. affective and motivational variables) that play an important part in the social and interpersonal activities of each student.

Let us look now at how behavioural matters have been used to change students' social interactions. Three approaches can be identified: contingency management, modelling, and coaching (Asher 1978). Contingency management emphasises rewarding positive behaviours and ignoring or punishing negative ones. Modelling focuses on the teacher providing a model of competent and appropriate behaviour and the student copying it. In the coaching approach, the teacher provides information about appropriate skills and behavioural examples, and the student applies these skills to other social situations. Training focuses on specific social skills (e.g. eye contact) although some recent studies have taught a cluster of skills such as talking with peers in a group.

While the behavioural approach to social and interpersonal skills training has been widely adopted, it has not meet the criteria established by Baer *et al.* (1968) who saw the need for applied behaviour analysis research to produce generalisable behaviour change: beyond the training tasks; to a variety of situations; and that can be maintained over time. Despite the efforts of writers such as Stokes and Baer (1977) and others, there has been little success in achieving any of these three criteria. In a review of fifteen years of applied behaviour analysis studies in teaching early education social skills, Chandler *et al.* (1992) found that most studies failed to demonstrate either generalisation and/or maintenance of trained behaviours. In identifying those practices most commonly associated with successful generalisation, Chandler *et al.* (1992) identified four common strategies. These involved

- addressing functional target behaviours
- specifying a fluency criterion
- using indiscrimant contingencies
- using mediation techniques.

Chandler *et al.* (1992) concluded that the focus of future research must be on maintenance and generalisation of behaviour gains, echoing the statements of Baer *et al.* (1968), twenty-four years previously.

COGNITIVE BEHAVIOUR MODIFICATION

The failure of the behavioural approach to produce lasting and generalisable behavioural change, together with its failure to accept that the cognitive experiences of the student can affect success in learning and problem-solving, led to the development of cognitive-behavioural techniques. Sapp and Farrell (1994) identified the foundations of the approach as follows:

> a student's cognitions (thoughts), affect (emotions), and behavior (actions) cannot be treated individually because they are overlapping processes. Cognitive-behavioral interventions apply cognitive (thinking), affective (emotive) and behavioral (actions) techniques to help students in the classroom.
>
> (Sapp and Farrell 1994: 20)

The involvement of the person in behavioural approaches provided the mechanism to link the student with observable outcomes of learning and problem-solving.

Contemporary cognitive-behavioural methods have been applied to a broad range of social-emotional problems including aggression, depression, and anxiety (Finch *et al.* 1993), coping self-statements (Kamann and Wong 1993), delinquency (Hains and Hains 1987), anger control (Hains and Szjakowski 1990), test anxiety (Sapp 1993), and general social skills training (Taffe and Smith 1994).

Let us now look at some specific programmes that have produced lasting change. Hains and Szyjakowski (1990) used a cognitive-behavioural approach to teach anger control through a three-phase process: con-ceptualisation, skills acquisition and rehearsal, and application. In the conceptualisation phase, students were taught to identify irrational thoughts that resulted in stress and anger, and then to change these thoughts by monitoring their thought processes. In the skills acquisition and rehearsal phase, students learned how to challenge their irrational thoughts through self-questioning. Some examples of the coping statements included: 'I would like to get angry. This really annoys me, but I do not have to get angry. This is not nearly as serious as it appears to be. I can cope with the situation' (Sapp and Farrell, 1994: 22). In the final application phase, students practised their coping skills in role-playing situations, homework assignments, and in small group discussions.

Another cognitive-behavioural approach used by Hains (1992) was based on a four-step approach (Table 9.1) which requires students to identify the angry feelings they are experiencing first, and then to brainstorm alternative approaches for dealing with them. Alternatives are then ranked and the student tries out some of the alternatives. Hains recommended that the activities are carried out in small-group situations.

Cognitive-behavioural approaches have also been used successfully to teach coping skills to students (e.g. being able to deal with criticism) (Kamann and Wong 1993). The training programme involved the use of cue cards to outline the three stages in the coping process (Table 9.2).

In addition, students were taught a number of coping self-statements for

Table 9.1 Problem-solving approach for anger control

Step	Procedure
1	Identify the situation producing the anger and accept the angry emotions that are occurring.
2	Think of alternatives for handling the anger.
3	Rank two or three alternatives for handling anger.
4	Test out the two or three alternatives chosen. If all of the alternatives fail, return to Step 2.

Table 9.2 Stages in the coping process

Stage	Procedure
1	Assessment of the situation Label and plan
2	Recognising and controlling the impulse of negative thoughts Recognising that negative thoughts hurt my work Controlling by replacing
3	Reinforcing Pat yourself on the back for a good job

each of the steps such as, 'What is it that I have to do?' (assessment of the situation); 'I'm saying things that don't help me ... I can stop and think more helpful thoughts' (recognising and controlling). Importantly, once the cue cards had been discussed and students were aware of the procedures, no further instructions were given. This allowed the student to adapt class statements to become their own self-statements. Results of the programme indicated that students were able to develop coping self-statements although negative self-statements were not eliminated entirely.

An issue that arose from this approach, which had direct importance in the selection of a training strategy approach, was that older students (Grades 5 to 7 – ages 11–13) could use the strategy effectively, while younger students (Grade 4) could not. The issue of the need for a level of cognitive development in students, before they were able to use such strategies effectively, needed to be borne in mind. Kamann and Wong (1993) suggested that the use of picture cues, and breaking the self-talk procedures into smaller steps, would be most effective with younger students.

The expanding use of cognitive-behavioural approaches reflects a growing awareness of the need to have students recognise that they have the cognitive ability to make decisions about their behaviour, and to have some control over it. The teacher's role is to facilitate students' self-examination of their actions and to assist them to select appropriate alternative behaviour.

THE SELF AND COGNITIVE TRAINING METHODS

The discussion on self-examination raises the need to consider three aspects of self-perception which are essential in any discussion of cognitive and metacognitive approaches to social behaviours. These are self-concept, self-efficacy, and self-esteem (Gordon *et al.* 1996). Self-concept refers to the beliefs that a person has about themselves as a total person, and the way in which he/she interacts with the world. Self-efficacy refers to the individual's belief about competency for a given task and is a sub-set of self-concept. Gordon *et al.* (1996) suggested that students who have positive self-efficacy are confident in their ability to do the task, enjoy the challenges of learning, and have an expectation that others will listen to their views. Self-esteem relates to the individual's evaluation of their self-concept, how they measure their level of needs satisfaction, and the degree to which they like themselves as an individual.

The role of each of these three aspects of self is important, as any change in social behaviour needs to be matched by a change in self-concept, self-esteem, and self-efficacy. Changing behaviour alone may not change these self-perceptions thereby leaving the student with no empowerment or involvement in the process of behaviour change.

Social-cognitive strategies

Social-cognitive strategies include problem-solving at the interpersonal and social levels, self-control of impulsive and aggressive behaviours, internalised locus of control, and the development of appropriate attributions (R.E. Kennedy 1984), reflection (Gallagher 1994), planning (Ashman and Conway 1993c), moral reasoning, and social perspective-taking skills (Guerra and Slaby 1990). While many of these strategies have also been used in research on academic content, they are of considerable importance in social behaviour and their presence or absence can distinguish between non-delinquent and delinquent students (Hains and Herrman 1989).

The term 'social problem-solving skills' refers to the generation of alternative solutions to problems of social interaction, the evaluation of possible consequences, and the choice of an effective solution (Dubow *et al.* 1991). Social problem-solving sequences have been taught in a variety of settings. Guerra and Salby (1990) list a common sequence (Table 9.3), in this case, for the management of aggressive behaviours. The steps would be introduced over several sessions with students progressing as each step is mastered. In the Stop-Think-Do programme (Petersen and Gannoni 1989),

Table 9.3 Social problem-solving model steps

Step	Procedure
1	Is there a problem?
2	Stop and think.
3	Why is there a conflict?
4	What do I want?
5	Think of solutions.
6	Look at consequences.
7	Choose what to do and do it.
8	Evaluate the results.

the sequence is reduced to the three steps identified in the title of the approach. Although the number of steps appear less, the actions to be completed remain the same.

Attributional training attempts to change the reasoning behind success or failure. In other words, changing a student's incorrect attribution of success and failure from external forces (luck or an easy task) to those under personal control (effort and ability). Craven *et al.* (1991) argued that changing a student's attributions can enhance their effort, motivation, achievement, and academic self-concept.

Reflection involves students undertaking a number of cognitive processes including reviewing, reconstructing, re-enacting and analysing one's own performance (Gallagher 1994). The approach has been used successfully in self-instruction training for students with poor social and cognitive behaviours (Bash and Camp 1985).

The development of students' planning skills is considered important because it places emphasis on students working systematically through a planned sequence of actions and monitoring (metacognitive) steps to achieve a behavioural goal. For a plan to be effective, each student must be involved in making decisions about the behavioural goal and then developing a plan that meets their individual needs (Conway and Ashman 1992). An example of the development of an individual behaviour plan, together with the dialogue of teacher and student, is provided in Ashman and Conway (1993c). The use of plans and planning with students is discussed in detail later in the chapter.

Students with behaviour problems experience difficulty with a variety of specific cognitive strategies. While adolescents with depression have been shown to have a significantly lower level of self-concept and self-confidence than regular adolescents, they do not differ from regular adolescents in their social problem-solving ability or understanding of interpersonal behaviour or cues (P. Martin *et al.* 1993). Similarly, adolescent delinquents who are high performing in terms of behaviour management and who are non-aggressive, have better problem-solving skills than those who are low performing in terms of behaviour management (Hains and Herrman 1989). These types of social-cognitive skills will be discussed further in the following sections, both in terms of training approaches and programmes for students with specific behavioural disorders.

Training in social competence

Social competence training is a term that has been used to identify interventions that promote students' social skills or social competence (Beelmann *et al.* 1994). Social competence is the preferred term as it allows for a broad range of approaches to be considered. Beelmann *et al.* (1994) identified four social competence training concepts:

1   *Social problem-solving* focuses on the development of competencies such as generating alternative solutions and consequential thinking.
2   A *social skills approach* assumes that students lack the necessary skills to interact successfully with other students. Training tends to focus on concrete motor responses using modelling and reinforcement, or the improvement of social adjustment through training competencies and/or modifying inappropriate social cognitions.
3   *Social perspective taking* focuses on seeing an interaction from another person's perspective.
4   *Self-control training* focuses on evaluating one's own behaviour prior to carrying out the behaviour.

While these four approaches could be considered to cover the spectrum of social competence training, many variations exist. Prior to discussing these, a number of other important aspects of social competence training raised by Beelman *et al.* (1994) should be considered, including the use of monomodal and multimodal training programmes, and the influence of age and gender.

Monomodal and multimodal interventions

Beelmann *et al.* (1994) suggested a distinction between monomodal and multimodal interventions, particularly as many interventions focus on a combination of strategies and a blending of behavioural, cognitive, and other training components. In their analysis of the literature in the area, Beelmann *et al.* (1994) found that multimodal social problem-solving programmes showed the greatest impact on social-cognitive and social-interactive skills. Self-control programmes produced strong gains in social adjustment and self-related cognitions and affects.

Behavioural difficulty

Beelmann *et al.* (1994) found that socially deprived students showed the greatest gains in social-cognitive skills, possibly because the training programmes exposed those students to competencies that had not previously been available to them. In contrast, students who were withdrawn performed better on simple behavioural training programmes rather than more complex multimodal programmes that had a cognitive emphasis.

Age and gender

In terms of age of students, the study demonstrated the importance of developing programmes that met the cognitive developmental levels of students. Younger students operated best under monomodal programmes that taught specific skills, with reduced emphasis on self-regulated cognitions, self-concept and locus of control. Older students coped better with multimodal programmes in which there was a greater emphasis on more complex cognitive structures such as self-concept and locus of control. The analysis also demonstrated that pre-school children had social skills deficits, while older students had problems with the social skills they already possessed. Hence, different programme emphases were needed across age groups.

Most social competence training programmes are aimed at boys. This may be due to the over-identification of social problems with boys, because they tend to act out more than girls, who may demonstrate withdrawn or shy behaviours and consequently be less likely to be noticed in class (Conway 1994). Programme planners should be aware of the differing needs of boys and girls in terms of motivation, and self-perceptions.

We now turn to examining the main approaches to social competence training, beginning with social problem-solving skills training.

SOCIAL PROBLEM-SOLVING SKILLS TRAINING

This approach is based on a social-cognitive development model and aims to develop each student's cognitive resources to control personal behaviour difficulty. Each student is considered to have a set of cognitive resources for dealing with specific situations as well as cognitive mediators (the organising factors) which determine student response patterns at any time. The training programme is intended to change the cognitive mediators and lead to changes in the student's responses to social situations.

General social problem-solving skills training programmes have been effective in: reducing the adjustment difficulties of students moving into middle school (Elias *et al.* 1986); the levels of depression in junior high school students (Glyshaw *et al.* 1989); and aggressive behaviours in adolescent juvenile offenders (Guerra and Slaby 1990).

A wide variety of social problem-solving difficulties have been identified in students with aggressive behaviour problems. These include

- defining social problems based on a perception of hostility
- setting a goal consistent with that perception of hostility
- searching for few facts
- generating few alternate solutions
- generating few consequences for an aggressive solution
- setting priorities in favour of ineffective solutions (i.e. aggression or hostility).

(Guerra and Slaby 1990: 270)

Guerra and Salby (1990) taught social problem-solving skills to adolescent aggressive offenders in detention using a cognitive mediation strategy in small group situations. The programme was based on developing four specific information-processing skills:

1   Focusing on relevant and non-hostile cues when defining a social problem and setting a goal.
2   Searching for additional information.
3   Developing a variety of responses and consequences.
4   Listing possible responses in terms of their effectiveness in providing goal-directed, legal, and non-violent outcomes.

The technique uses an eight-step social problem-solving sequence (refer again to Table 9.3) taught over twelve sessions, in which students talk about how to identify problems, and to differentiate between 'hot-headed' and 'cool-headed' (Guerra and Slaby 1990: 272) responses. Instructors use hypothetical social problems throughout based on a prior survey of common aggressive problem situations identified by the students.

Results of Guerra and Salby's study demonstrated that students increased their ability to solve social problems, and reduced their support for aggressive behaviour statements such as 'aggression increases self-esteem'. Post- intervention reports from staff not involved in the study noted reduced aggressive, impulsive, and inflexible behaviours.

Another approach suitable for juvenile offenders involves a five-step social problem-solving procedure for use when confronted with dilemma scenarios. The strategy developed by Hains and Hains (1987) (see Table 9.4) followed similar steps to those described by Guerra and Slaby (1990).

However, unlike the approach used by Guerra and Slaby, the Hains and Hains (1987) training strategy is based on modelling responses to the complete sequence, with the instructor working through each of the steps and then asking the student to follow the same process, using the instructor's support. The student then completes a second scenario followed by instructor feedback. In the Hains and Hains study, all adolescents showed improvement in problem-solving on the dilemma tasks and at the post-test; some were able to

Table 9.4 Five steps for social problem-solving

Step	Procedure
1	What exactly is the problem here? (Define it clearly. What factors are involved?)
2	What are all the possible decisions that can be made to solve the problem?
3	If any of these decisions are made, what possible outcomes could ensue? (What might be the consequences?)
4	Weigh the importance of the possible outcomes or consequences. (Which is most important to you?)
5	Make a decision.

generalise the strategy to untrained problems after training. Improvement was also shown in their overall behaviour within the institution.

Interpersonal cognitive problem-solving

One approach that emphasised the role of thinking processes was developed as a specific training programme under the title 'I can problem solve' (Shure 1992). The approach concentrated on three thinking skills:

- alternative thinking (i.e. generating multiple alternate solutions)
- consequential thinking (i.e. seeing the immediate and long-term implications of each solution and then using the information in the decision-making process)
- means-end thinking (i.e. planning a series of actions to achieve a goal, recognising obstacles and working around them, and working within a realistic time framework).

While some of these skills are similar to those discussed earlier, there are a number of additional features, including the recognition of obstacles, and working within a time frame, that distinguish this approach from others.

The 'I can problem solve' (ICPS) approach has been designed as a curriculum with three volumes covering pre-school, infant, and primary grades. The volumes contain individual lessons, with details on lesson content and presentation. Each lesson is divided into pre-problem-solving skills (i.e. learning the problem-solving vocabulary and language; identifying with own and others' feelings) and problem-solving skills (i.e. alternate solutions; consequences; solution-consequences pairs; means-ends thinking). Lessons are held in small groups for about twenty minutes a day for at least four months.

Five principles underlie the approach.

1   Both the child and the teacher must identify the child's view of the problem.
2   Understand and deal with the real problem. A behaviour (such as hitting) may be initially identified as the problem when it is actually the child's solution to a personal perception of the problem (e.g. to repossess something from another child).
3   Once the real problem has been identified, the teacher must not alter it to fit his or her own needs.
4   The child, not the teacher, must solve the problem.
5   The focus is on how, not on what, the child thinks.

An informal evaluation of the ICPS approach was conducted by Rooney *et al.* (1993). Some teachers reported ease of use because the programme fitted into their curriculum focus. Others reported some difficulty with the ideas recommended in units and with fitting the programme into the class timetable, given the pressures of teaching academic content at the senior elementary level. Rooney *et al.* (1993) noted that both issues can be addressed within the ICPS approach by combining lessons and teaching the content in longer but less frequent lessons. Teachers reported increased student involvement in lessons, and an increased willingness to generate solutions to problems. In addition, teachers thought that the programme had promise as part of a parent-training programme at the pre-school level. The question that we would ask of teachers is whether a packaged programme is the best way to teach social problem-solving skills.

Another classroom approach, developed by Conte *et al.* (1995), is to use coaching/role playing and information sharing in which the situations targeted for the intervention can be predetermined. These include

1   Knowing how to respond when the teacher asks a student why he/she is having difficulty reading.
2   Knowing how to ask for directions when you get lost.
3   How to approach a classmate who you would like to make friends with.
4   How to ask a person about his/her beliefs or culture when they are different from your own.
5   How to join a new club at a new school you are attending.
6   How to cope with a new school setting.

(Conte *et al.* 1995: 89)

The coaching/role playing techniques use a teacher outline of the strategy, followed by class discussion, and a small group role play. The role plays are performed for the class and a debriefing session follows. The information-sharing aspect of the programme is based on the Metacognitive Approach to Social Skills Training (Sheinker and Sheinker 1988), and follows the sequence of self-evaluation, group evaluations, and comparisons of others' perceptions with the individual student's own perceptions.

Results of the Conte *et al.* (1995) study showed that within a whole-class intervention, coaching, role playing, and information sharing can produce change in the social problem-solving skills and in the social acceptance of students.

SOCIAL SKILLS TRAINING

While many of the approaches discussed earlier in this chapter focus on social skills training, the constant reference, in the research literature, to social skills training in classrooms warrants a separate discussion. The relationship between learning difficulties and social skills difficulties has long been recognised, and while there have been attempts to have social skills difficulties recognised as a learning disorder, the relationship between the two concepts remains an important issue for both teachers and researchers (Conte and Andrews 1993). Many intervention programmes for students with social skills difficulties are conducted in withdrawal settings (i.e. away from the setting in which the social skills difficulties occur) (see review in McIntosh *et al.* 1991). The debate about whether behaviours learned in a withdrawal setting will transfer remains contentious.

Three approaches to social skills training are considered below. One follows a group-based social-cognitive training approach using social problem-solving skills (Kolko *et al.* 1990); one integrates behavioural approaches with a co-operative learning strategy (Fad *et al.* 1995), and the final approach uses a rational behaviour skills method combining self-analysis, self-monitoring, and rational thinking (Maultsby 1990).

A group-based social-cognitive skills training

Group based social-cognitive skills training has been used to improve conversational behaviour, social competence, and to reduce aggressive behaviours. A number of training techniques have been incorporated, including social perception, knowledge of social rules, peer group behaviour, and group-based games and tasks (see Kolko *et al.* 1990).

In a comparative study of elementary-aged students receiving psychiatric care, Kolko *et al.* (1990) trained one group using social-cognitive skills training (SCST) and a comparative group using social activity training (SA). The SCST was conducted in small groups over fifteen hourly sessions. Training was designed to assist the students to understand the situational characteristics and consequences, to select appropriate responses in problem situations, and evaluate their performance. Targeted skills included social involvement, appropriate gaze, awareness of physical space, voice volume/inflection, openers/compliments, making requests (positive assertions), responding to provocation (negative assertions), and appropriate non-aggressive play and sharing.

Training followed a consistent format in all sessions. Group rules and the skills learned in the previous sessions were reviewed at the beginning of each session. New skills were introduced by providing a rationale for their use and group members were questioned about their understanding of the skill components. The group was then shown five video-taped situations in which the skill was portrayed either correctly or incorrectly. Discussion and role plays were also included, with some being taped for further discussion by the group. Importantly, training included opportunities for afternoon and night staff to reinforce the display of appropriate behaviours in situations outside the training sessions.

The SCST group demonstrated significant improvement over the comparison SA training group in terms of self-reported loneliness, staff social problems ratings, social competence on role plays and observations of social skills during free-play interactions. They also showed improvement in both social and interpersonal behaviour and one-year later, those in the SCST group continued to show appropriate social skills such as sharing, positive assertion, and appropriate play.

Reasons for the gains can be attributed to four factors previously identified in the literature. First, the targeted skills were identified by staff, improving the likelihood that they would be supported beyond the training situation. Second, the emphasis in training was on verbal interaction skills that would allow the child to enter groups more effectively, play in the groups, and provide social reinforcement to members of the group. Third, the techniques enhanced students' status within their peer group. Finally, the skills acquired by the students were reinforced by non-intervention staff in alternate situations, thereby strengthening the value of the newly acquired positive behaviours.

A behavioural and co-operative learning approach to teaching social skills

Fad *et al.* (1995) recommended the use of a co-operative learning approach in teaching social skills to pre-school children. The approach has four main steps and a series of sub-steps as shown in Table 9.5.

Although not tested in a study, the approach does demonstrate the importance of targeting appropriate skills and ensuring that teachers have a thorough understanding of the importance of the assessment-planning-instruction-evaluation cycle, discussed in Chapter 1, and emphasised throughout the following chapters.

The cognitive aspect is evident in the group interactions and reflections made by the students on the skills they learned in groups. The concept of assigning group members specific tasks assists in ensuring that all students

Table 9.5 Four steps for using co-operative learning to teach social skills

Step	Procedure
1	Target special social skills • use a behaviour rating scale • rely on teacher observation • identify skills necessary for success in mainstream environments • ask students which social skills they think are important
2	Define the skills behaviourally • place skills in a logical hierarchy • place objectives in a priority list • task analyse the behaviour • describe student behaviours
3	Design and implement the co-operative activities • define both academic and social goals • provide direct instruction in the social skills • assign a specific role to each group member • create positive group interdependence • develop a reinforcement plan
4	Process and evaluate • review the criteria for success • provide opportunities for students to self-evaluate • suggest strategies for generalisation • provide teacher evaluation of social skill performance

can play different roles in the group, each using different social skills.

While the approach may seem to be too teacher controlled, and lack spontaneity in implementation, it would be successful for teachers beginning a cognitive social skills programme with young children who may not be able to apply their limited cognitive problem-solving skills without teacher direction.

A rational behaviour skills approach to teaching social skills

Rational behaviour therapy (RBT) is a neurobehavioural approach which targets thinking behaviours, feeling behaviours and behavioural responses to the environment, and which encourages self-monitoring (Maultsby 1990). Maultsby records the successful use of the approach in classrooms, criminal justice programmes and in substance abuse programmes. Patton (1995) has also suggested its use in teaching behaviourally disordered or emotionally disturbed students.

The approach operates over seven sessions as shown in Table 9.6. The approach may take longer than seven sessions as the students must master the skills of each session (topic) before proceeding to the next. For each lesson, there is an objective, a scripted goal and learning activities. Techniques used

Table 9.6 The rational behaviour skills training programme

Session	Content
1	How the brain works to create emotions
2	The anatomy (or ABCs) of an emotion
3	The five rules of rational behaviour
4	Rational self-analysis: the basics
5	How to write a rational self-analysis
6	How to do rational emotive imagery
7	Self-monitoring of rational skills

in the sessions include controlling thoughts and emotions, using relaxation techniques and imagery, and self-monitoring.

The difference between the rational behaviour skills approach and the co-operative learning approach can be seen in the former's focus on emotions and self-control of them, as contrasted with the teacher-controlled introduction of specific teacher-selected social skills in the latter. The important point is that the selection of a specific approach to social skills training should depend on the needs of both the teacher and students in that particular situation, and not seek to implement a fixed format regardless of the needs of the situation.

SELF-MONITORING STRATEGIES

Self-monitoring is a crucial part of most contemporary cognitive education programmes as it increases attention and alerts the learner to potential problems which might compromise the success of a learning or problem-solving activity (see R. Reid and Harris 1993). Self-monitoring has also been an important element in many strategy training programmes designed to assist students with learning difficulties, many of whom have behavioural difficulties as well. One of the most common behavioural problems found in the classroom is maintaining on-task behaviour. Hence, there is a logical need to increase both academic and social skills at the same time.

R. Reid and Harris (1993) trained self-monitoring and attention strategies to students with learning difficulties. Students were taught about the importance of this and what paying attention meant in a spelling lesson. They were then taught to ask themselves when they heard a taped tone, 'Was I paying attention?' and to note the result on a record sheet. On-task behaviours were listed on the sheet as a cue.

While students increased their on-task behaviour following training, their spelling performance was significantly lower than for students who were taught only spelling strategies. Reid and Harris explained that the poorer performance was due to the intrusive nature of the strategy and this was supported by student interviews. The results also supported earlier findings that increased attention does not necessarily mean increased academic performance and that on-task behaviour does not necessarily mean increased cognitively engaged time. The results of this study emphasise the need for strategy training to be consistent with students' existing strategic behaviour, and with the prime focus of the intervention.

ANGER CONTROL

In the previous section, the focus was on specific strategies and their use in meeting the needs of students with a variety of social behaviours. In this section, anger control will be considered in relation to the variety of cognitive techniques available. Two main approaches to anger control have been identified which, although conceptually different, have been effective as interventions (Deffenbacher *et al.* 1994).

The first are those that focus on teaching increased emotional control through reduction of the cognitive, psychological and emotional components of anger. Reduction in these three components allows the person to access their existing skills and problem-solving free of the blocking effects of heightened emotional arousal. The second group are those intervention approaches focusing on social skills training through increasing positive interpersonal skills that assist in handling difficult social situations. Both approaches are considered to be highly structured and sequential.

Three specific anger reduction group training strategies have been suggested (Deffenbacher *et al.* 1994): inductive social skills training (ISST), skill assembly social skills training (SASST) and cognitive-relaxation coping skills (CRCS). CRCS training uses a cognitive-relaxation approach in which imagery is used to reduce arousal and then transferred to the environment. Four relaxation techniques can be used: relaxation imagery using a personally selected image; cue-controlled relaxation using terms such as 'relax', paired with relaxation; relaxation by consciously reducing muscle tension; and breathing-cued relaxation.

The SASST training develops specific skills in each session and then sequences them together throughout the training. In this case anger is considered a result of miscommunication, misunderstanding and communication skills that increase conflict, and training concentrates on overcoming these. In the SASST training, anger again is described as the result of personal communication and provocation. Students are taught that by changing their communication patterns they can increase anger control. In this approach, group members are told that they have to develop the effective communication skills themselves.

Deffenbacher *et al.* (1994) compared training outcomes from the three strategies with first-year psychology students, using small-group one-hour weekly sessions over eight weeks. Results of the study demonstrated that all three approaches reduced a variety of anger types including general anger and anger across a variety of situations.

A number of important issues arise from the Deffenbacher *et al.* (1994) study, including the difficulty that some programmes (e.g. ISST) do not address personal anger as opposed to anger in interpersonal situations, and that although anger reduction programmes do provide assertiveness-type skills, there is no post-intervention evidence of increases in assertiveness. The study, however, does illustrate the importance of adopting a variety of approaches to meet the needs of students with high anger levels.

THE IMPACT OF AFFECT ON SCHOOL PERFORMANCE

Affective (emotional) variables, such as moods, feelings, temperament, motivation, and resultant stress, play an important part in the application of social-cognitive skills. While affect is a commonly discussed aspect of human problem-solving, it is likely the least investigated (McLeod and Adams 1989). While students can be trained to use specific strategies when interacting with another student, the application of that strategy may depend on whether the student is motivated to do so at the time. Hence, there is a need to teach some aspects of attributions and reasoning about affect prior to training pro-social skills (Carlo *et al.* 1991).

Mood states

Students can experience negative emotions, mood changes, and concern for their well-being when confronted by difficult tasks (Boekarts 1993), and positive and negative mood states can affect information-processing performance (Bowers 1991). When a student is happy and has a positive mood state, intellectual performance can be enhanced and later recall of positive features of the information is also enhanced. Students with poor mood states have been found to take longer to process information and often look for negative aspects of the material. Knowledge and control of mood states and emotions should then assist students in cognitive activities (Boekarts 1993).

Studies have shown that by the end of primary school, students experience stress in social conflict situations, as well as anger and sadness in response to social conflict, and avoidance behaviour is a common strategy in social conflict situations (Boekarts 1993). Although the ramifications for intervention should be clear, many social behaviour programmes fail to address these issues directly, believing that tackling specific social-cognitive skills will result in indirect changes in emotions, mood and stress levels.

Temperament

Temperament is another affective area that has received considerable attention in the psychological literature, but comparatively little in the intervention literature. Temperament refers to 'individual differences in behavioral tendencies that are present early in life and that are relatively stable across time and a variety of situations' (Martin 1994: 120). As the environments that young children are exposed to are varied (school, home, peer groups), some instability in temperament can be expected as students develop through their school years. R.P. Martin (1994) discusses the effect of environmental stress on behaviour problems as being at five levels: therapeutic, benign, modal, stressful and pathological.

At the therapeutic level, the environment is supportive of individual behavioural differences and positive support for learning occurs. At the benign level, the environment does not create behaviour problems, nor does it provide a positive support for learning (i.e. it is neutral). At the modal or typical level, short-term stress can be expected, as would occur in most classes or families. At the stressful level, chronic stress is encountered, while at the fifth, pathological level stress is extreme and the pressures on the child, class and family are beyond the level at which these environments can cope. As environments change, so do the environmental stress levels and, consequently, so do temperament levels and problem behaviours. In ecological terms, there is a misfit between the environmental demands and the disposition of the students (e.g. the teacher wants silence, individual, at-desk work and the student wants to move around and talk). The resulting misfit between environmental demands and the student's temperament will result in stress for both the teacher and student, and end with the behaviour (and student) being labelled a problem.

The importance of considering temperament in the management of specific students is most clearly illustrated in the cases of students with Attention Deficit Hyperactivity Disorder, or those who are inhibited and socially isolated. In both cases, the temperament levels affect the student's ability to join in, and their temperaments discourage other students from accepting them. Where intervention programmes can be designed to encourage other students to interact with them, the temperament constraints may be reduced.

Temperament has been shown to be a predictor of academic performance and classroom behaviour, through three of its dimensions: activity, distractability and persistence (see Orth and Martin 1994). Many studies have looked at the three dimensions together under the term Task Orientation with a continuum from high task orientation (low activity, low distractability, high persistence) to low task orientation (high activity, high distractability, low persistence).

In a study of temperament, problem-solving performance and academic ability, Orth and Martin (1994) taught students five problem-solving tasks, either through computer-directed instruction, or teacher-directed instruction. High task orientation students were equally successful with both approaches because of their disposition to attend to the task, regardless of its format. In addition, their level of off-task behaviour was low. Students in the low task orientation group were significantly more likely to engage in off-task behaviour in teacher-directed sessions, than in computer-directed sessions.

The reason may be due to temperament factors, such as the one-to-one instruction of the computer, the immediate feedback and the instructional format. This contrasts with the waiting for materials, waiting for assistance and lack of immediate feedback that can occur in teacher-directed sessions. The problem-solving ability of the groups, however, was not different for either method of instruction or temperament level. Orth and Martin explained this unexpected result as being due to the use of problem-solving tasks rather than academic achievement tasks. As strategy development was stressed in both groups, group differences following instruction would not be expected to be as great.

The other important result of the study was the relationship between temperament and off-task behaviours. Teachers were able to accurately identify both the temperament characteristics of students and their level of off-task behaviour. Students rated as more active, and distractable and less persistent, demonstrated greater levels of off-task behaviour. Hence, teacher ratings of individual temperament levels are consistent with actual student behaviour patterns in class. This finding also has implications for incorporating issues of individual temperament levels into instructional programmes.

MORAL REASONING AND METACOGNITION

Following from the issues of affective skills, the relationship between metacognition and moral reasoning presents another dimension to the concept of behaviour and student selection of options that are perceived as acceptable or not. A number of connections have been found between metacognition and the development of moral reasoning (judgement) and moral behaviour (ethical behaviour) (Swanson and Hill 1993). Moral metacognition has been found to relate to high moral reasoning and high moral behaviour. In addition, consistent with many other studies of metacognition, an age factor has been found.

While younger students are aware of their own thinking (metacognition), only in older students is there a consistent relationship between awareness and observable behaviour. This is important as older students will have a greater repertoire of strategies for moral action, and should be able to use them in guiding their decision-making. Younger students, and those without these skills, such as students with behaviour problems, will be at a disadvantage in making decisions about ethical behaviour.

SOCIAL-COGNITIVE SKILLS AND STUDENTS WITH BEHAVIOUR PROBLEMS

To this point, consideration has focused on specific approaches and specific behaviour problems. In the following sections, the use of cognitive social skills at different school levels will be discussed. The main focus is on the relationship between social-cognitive skill programmes and school social and academic performance.

How do these approaches differ from the traditional behavioural approach? Two major differences exit. First, the behavioural approach is based on reinforcing responses, while the cognitive approach is based on reinforcing process. In the behavioural approach, students are externally reinforced until the desired behaviour is demonstrated, and then reinforcement ceases. Within the cognitive approach, students are consistently encouraged to think about alternate solutions, their chosen solution, and its effectiveness.

The second relates to the issues of generalisation discussed at the beginning of the chapter. While the behavioural approach seeks to teach generalisation and maintenance of a behaviour after it is learned, the cognitive approach seeks to teach students to become independent of external mediation during the programme. At the point of independence, students are able to make their own rules and apply them to both academic and social skill activities.

Early education settings

Throughout this chapter, and in the preceding chapters on the application of cognitive strategies in academic content, we have highlighted the importance of stages of cognitive development. At the early education level, students are beginning their understanding of social skills and the need to manage their behaviour, or to have their behaviour managed by teachers. Students learn that appropriate social behaviour is as prized as appropriate academic behaviour.

One of the most common techniques used to maintain appropriate behaviour in classrooms, from early education to secondary school, is the use of class rules. At the early education level, cognitive preparedness for understanding of rules is not adequately developed. Hence, any rules that are developed need to be considered in relation to activities that children understand. Rules made for the teacher's control benefit, but not understood by students, will not enhance students' learning.

As young children do not have well-developed social skills, training programmes for young children may need to be more structured and proceed through more sub-steps. One approach is through the use of cognitive mediation (Haywood and Brown 1990). Within a cognitive/mediational approach, behaviours that are disruptive are seen as cognitive problems to be solved, rather than as misbehaviour. A sequence of strategies used to teach desirable behaviour is shown in Table 9.7.

Where a behaviour becomes a problem and cannot be managed through unobtrusive measures such as glances or warning signals, a more specific management strategy may be needed. A cognitive/mediational approach could be employed following a sequence similar to the one shown in Table 9.8.

The effects of a cognitive approach on young children begins with the unlearning of the previous behaviour management approaches and the development of a sense of responsibility for their own behaviour. As they begin to sense their control, they can monitor their own actions in terms of the classroom rules, and can think through the consequences of their actions. Haywood and Brown (1990) give the example of a child who deliberately spilt milk on the desk. After exploring the consequences of the behaviour, the student decided that drinking the milk had more positive consequences than spilling it (i.e. cleaning it up). In this way, the student saw that she had control over the situation.

While structured programmes certainly assist in the social-cognitive development of young children, sometimes the least structured experiences can achieve the greatest gains. One such strategy is the use of plastic house guttering as a resource (Dinwiddie 1993). Dinwiddie introduced plastic guttering into play sessions to enhance teaching of the science syllabus. As students began to explore alternate uses of the guttering, other benefits emerged including social-cognitive skills. Gutters were almost always a social activity, with students co-operating in placing the long lengths, jointly developing and brainstorming activities using the guttering, and solving problems they had raised. The outcome was that a cheap resource, bought for an academic purpose, developed into an important part of the social-cognitive curriculum.

Table 9.7 A cognitive/mediational approach to teaching desirable behaviour

Step	Strategies
1	Model the desired behaviour.
2	Make certain that the children know and understand what behaviour is desired.
3	Mediate the reasons for desiring a particular form of behaviour.
4	Reward appropriate behaviour using task-intrinsic rewards.
5	Maintain a challenging cognitive pace.

Table 9.8 A cognitive/mediational approach to disruptive behaviour

Step	Procedure
1	Interrupt the disruptive behaviour quickly. Cognitive intervention cannot occur while the behaviour continues.
2	Ask the child to define the problem. The child's definition can assist in seeing the child's perspective of the problem and why it is a problem.
3	Ask the child what else may be done to achieve the objective.
4	If the behaviour is acceptable in other situations (e.g. running, talking), ask when would be a good time to do it and suggest an agreement to do it then.
5	Suggest role taking. Have the child consider what it would be like to be the one who was disadvantaged by the behaviour such as the one who was hit, or who had the toy pulled away.
6	Ask the child about the activities that should be occurring at that time, perhaps by checking the daily planning board.
7	Discuss with the child and other children in the group, the rules that cover that situation.
8	Have the group problem-solve the issue to see their possible solutions. Avoid making the child a scape-goat, by focusing on the issues.
9	Work towards more cognitive and independent solutions. If children do need to have their behaviour managed by the teacher because they are unable to think through the behaviour and solutions, this should occur. However, as soon as possible, the child should be involved in cognitive solutions.

School settings

One of the critical issues in the management of social behaviours in schools is what to do with students who refuse to co-operate with school rules, or who do not have the academic ability to keep up with grade-level instruction. The term 'at-risk students' has often been applied to this group. Among the social-cognitive weaknesses this group display are low self-concept; negative attitudes to school; poor planning skills; inability to construct alternate solutions; and difficulty in interpersonal skills (see Lockhart and Hay 1995).

A number of alternate programmes have been undertaken that specifically address some of these social-cognitive issues. The two examples discussed below reflect approaches to meeting the needs of students who are enrolled in regular classes in schools. One focuses on primary-aged students who have been identified within their schools as being at-risk because of their school behaviour (Dupper and Krishef 1993). The other (Lockhart and Hay 1995) discusses the implementation of a self-esteem programme for adolescent girls at risk of suspension due to inappropriate behaviour.

Dupper and Krishef (1993) selected Grade 6 and 7 (aged 12–13) students who had one or more disciplinary referrals for behaviours such as defiance, fighting and insubordination, and who had two or more conduct reports of 'needs to improve' or 'unsatisfactory'. The social-cognitive skills training programme had three main process goals:

1   To provide group members with a greater cognitive awareness of provocative school situations, and their unproductive verbal and non-verbal responses to such situations.
2   To teach a sequential problem-solving process to group members.
3   To provide group members with an opportunity to discuss and practise specific school survival skills within the group through the use of modelling, role playing, group feedback, and homework.

(Dupper and Krishef 1993: 135–6)

The programme operated through three phases, over ten one-period weekly sessions. The initial five sessions taught many of the skills developed in the Transactional Analysis approach (Berne 1961) in order to teach awareness of their interpersonal difficulties in the school. The following two sessions concentrated on the use of a problem-solving process, while the remaining three sessions (phase 3) concentrated on specific school survival skills and adaptive school behaviours. Throughout the three phases of the training programme, the three goals discussed above were stressed.

Outcomes for the students in the programme included an increase in internal locus of control, and an increase in ability to control impulses and behaviour. As the measures of impulse and behaviour control were taken by classroom teachers, Dupper and Krishef (1993) concluded that there had been generalisation from the training programme to classrooms. In any training programme that sought to change the acceptance of students with discipline problems in school, demonstrating changes in teachers' perceptions was an essential part of that programme. It also demonstrated the importance of focusing on remediating student social-cognitive deficits, rather than on negative suspension procedures.

In a study of at-risk adolescent girls, Lockhart and Hay (1995) implemented a programme designed to develop four social skill behaviours: interpersonal communication skills; appropriate assertion; building co-operation; and problem-solving, planning and decision-making. Students were identified to be at-risk if they had difficulties in two or more academic skill areas (e.g. not achieving to potential, making little effort to complete tasks) or in social skill areas (e.g. truancy, disruptive).

The programme was conducted over three phases: one full and two half days per week for five weeks; followed by a full-time residential six-day camp; followed by a further five weeks of school-based activities. The initial five weeks concentrated on team-building, problem-solving, study skills, communication skills and self-identity activities. The second stage included outdoor activities in which the earlier skills were applied to tasks such as abseiling. The final phase concentrated on goal-setting, assertiveness training, self-identity and future planning. The use of reflective procedures, through student diaries and individual and group reflective sessions, provided the opportunity to develop personal consideration of outcomes. The study also reflected the importance of collecting data throughout an intervention, rather than only at the pretest and post-test stages.

Results of the study demonstrated significant improvement in self-concept as measured by the Self-Description Questionnaire SDQ-II (Marsh 1990b). In addition, analysis of students' reflective diaries demonstrated a change over the intervention period, from negative and aggressive statements about schools and personnel at the beginning, to self-evaluative and personal comments at the end. Lockhart and Hay (1995) reported that by one-third of the way through the intervention, diaries began to reflect a self-awareness of the benefits of planning, the need to use effort, and the fact that they, as individuals, had something to contribute to the group. In terms of the students' behaviour in class, interviews with teachers indicated an increased willingness to ask for help, to complete homework, and to attempt work. Levels of disruption in class were reported to have decreased by 50 per cent on average. Two years after the programme, students were reported to have continued in school and were no longer at risk of failure.

SUMMARY

The key outcomes of the intervention, as noted by Lockhart and Hay, provide an important summary to this chapter. They concluded:

> the critical issue is not the challenging activities themselves, but more importantly, how the students process their successes and failures that is important. The linking of planning, verbalisation, and reflective writing to attribution retraining as well as the teaching of specific social and study skills is thought to be the reason why the program was successful.
>
> (Lockhart and Hay 1995: 66)

The development of social-cognitive approaches to meeting the challenges of students with behaviour problems has been based on the concept of processing understanding of why successes and failures occur in inter-personal and intrapersonal social skills. The specific combination of social-cognitive training approaches required to meet the needs of specific behaviour problems, specific student stages of development and specific school needs will vary. The common link is their focus on students' understanding of the cognitive processes involved.

STUDY TASKS

9.1 In note form, list the main points covered in this chapter. Be especially attentive to the use of cognitive concepts in behaviour change programmes.

9.2 Prepare a cognitive-behavioural intervention to change an undesirable social behaviour of one of your friends. Use the descriptions in the chapter to help you define the behaviour you want to change, identify the thought processes that need to be changed, and set out the process carefully.

9.3 List the various social skills training methods identified in the chapter. In a table, note the similarities and differences in focus, intervention process, and cognitive skills addressed. Think about which skills for each programme may be best suited.

9.4 Choose a number of television programmes from your weekly viewing schedule (presuming you have one) and look for examples of successful and unsuccessful social skills training. You may be surprised what you find on TV! Keep a log of the behaviours that seem to be addressed and how the characters try to influence change. Then identify ways in which effective change might have occurred.

ADDITIONAL READING

Kauffman, J.M., Mostert, M.P., Nuttycombe, D.G., Trent, S.C. and Hallahan, D.P. (1993) *Managing Classroom Behaviour: A Reflective Case-based Approach*, Boston, MA: Allyn & Bacon.

Linehan, M.M. (1993) *Cognitive-behavioral Treatment of Borderline Personality Disorder*, New York: Guilford.

Schwebel, A.I. and Fine, M.A. (1994) *Understanding and Helping Families: A Cognitive-behavioral Approach*, Hillsdale, NJ: Erlbaum.

Chapter 10

Cognitive education and the school community

In previous chapters we examined the concepts of cognitive theory and their applications to educational practice in the two areas that constitute the substructure of cognitive education: assessment of human skills and thought processes, and instruction. As may be apparent, cognitive concepts can be combined and recombined to emphasise various aspects of thinking or problem-solving. You might consider cognitive theory as an intellectual larder of ingredients, and the researcher or practitioner as the chef. In a real kitchen, a chef can choose from a range of ingredients to create a number of culinary products. For example, the same ingredients can be combined to produce pancakes, muffins, or a cake. Brioche, croissants, bread, pizza bases, and pastry come from more or less the same ingredients. Hollandaise sauce, soufflés, and bavarois also have the same basic constituents. So, cognitive researchers and practitioners have chosen from the same group of compo nents to produce a wide range of educational applications.

In the final analysis, however, the potency of cognitive education will be realised only if there is a much more active attempt to validate procedures and models, and disseminate research and practice throughout all levels of instruction, training, and education. In this chapter we deal with the expansion of cognitive education and its benefits through training and systematic applications.

First, we briefly consider the nature of research, then review some key conclusions drawn from the foregoing chapters which emphasise the importance of ensuring that connections are made between each of the elements of the instructional cycle. We reconsider the need for a paradigm shift in education as a result of the substantial changes that are occurring in our world. Finally, we suggest system-wide acceptance and use of cognitive education methods, and consider how training and collaboration within the school community can lead to the widespread use of cognitive education methods.

EVALUATING COGNITIVE RESEARCH AND ITS APPLICATION

Research is an activity directed to the discovery of facts and is part of the domain of scientific inquiry. Among its many dictionary definitions, science is concerned with a connected body of demonstrated truths or observed fact which are systematically classified or linked by general principles or laws. Science also embodies trustworthy methods of the discovery of new truth within any specified domain. In other words, science is examinable knowledge, based upon truths or fact. The goal of all scientific endeavours is to explain, predict, and/or control phenomena. It is supported by the assumption that all behaviours and events are orderly and have discoverable causes. Progress toward the goal involves the acquisition of knowledge and the development and assessment of theories and concepts.

When attempting research in the social and behavioural sciences, we are faced by many constraints because of the difficulty of explaining, predicting, and controlling situations which involve human beings. Observations are difficult to conduct, measurement of behaviour is difficult, and ensuring that the conclusions and implications of research are unflawed is also difficult. One of the half-truths encountered by those working in the education field has been the belief that 'real' research must be high-powered, statistics-driven experimentation. This is far from reality as 'good' research and the application of the scientific method can be found in surveys, interviews, and observation as it can be in laboratory experiments. Nevertheless, the process through which many educational researchers pass in their investigatory endeavours will be very familiar to colleagues working in other sciences, such as botany or physics, and it is sometimes difficult to perceive the application of some research activities.

Service providers in education, therefore, have often been critical of academic literature and experimental research which seems to have little relevance to what occurs in the classroom, or in other learning contexts. It is not difficult to understand this position when confronted with reading material on in vitro primaquine sensitivity in Asiatic Indians from Gularat, or the intellectual functioning of neurological and myxoedematous cretins. Often, however, the criticism is based upon the impracticality of research endeavours, rather than the impracticality for the teacher or educational practitioner to implement the findings. Sometimes their criticisms are light-hearted, reflecting a live-and-let-live demeanour, while at other times they are of serious intent when both researchers and service providers are competing for funding from common sources. Regardless of the purpose, much of the criticism of research reflects the perceived chasm between what commonly occurs in tertiary institutions in the name of research, and what takes place in the field, in the name of education practice.

Reading the history of research on cognition fits rather too comfortably into the description of detached, isolated research practices and the criticisms of impractical outcomes presented immediately above. The overwhelming bulk of the research literature has an experimental flavour: it is often located in laboratories or clinical settings where there is one researcher or assessor, and one or perhaps two students. That a considerable number of intervention studies are still sited in withdrawal settings and laboratories is a concern if the objective of research is to develop instructional or remedial procedures that can be applied to a diverse set of learning situations such as regular classrooms.

Let us hasten to add here that we are not opposed to experimentation or laboratory research. We are, however, concerned that what has been discovered from much of the basic research has been suggested – unrealistically – as solutions to problems that confront teachers and clinicians in their applied settings. In 1983, Pressley *et al.* drew attention to the difficulty in translating laboratory-generated strategy training techniques to secondary school classrooms. They found that the students were decidedly unresponsive to their training attempts and degenerating classroom behaviour clearly inhibited the smooth progress of their study. In more recent publications, Pressley *et al.* (1989c) and Pressley and Woloshyn (1995) offered suggestions about cognitive strategies in a number of teaching areas (e.g. reading comprehension, spelling, writing, science, mathematics). While they suggested that the recommended strategies are applicable to the primary school curriculum, and have been shown to be effective in a number of empirical studies, there remains a clear lack of well-substantiated strategies that teachers can use in the classroom. The difficulty is exacerbated when empirical researchers fail to use the existing classroom environment and resources. Additional staff (i.e. trainers) are typically outside the regular teachers' grasp and there is little likelihood that other classroom teachers can reproduce the same augmented teaching environment.

Let us turn our attention to some common themes that emerge from the literature. We deal first with the implications of research in assessment and, later, research in training and instruction.

Looking for connections in assessment of teaching and learning

If we put to one side the body of basic research that has provided indications of the relationship between concepts (e.g. memory and metamemory), the body of substantiated research in the field of cognitive education is not vast. We can, however, make a number of general comments that draw together some of the themes that have emerged in the literature. These relate to general beliefs about the way in which thinking and problem-solving occur, and the nexus between assessment and instruction.

First, it is generally accepted that many factors influence a person's performance in any learning context. We have summarised these as four agents: the learner, the teacher, the setting, and the curriculum (see Chapter 1).

They include the learner's intellectual characteristics, personality, emotional state, learning history, and cultural and family influences; the personal and professional characteristics of the teachers that influence the way in which that person provides instruction and/or facilitates learning; the environment (class or work group) in which learning occurs; and the information to be learned which is the curriculum taken in either a broad or narrow sense.

Second, cognitive education reflects a learner-centred, rather than teacher-centred approach to education. In other words, there is a commitment to understanding how and why the individual interacts with the learning environment and those in it, to maximise the efficiency and effectiveness of learning and problem-solving.

Third, assessment and instruction must be closely linked as part of an instructional cycle which includes assessment, preparation, instruction, and evaluation. Assessment, therefore, must be multidimensional in nature to provide information about each of the four agents, and not just simply what the individuals know and how they can learn most effectively. Hence, assessment must inform us about each of the five areas below.

The learner's existing knowledge base

Assessment of the learner's existing knowledge base means knowing, for example, about academic facts (terms and knowledge in reading, mathematics, science, chess, sailing, the calorific value of foods, what esters are, movie stars, plays, music, technology, and so on). Teachers, clinicians (and test publishers) have focused on a small number of domains, notably reading and mathematics but also several other areas in the more extensive testing systems as in the Wide Range Assessment Test (WRAT) and the Woodcock-Johnson. Testing should provide a description of what a student knows so that instruction can build upon that knowledge. In behavioural terms, this could be seen as identifying the prerequisite skills and the next appropriate teaching step in a task analysis. It also assists in identifying any gaps in prerequisite skills that may need to be retaught.

The learner's knowledge of how to learn

Most assessment methods fail to appraise how students attempt a task, deal with a problem and find the solution. Interactive assessment can provide useful information but the extent to which this information can be applied to instructional design will depend upon the skills of the tester. Interactive assessment often proceeds without a clear understanding of what processes to mediate and is usually undertaken on a child-by-child basis. Of course, advocates of interactive assessment would say that this is precisely what is needed, as the purpose of assessment is to establish the dimensions of the learner's cognitive schemata. Care must be taken, however, to clarify the purpose of the assessment from the outset so that the teaching phase does not become the *raison d'être* of assessment; it should lead to quality teaching based on identified needs. What interactive assessment must show is how learners go about the learning and problem-solving process to enable the teacher to plan and implement effective instruction.

The learner's processing capabilities

It is difficult to know whether the learner's processing capabilities are related to hardware (structural) or software (knowledge and experience) aspects of a person's cognitive capabilities. Information processing test batteries such as the Das-Naglieri•Cognitive Assessment System (DN•CAS) and Kaufman Assessment Battery for Children (K-ABC) can play a role in elaborating the learner's preferred processing style, together with processing strengths and weaknesses. A variety of approaches have been suggested as the best method of teaching processing skills, such as remediating the processing weaknesses as the priority (as suggested by Kirby and Williams 1991), basing instruction on only the learner's strengths (as recommended by A.S. Kaufman *et al.* 1983), by teaching processing skills in isolation and then within academic tasks (as suggested by Das *et al.* 1994), and embedding process training within the curriculum context (as urged by Pressley 1994). The last approach has been the only one to receive widespread support in the literature because of the importance of relating processing skills to content skills as required.

The affective dimensions of the individual

This is perhaps one area that teachers, clinicians, and many researchers have avoided or, at least, overlooked despite a volume of research that has directly linked self-perception and self-efficacy with academic achievement (see Lockhart and Hay 1995). While several self-perception measures developed many years ago remain in use today, those like the Coopersmith (Coopersmith 1967) and Harter scales (Harter 1982) have been expansively criticised for their unidimensional approach to self-perception. In other words, they provide only a single measure of self-concept rather than several measures that reflect the individual's differing perceptions of competence in academic and non-academic areas. The Perception of Ability Scale for Students (PASS: Boersma and Chapman 1992) and the Self-Description Questionnaires (SDQ-I, SDQ-II and SDQ-III: see Marsh 1990b). (The Boersma and Chapman PASS should not be confused with the same Das *et al.* 1994 acronym.)

The learner's reactions/responses to the learning environment

Co-operative and collaborative learning, and peer tutoring emphasise the learning environment, but rarely (if ever) do investigators in these areas assess the nature of the context in which learning occurs and its effect on the teaching programme.

We are not suggesting that every child, or even every child who is experiencing difficulty in school, be subjected to a huge battery of tests that provide information on all five domains mentioned immediately above. Knowledge of some domains, however, can be collected informally and we have suggested ways in which different aspects of assessment can be integrated into an assessment-intervention model (see Figure 10.1).

If, as we suggest, assessment is vital to the preparation and intervention phases of the instruction cycle, what are some important considerations in the cognitively oriented instructional phase?

Looking for connections in instruction

In the same way that research and educational practices have guided assessment, there are some general principles that emerge from the cognitive education literature that address what should be taught and how. There are several domains of knowledge that learners must develop regardless of their age or ability (see Figure 10.2), although each domain will develop through exposure to a range of teaching-learning environments.

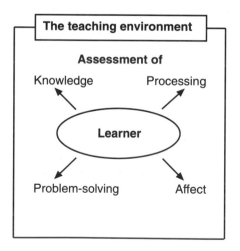

Figure 10.1 Aspects of the learner's characteristics which are important for instructional design

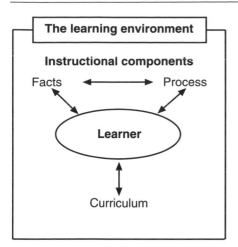

Figuro 10.2 Aspects of the instruction required for effective learning and problem-solving

Knowledge of facts

Facts are the building blocks of acquisition and problem-solving and the brief of formal education is to expand the learner's knowledge of the world. In the early school years, students learn these facts through a wide range of activities which might include didactic (chalk-and-talk) teaching or through discovery learning or informal learning outside of school. At the secondary school level, facts are often presented in a more structured way through systematic, often prescribed, curricula or syllabuses. History indicates to us that teachers know how to impart knowledge effectively.

Knowledge of process

Perhaps the most fundamental principle of cognitive education is the need to teach learners how to be strategic. This means learning about the use and effectiveness of strategies that help organise information (e.g. memory strategies), the importance of metastrategies that include the monitoring and regulatory aspects of conscious thought, and priority-setting, planning, and decision-making skills.

Those interested in teaching specific strategies within one or many academic areas need only to gain access to PsychLit or the ERIC databases in a university library to collect scores of examples about how to improve students' strategic behaviour.

A major problem we have perceived over the years is the general lack of a systematic approach to teach children about metastrategic behaviour, and especially planning. The common assumption that teachers appear to make is that the student will learn about these processes vicariously or informally through trial and error (or through osmosis). Even gifted children may not know much about the process of planning (see Ashman *et al.* 1994) and students who have a learning disability or developmental disability will definitely lack planning competence (see e.g. Todman and McBeth 1994).

Knowledge of the link between process and content

Researchers and writers have emphasised the importance of declarative and procedural knowledge in any domain and the need to link process with content (see Pressley 1994). The issue is not so much whether process and content (facts) should be linked but how this can be done successfully.

Cognitive education researchers have been prodigious in their study of some academic areas, such as reading and mathematics, in which the skills required could be considered 'basic'. We use the term basic in a relative way, recognising the complexity of the reading process and other fundamental skills. It seems a relatively straightforward task to deconstruct some reading skills especially when there is an obvious link between process and skill. For example, researchers have established a strong relationship between successive processing and phonic word decoding, at least at the beginning stages of reading (Das and Conway 1992). However, it is difficult to know what role simultaneous and successive processing, for example, play in the development of social and interpersonal skills, calculus, algebra, French grammar, Japanese syntax, religious education, physical education, recreation and leisure, getting a good score on a pinball machine game, throwing a 250 in ten-pin bowling, writing a marketable computer program, essay writing, sailing, report writing, publishing in a professional journal of high repute, learning how to be a good plumber or brick-layer. The cognitive processes are essential, but their role, and the relationship between process and performance is often far from clear.

In addition to the importance of instructional procedures as part of any teaching-learning situation, there are other fundamental changes that are required. Cognitive education can operate at the level of the teacher (whether this is in school, a tertiary institution, flight instruction training, or trade programme). However, cognitive education will be more effective if it is implemented at the level of the institution rather than instructor. For example, when cognitive strategies are used across a school or schools, there is increased opportunity for staff development and support (Greenberg 1995). We shall expand on this issue a little later.

Future classroom research

Without doubt, many cognitive education researchers are moving toward classroom-based research. However, the traditions that have guided intervention research over the past century may not be applicable to a research context in which there are innumerable, uncontrollable influences. Simply observing the range of interactions that occur in any regular or special education classroom will reinforce a view of an ever-changing, even volatile environment. How can research, therefore, be undertaken to validate the effectiveness of any teaching-learning process? In one sense, there is a need to reconceptualise the nature of research that is undertaken in applied/field settings. The increasing acceptance of ethnographic and observational research methods attests to a recognition that experimental methods may be inappropriate.

One question that needs the consideration of education researchers is whether it is defensible to pursue controlled experimental studies in a context in which the assumptions of experimental research can rarely, if ever, be fulfilled. Paris (1993) seems to have placed a bet 'each way' when he drew attention to the difficulty of experimentation in applied settings. He suggested that there was a need for a reconsideration of the accepted conventions and practices that have governed earlier experimental work in education. He suggested that there are a number of conceptual, implementation, and design issues that researchers must accept about classroom-based intervention research of the form typically undertaken by cognitive educators (Table 10.1).

If we combine Figures 10.1 and 10.2, and link them to the issues that Paris (1993) raised, we derive a general assessment-instruction model that highlights the interactions that occur between assessment, instruction, and the learner (Figure 10.3). In that figure, data that need to be collected via relevant assessment methods include the learner's knowledge base, processing and problem-solving capabilities, and affective response to the teaching-learning situation. Instruction is a fully interactive model linking the knowledge base (facts and processes) the curriculum, and the learner's interactions with the instructional procedures that ensure that learning occurs. The environment interacts with both the assessment and instruction components of the model to provide either support or hindrance.

To bring such a model of assessment and instruction into effect, it must be introduced to, and incorporated into, the education community. We now turn our attention to a number of ways in which this can be achieved.

COGNITIVE EDUCATION IN THE COMMUNITY

A number of major changes have taken place since the mid-1970s that will have a major impact upon the way in which educational services are delivered. First, there has been a change in the bases of power internationally. At one time – not too long ago – governments were the power-brokers that held political and economic control. Now, multinational companies and huge corporations control international and intra-national finances, the media, and many essential services. This appears to have led to the introduction of

Table 10.1 Factors that affect the efficacy of research in applied settings

Conceptual considerations

Interventions operate in a context which has a teaching-learning history, in other words, the intervention cannot be the first mark on a blank sheet.

It is difficult to isolate the effects of specific components of a complex intervention to gauge their importance to the students' learning or problem-solving outcomes.

There is no absolute way to judge if one intervention method is better than another.

A successful intervention in one setting may not necessarily be successful in other locations or cultures.

Repeated use of an intervention may lead to positive or negative changes in its effectiveness.

Implementation considerations

Teachers impose their own personal character on so-called standardised interventions.

Interventions are subject to both teacher and learner influences.

Teacher effort, motivation, and commitment of time will influence treatment effects.

The components of an intervention may interact positively (to enhance impact) or negatively (to diminish impact) on other programmes that may be operating in the learning context at the same time.

Design considerations

Interventions may require a range of evaluation procedures to judge their effectiveness.

Both academic and affective interventions are relevant to student learning outcomes.

Intervention studies undertaken in applied settings may require greater researcher effort to generate useful outcomes than experimental studies undertaken in laboratory conditions.

There are ethical considerations about withholding effective interventions from students assigned to non-intervention research conditions.

Culture can affect the outcomes of studies.

---

economic rationalist policies in many western countries and governments, and the administrators of most public services, are realising the need to consider how they can continue to provide a range of human services, with limited funds, but with improved productivity.

Second, it should come as no surprise that the way in which we shall collect a considerable amount of information will be via microchip technology. The phenomenal expansion of the World Wide Web has required a change of perception about computers; where information is available; and from whom we can obtain it. It is possible to browse universities and university programs, do personal banking, purchase goods, and book airline

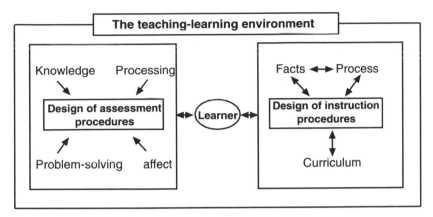

Figure 10.3 A general assessment-instruction model that highlights the interactions that occur between the assessment, instruction, and the learner

flights (to name just a few services) using a fibre optic or modem version of window shopping. CD-ROM technology, Internet connections, and open learning programmes on public television already allow students to study off-campus with minimal recourse to the printed word on paper, and there is little doubt that there will soon be a change in the way in which we think about teaching and learning simply as a result of technological inventions.

Samuels (1995) argued that the important commodity of the twenty-first century will be knowledge and innovation rather than commodities. This will demand changes in the field of education because of

- a community awareness of the need for better schools and other centres of learning than currently exist
- the need for educators to be more accountable for students' educational outcomes
- the need for educators to respond to innovation in communication technology.

Samuels argued that workers will need to be involved in lifelong learning that will enhance their thinking and planning skills, their ability to work in teams, and to adapt to the changing circumstances within their environment.

Some writers have suggested that there is a need to reach out toward change, rather than allowing it to approach and engulf. Skrtic (1991), for example, argued for a power shift in school organisations. He claimed that schools must undergo fundamental changes in the way in which they are structured to empower classroom teachers to contribute more to the school decision-making process than they do at present. He referred to the ideal school organisation as an adhocracy – rather than bureaucracy – in which teachers operate spontaneously to create innovative solutions to old and new problems. A shift in the organisation of schools will require that all school personnel

become creative, effective communicators and efficient problem-solvers.
Teachers in all contexts (formal and informal), therefore, will need to

- attach importance to some fundamental goals that relate to effective teaching and learning
- learn the skills so that they can use and model them
- ensure that students develop the same skills so that they are empowered to become independent learners and problem-solvers.

Similarly, parents need to understand the philosophy and also learn the skills so that they can support their children. We are especially concerned to ensure that cognitive education methods be seen as relevant both to the classroom and to informal education, that is, the lifelong process of acquiring attitudes, values, skills, and knowledge from daily experiences and the educational influences inherent in them. Cognitive education can provide teachers and parents with the skills they will need to teach children how to become flexible thinkers and independent learners and problem-solvers (Samuels 1995).

TRAINING FOR COGNITIVE EDUCATION

There are three main strategies that will lead to greater use of cognitive education theory and practices. There is a need to generate an awareness and knowledge of cognitive education; facilitate greater communication and collaboration within teaching-learning communities; and encourage the use of cognitive education methods in both formal and informal learning contexts.

The passage from novice to expert in any field begins with the accumulation of skills and knowledge relevant to the specialist area regardless of whether the expertise is as a bird watcher, racing-car driver, chef, sailor, motor mechanic, teacher, or psychologist. The rite of passage may vary with each domain but in the professions, it comes with the completion of training when the individual is considered to have embraced the beliefs and dispositions of the expert. Here, we consider the roles and training required for three specialist groups: teachers; counsellors/school psychologists; and parents.

Generating an awareness of cognitive education

Cognitive education has developed within the school education community largely as a response to the efforts of researchers and school practitioners to discover effective ways of teaching, learning, and problem-solving. Notwithstanding this, there remains relatively little knowledge about cognitive concepts and their application to teaching and learning. Hence, it appears that the initial thrust in achieving greater use of these new instructional technologies is through pre-service and inservice programmes for school personnel.

The role of the teacher is to transfer the knowledge and values of the society to its younger members. How a teacher fulfils this role is governed by training and experience. Much of the knowledge a teacher gains during pre-service training relates to the essential skills (at least, familiarity with them) that must be applied during practicum placements and, later, on obtaining employment. Years ago, two and three years of teacher training was the norm. In some cases, for those preparing to teach in secondary school, training consisted of a one-year, post-degree qualification, as it still does in some places. One might speculate whether the skills obtained during these one to (now) four years of pre-service training equip new teachers with any greater level of knowledge or expertise than they received in the past.

Feedback from recent education graduates will identify their common concerns about high priority needs, such as student behaviour management, and the adequacy of their preparation. Graduates need skills that can be applied directly to their classroom such as

- teaching strategies
- knowledge of content
- classroom management skills
- use of relevant resources
- ways of developing professional contacts
- managing the volume of work or stress that will become part of their experience in their first and second years of classroom teaching.

Lacking in exit surveys are comments related to the new teacher gaining a greater awareness of how students learn, how to identify students' learning styles and preferences, how to integrate process knowledge with content knowledge, or how to meet the needs of individuals while satisfying group needs at the same time.

Elements of cognitive education are introduced in most pre-service teacher education programmes, albeit often only as concepts that have no link to practice or – in the case of some classroom techniques such as co-operative learning, or reciprocal teaching – as procedures that students may see in operation while they are on practicum (but generally only at the primary or elementary grades). However, even if cognitive education was a fundamental aspect of training, the teacher trainee's exposure to instructional practices in many schools, may render this knowledge irrelevant.

Lundeberg and Fawver (1994) attempted to develop the cognitive growth of students attending an educational psychology course in which a case discussion format was used to increase cognitive awareness. The small-group discussion used many of the strategies presented in Chapter 7 (e.g. discussion, questioning, reasoning, and reflecting) while the instructor provided guidance and framed initial questions. A number of changes occurred in the student teachers' beliefs about learning and instruction (see Table 10.2). These reflected an awareness of the role of students in the teaching-learning process and the need for teachers to assist in students' cognitive development, rather than expecting it to develop unassisted while they concentrated on the curriculum. Such changes in pre-service teachers' perceptions may assist them to consolidate their roles as future classroom teachers and encourage them to make the changes necessary to become good cognitive teachers rather than maintaining their previous beliefs.

Despite the changes achieved by Lundeberg and Fawver (1994), acculturation as a teacher comes primarily from other practising teachers rather than from the role models presented by their lecturers. A major problem in teacher education has been to sustain the beginning teachers' idealism about theory and process in the face of the professional's pragmatism when they are assigned to schools for teaching practice (practicum) placements. Andrews and Wheeler (1990) argued that the teaching strategies that students select and use at university are quickly eliminated by classroom experience. Why is this so? One answer may be the continuing adherence of generations of teachers to a collective oral tradition about how classroom instruction takes place. While there are no doubt more complex explanations, it is the master–apprentice relationship that establishes the attitudes, beliefs and teaching practices of the new teacher. School staffroom discussions about working memory, cognitive strategies, metacognition, planning, procedural knowledge, interactive assessment, assessment of cognitive processes, internal speech, mediation, and cognitive modifiability would be extremely rare.

Other school personnel also need to be aware of cognitive education methods. School psychologists, educational psychologists, and school counsellors, for example, provide a wide range of services to students and school

Table 10.2 Changes in pre-service teacher trainee beliefs about learning and instruction

Old beliefs	New beliefs
Students receive knowledge	Students construct knowledge
Teacher/text is the authority	Students create meaning
Teachers impart knowledge	Teachers encourage thinking
Learning should be fun	Learning should be challenging
Thinking develops naturally	Teachers can facilitate thinking
Discovery learning is best	Discovery learning needs guidance
Just teach the lesson	Teaching involves many decisions
'Black and white' thinking	Flexible thinking with many answers

personnel in primary and secondary schools that could draw on cognitive education principles. Ashman *et al.* (1993) described these clinical roles as

- group, individual and career counselling and counselling of specific groups
- preventive guidance programmes
- counselling of parents and families
- testing and test interpretation
- behaviour management
- interpersonal and social skill training
- consultation about student progress, case management and referrals
- inservicing school staff
- providing personal and professional assistance to school personnel.

In teacher training, acculturation takes places in the school. In the training of clinical personnel, it is not so much acculturation, but what might be called 'professionalisation' that occurs over the one, two or more years of training in universities or in practicum placements. Some of those who become psychologists or counsellors have been classroom teachers and so, for them, professionalisation involves a transition from one set of attitudes and expectations to another.

Certainly the roles of teacher and clinician are distinct although many of the educational goals are the same (e.g. providing the most effective teaching and learning experiences for all children). For the clinician, professionalisation not only involves learning a large set of new skills such as testing, counselling theory and practice, and atypical development, but also includes a belief in supporting others to help overcome students' learning problems. However, it has only been since the mid-1980s that this supporting role has included mutual problem-solving activities. None the less, many school-based professionals do not have a strong background in consultation (Curtis and Meyers 1988) and this may be traced to pre-service training and continuing professional development where consultation skills training is still infrequent (Phillips and McCullough 1990).

Facilitating greater communication and collaboration

Presently there is a gradual change in the role of the clinician with a greater emphasis being given to consultation and in-class involvement than before. Clinicians can play a significant role in changing the way in which classroom and special education teachers view the information that is collected through assessment. For example, when teachers refer children to a counsellor or school psychologist, they want suggestions about how to assist the child within the context of the classroom. The clinician may then make the link between the data collected during formal assessments, other information gained from the teacher through observations of students' classroom behaviour and examples of their work, and potentially successful cognitive education interventions.

Parents are also part of the school community but few are involved in the formal process of education. Most parents have derived their role perceptions from their experience as children in their own families, and from the trial-and-error encounters of their daily lives as parents. The experiences gained from raising one child help in rearing the next and for foreseeing the inevitable problems that occur as children grow and develop.

Few parents have been prepared formally for their parenting roles, and fewer still would admit to the role of professional child-rearer and mediator. Most will express the view that parenthood is simply another role in addition to that of husband/wife, career person, cook and kitchen-hand, and perhaps even socialite.

A person's experience as a child appears to be the main source of education for parenthood. The time-honoured child-rearing practices that our grandparents taught our parents, who eventually taught us, will be passed down with some variations to the next generation to suit the forthcoming social, cultural, and economic context. When children are raised with every imaginable toy, their own children may well be similarly showered with toys and computer games and, no doubt, these children will adopt similar child-rearing practices and beliefs about the nature of the world as it is currently portrayed by their mother and father.

There is no more compelling evidence of the impact of parenting practices on children than the data about the transfer of family violence and child abuse practices across generations (see e.g. Milner et al. 1990). However, while there is considerable attention being given to the issue of children's emotional education (and justifiably so), there is little being given to the parents' role as an educator.

The traditional roles of parents have been changing over the years. The structure of many families has transformed from one in which the mother undertakes home duties and the father is the 'breadwinner', to families in which the roles are not defined by gender: many mothers follow a career while providing the foundation of care for the children; many fathers share the household and child-rearing duties. More demanding for the child-rearer are those families in which there is only one parent, and where there may be a number of 'uncles' or 'aunts' who are also involved, for limited times, as surrogate parents. For example, in 1985 only 7 per cent of children in the US lived in families in which there was a working father, housewife mother and two or more school-age children. In 1988, nearly 25 per cent of all US children lived in a single-parent family (Davis 1991).

Some writers (e.g. Lombano and Lombano 1982) have argued that there has been a shift in the sociological structure of the home and school which has undermined parental involvement in their children's education and made it virtually impossible for parents to maintain daily contact with their children's education programme. What is perhaps more important is the awe that some parents have of educational processes and the reverence with which they hold the status of the school. In the United States, the Education for All Public Law has implied an essential role for parents in the education of their children, however, this is more an ideal than a practice, except for children who are experiencing learning difficulties for which parent involvement in the IEP process is subject to local interpretation (Idol 1983). In Australia, most parents do not participate in the school life of their children and have an incomplete understanding of how the children are taught, the curriculum, and even their rights as parents.

Parents can play a variety of roles in the education even though few have any active involvement with their children's school. At least some have abdicated the role of educator to the school and seem indifferent to their children's behaviour or learning (Boyer and Horne 1989). While there are many schools where parent involvement is actively sought, there are others where parents are not encouraged to participate and information about children is withheld, especially if the child is well above average ability (see e.g. Tolan 1987). Many parents do not know how to respond to situations and reluctantly accept the notion that it is the school, not the parents, who is responsible for the education of their children.

The 'submissive' role of parents, of course, is not universal. Some parents actively seek involvement in the children's education (Davis 1991; Lombana and Lombana 1982) especially when they have a child with a disability. In other situations, collaboration between parent, teacher and specialist has proved to be very successful (Sheridan *et al.* 1990). In these cases (as no doubt it may be with other parents), the major complaint of parents and teachers alike is of a lack of communication. Roos (1985) states this quite well:

> I was fortunate in having established myself as a professional in the field of mental retardation before I became a parent of a retarded child. Things did not go smoothly, though. Surprisingly, my wife and I embarked on a long series of catastrophic interactions with professionals which echoed the complaints I had heard so often from other parents.
>
> (Roos 1985: 13)

In situations like this, it appears that the ability to communicate is clouded by role perceptions and the 'we–them' dichotomy.

In summary, it appears that there are a number of impediments to parent–professional collaboration. Vosler-Hunter (1989) has described three general classes. These include past negative experiences that both parents and professional people may have had when dealing with the other group, the environment in which the interactions occur, and the psychological barriers that each erect. All these factors mitigate against effective collaboration.

Parents can be used very effectively in a cognitive-education framework. This is most clearly demonstrated in the early education programmes such as

COGNET and Bright Start. Both programmes place considerable reliance on parent involvement, as much early learning takes place in the home, with parents acting as the teacher. In a review of cognitive approaches to education, Haywood (1990) noted that parents have both a right and a responsibility to be directly involved in their child's education. Parents play a complementary role to the cognitive approaches of the classroom, by providing the bridge (or connection) between cognitive skills and everyday life activities.

For parents to play an effective role in cognitive education, there is a need for systematic training, similar to teacher training, so that they are aware of the classroom approaches and how they can facilitate them at home. COGNET (1995) includes parent training in each of the Building Blocks of Thinking and the Tools for Independent Learning (see Chapter 8) so that parents can focus their child's attention on these during everyday activities such as doing jobs around the house or garden, shopping, or planning a birthday party. In addition, teachers send home weekly handouts to keep parents informed about the classroom COGNET programme and also to suggest activities for the home. In some schools parent advisory boards liaise with teachers or establish parent volunteer programmes to assist teachers in the classroom. These procedures assist in building the bridge between school and home to consolidate a cognitive approach to learning.

Impediments to collaboration

There appear to be a number of impediments to the development of effective collaboration and consultation between parents, teachers and clinician that may limit the expansion of cognitive education initiatives in the school and home. Notwithstanding this, over several years many writers have attested to the effectiveness of collaboration and consultation (West and Idol 1987) and have proposed a number of formulae for establishing collaborative ventures within individual schools or school systems.

The foundation for collaboration must come from

- the belief in relationships of openness
- trust and support among the school community
- parent involvement in the school decision-making process
- a belief in the need for personal development
- the evolution of the curriculum to serve the needs of all students.

These points constitute a definition of the collaborative ethic. However, while these characteristics can hardly be challenged as being appropriate, many educators suggest that they are typically missing in most schools.

Several writers have outlined how the collaborative ethic can be established within schools. Nevin *et al.* (1993), for example, referred to the need to establish heterogeneous schools which

- accommodate the unique educational needs of students through responsive and varied instructional options
- include all school personnel and members of the wider community in the decision-making process, depending upon who is affected and who has skills and expertise valuable to the decision-making process or is interested in the process
- have academic achievement and the mastery of social and life skills as programme objectives.

At the heart of the collaborative ethic is the concept of equality (see e.g. West and Cannon 1988) although we prefer the term 'reciprocity', as it implies the acceptance of the position of others. Assigning ownership of the problem to an individual establishes a hierarchy and implicit blame for the problem under consideration. In a collaborative relationship, it is the partnership that must own the problem, not the individual. If a specialist or a parent is to help guide the process, they must come to offer words such as, 'What must we do to overcome the problem?' rather than asking, 'What do you need to do to overcome the problem?'

A second consideration in establishing the collaborative ethic is ensuring that there are common goals for school community, staff, and student development, and problem resolution. Not all problems require a collaborative effort but there is a tendency among professionals who judge the value of collaboration to be great, to seek collaborative resolutions under all circumstances. In a school where the collaborative ethic is not completely accepted (this may be most schools), it is counter-productive to require collaborative solutions. Perhaps it is better to ask, 'Is collaboration a realistic approach to problem-solving in the present context?'

From a general overview of the development of professional skills, it appears clear that few members of the school community receive training in collaboration (Davison 1990; Dougherty et al. 1991; Fine et al. 1979; Idol and Baran 1992; Piersel and Gutkin 1983). Few pre-service teacher training programmes include specific subjects, units, or modules in communication skills and processes that characterise collaboration activities. Some teacher educators may talk about team-teaching, and some students on teaching practice may observe co-operative teaching lessons or classrooms in which two teachers are working together. However, the overwhelming majority of education students at the undergraduate and graduate level will have minimal knowledge and few skills to facilitate collaboration.

Clinical trainees may fare somewhat better as their training is often undertaken at the postgraduate level during which they are likely to have time to devote to remedial education in which cognitive methods prevail (at least at the level of mild learning difficulties). Hence, the clinician may provide an important link in the education chain to promote greater awareness of cognitive education in teachers and parents.

Inservice training is also needed to familiarise experienced teachers, clinicians, and parents with cognitive education theory and practices. The amount of time available for professional development in schools is relatively small. With the restrictions that are often placed on inservice activities by employers and teachers' unions, most teachers will have very few pupil-free or non-contact days each year in which to schedule staff development. One, or part of one, of these could easily be put aside to one or a number of cognitive education methods and interested parents could be invited to attend.

Encouraging cognitive education in formal and informal education

In this chapter we have emphasised the need for the development of cognitive methods. At this stage, it would be useful to consider how effective training may be presented. It is often difficult to change teachers' methods of instruction to allow students to take responsibility for independent thinking and problem-solving. In the same way that students must be taught to be strategic and metastrategic, teachers also need to acquire a knowledge of strategy use and application.

Most teachers have developed and consolidated their current instructional methods in a single teacher classroom and have learned to deal (or not deal) with students' individual differences without formal assistance from others. The routines and pressures of the working day, the perceived 'success' with the majority of students, and the established system-based procedures contribute to the continuation and existing practices and a resistance to change (Witt 1990). Changing the culture of education to include cognitive methods appears to be essential, but it is also perhaps the most difficult change to make.

The transfer of cognitive strategies from teachers to students requires a systematic approach. Three dimensions of cognitive learning and transfer have been identified by M.M. Kennedy (1991).

- *Connectedness* refers to the extent to which an idea is embedded in a larger network so that it is easier to access when needed.
- *Flexibility* refers to the ability to use an idea in a number of contexts, rather than in the training setting only.
- *Perceived meaning* relates to the student's understanding and appreciation of the usefulness of knowledge and its social and cultural contents.

These skills have also been identified in interviews with teachers implementing cognitive instruction within their teaching programmes (Pressley *et al.* 1989b). Teachers commonly agreed on a number of common features of good strategy instruction including:

- Direct modelling and explanation are essential components.
- Extensive practice in the use of the strategies is essential.
- Strategy teaching and the use of strategies must occur across the curriculum.
- Extensive information needs to be provided to students on when and how to apply strategies as well as the benefits of effective strategy use.
- Transfer of strategies is not automatic, but requires teaching.
- Only a few strategies should be introduced at a time.
- There needs to be explicit reinforcement of strategy use at first.

While many programmes have recognised the benefits of training staff in the skills necessary for successful strategy training in classroom, there has been little systematic research on the monitoring of staff development and its follow-up application in the classroom.

One landmark study of staff development was reported by Duffy (1993) who, over four years, taught teachers how to integrate cognitive strategies into their reading programmes. Duffy described a process that was not developmental as teachers' progress was recursive rather than linear, and affected by the four agents that influence learning outcomes (described in Chapter 1).

Duffy suggested that teachers pass through nine stages in training (Figure 10.4).

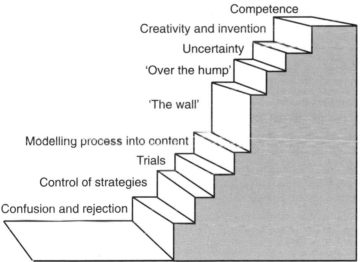

Figure 10.4 Nine steps in developing competence in cognitive education

Confusion and rejection

Many teachers are resistant to new teaching approaches when they do not have a prescription format (such as a textbook), and when they are required to develop their own materials based on strategic thinking and cognitive methods. Duffy reported that many teachers are reluctant to continue beyond the initial staff training sessions and require coaxing to try the new approach.

Control of strategies

During the initial training phases, teachers attempt to use the strategies without a full understanding of the reasons for using them. As a result, teachers control the strategies and often forget to involve students in their use. Hence, teachers do the thinking, while the students remain passive recipients of knowledge.

Trials

Teachers begin using strategies but often in isolation from the curriculum. They teach the students about them, then provide opportunities for regulated practice. However, teachers commonly do not demonstrate how the strategy can be used in other teaching-learning contexts.

Modelling process into content

At this fourth stage, teachers realise the importance of students being metacognitive and in control of the strategy. Teachers also see the importance of teaching the strategy immediately prior to its application in the lesson, rather than in isolation. In addition, teachers explain the use of the strategies to their students, illustrate their application, and show students how they can personalise the strategies for their own use in a particular problem. However, students remain unaware of the purpose of strategy use and do not generalise them to other tasks or situations.

'The wall'

Duffy considered this step to be crucial as it is the point at which teachers realise that strategy instruction is still embedded in the training context. There is no application of the training set of cognitive strategies. Students use strategies when cued and on tasks with which they are familiar. Successful scaling of the wall occurs when teachers make a fundamental change in their approach and release control of the strategies to their students.

'Over the hump'

At this stage, there is an awareness that strategy instruction involves more than teaching individual strategies. Strategy instruction becomes embedded in activities that students want (or need) to learn. Teachers become less concerned about having lists of strategies to use and are more concerned about encouraging students to become strategic independently. Students also become aware that a strategy is useful for solving a range of problems, rather than for only one specific task.

Uncertainty

Although teachers have made a major step forward, there is still a lingering doubt that they may not have implemented the approach appropriately. This represents the 'I don't quite get it yet' phenomenon and occurs where teachers begin adapting strategies and are unsure of themselves in doing so.

Creativity and invention

Teachers move to a level of self-confidence in making changes to strategies when appropriate. They change old strategies and develop new ones to suit the existing situation, and decisions about which strategies to teach are based on student needs. Duffy identified three conditions that are associated with this stage: teachers are no longer afraid of failure when teaching a strategy; they give control to the students; and they tolerate ambiguity.

Competence

Although Duffy did not label the ninth point on his continuum, teachers in his staff development programme perceived the likelihood of moving beyond the creativity and invention stage, especially when facilitating students' independent use of cognitive strategies in their day-to-day lives.

Duffy (1993) provided not only a training continuum along which teachers move as they become effective strategy users and facilitators in the classroom, but also an indication of how we need to proceed in providing preparatory and ongoing inservice training for teachers. As part of the evaluation process, Duffy asked teachers to assess the staff training procedures and four key elements were identified for effective strategy teaching.

First, teachers wanted training to occur in the classroom, not in an isolated staff development session, as they wanted to relate ongoing training to actual classroom needs. Second, they wanted trainer involvement over an extended period as changes in teaching style and student learning styles needed support until the teacher felt confident to proceed without this back-up. Third, teachers saw a need to ensure that there was a change not only in the way students learn to use strategies, but also in the way teacher education training occurred. Fourth, teachers wanted the theory and definitions of strategy training translated into the language of the classroom so that terms such as strategy also had a classroom-based meaning. Finally, teachers argued for the inclusion of affective and motivational aspects in staff training on strategy use. They viewed motivation as an important part of any teaching programme and recognised the need to encourage students to use strategies that are successful.

The studies of Duffy (1993), Pressley *et al.* (1989b) and Lundeberg and Fawver (1994) illustrate the importance of providing teachers with appropriate inservice training prior to their attempting to implement cognitive strategies in the classroom, together with ongoing, in-class support over an extended period of time.

SUMMARY

In this chapter we drew together many of the themes that have emerged from other chapters in the book and proposed a review of the relationship between the learner, assessment, and instruction. We have argued that there is a need to expand our view of assessment to include fact, process, the relationship between process and content, the learner's belief about the teaching-learning process, and reactions to the teaching-learning environment. We have also suggested that instruction must include content, process, and knowledge of the link between content (the curriculum) and process.

We have adopted a basic premise that cognitive education has the potential to improve the process of education taken in its broadest sense. This includes not only formal instruction at the school and post-school levels, but also informal learning that takes place on a day-to-day basis. To achieve this goal, there is a need to promote change within the education system. This means: (a) generating an awareness of cognitive education principles and applications: (b) ensuring the inclusion of cognitive education in pre-service training for school personnel; (c) incorporating cognitive education principles and practices in formal teaching settings; (d) encouraging collaboration between school personnel; (e) informing parents about the impact of teaching-learning and problem-solving processes; and (f) ensuring that the students themselves become advocates of cognitive education principles and practices.

Finally, we drew attention to some general ideas that might facilitate staff development in the cognitive education area. To a large extent, this involves changing teachers' attitudes and empowering them to use methods and techniques that will lead to increased student independence in learning and problem-solving, while still acknowledging the importance of teacher encouragement and facilitation.

STUDY TASKS

10.1 Select a specific topic in a curriculum area with which you are familiar (such as the respiratory system in Science) and then, for each of the learner assessment variables in Figure 10.1, identify specific assessment items that would be important as a teacher of that topic.

10.2 From the lists developed in Task 10.1, identify the teaching content that would be important as set out in Figure 10.2. Remember that you are looking for facts, processes, and curriculum content. How would this change if the student had a learning difficulty and was working below grade level?

10.3 Consider the issues of teacher staff development and outline what you would include in a staff development day that aimed to provide teachers with information on the benefits of using a cognitive approach to teaching and learning.

10.4 In the study conducted by Lundeberg and Fawver (1994), there was a successful change in the students' perceptions of the role of cognitive education in teaching. List how one of your subjects could be adapted to be taught in this way.

ADDITIONAL READING

Brock, P.A. (1994) *Educational Technology in the Classroom*, Englewood Cliffs, NJ: Educational Technology Publications.

Bruer, J.T. (1993) *Schools for Thought: A Science of Learning in the Classroom*, Cambridge, MA: MIT Press.

Mandinach, E.B. (1994) *Classroom Dynamics: Implementing a Technology-based Learning Environment*, Hillsdale, NJ: Erlbaum.

Tishman, S., Perkins, D. and Jay, E. (1995) *The Thinking Classroom: Learning and Teaching in a Culture of Thinking*, Boston, MA: Allyn & Bacon.

Toffler, A. (1990) *Powershift: Knowledge, Wealth and Violence at the Edge of the 21st Century*, New York: Bantam.

Valletutti, P.J. and Dummett, L. (1992) *Cognitive Development: A Functional Approach*, San Diego, CA: Singular.

References

Alberto, P.A. and Troutman, A.C. (1995) *Applied Behavior Analysis for Teachers*, 4th edn, Englewood Cliffs, NJ: Merrill.

Anderson, P. (1990) 'The main features of long term potentiation: a model for the formation of memory traces', in J.C. Eccles and O. Creutzfeldt (eds) *The Principles of Design and Operation of the Brain* (pp. 26–382), Berlin: Springer-Verlag.

Andrews, S.V. and Wheeler, P.J. (1990) 'Tracing the effects of reflective classroom practice', paper presented at the annual meeting of the National Reading Conference, Miami, Florida, November.

Arbitman-Smith, R., Haywood, H.C. and Bransford, J.D. (1984) 'Assessing cognitive change', in P. Brooks, R. Sperber and C. McCauley (eds) *Learning and Cognition in the Mentally Retarded* (pp. 433–71). Baltimore, MD: University Park Press.

Asher, S.R. (1978) 'Children's peer relations', in M.E. Lamb (ed.) *Social and Personality Development*, Hillsdale, NJ: Erlbaum.

Ashman, A.F. (1978) 'The relationship between planning and simultaneous and successive synthesis', unpublished doctoral dissertation, University of Alberta, Edmonton, Canada.

Ashman, A.F. and Conway, R.N.F. (1989) *Cognitive Strategies for Special Education*, London: Routledge.

—— (1993a) 'Examining the links between psychoeducational assessment, instruction and remediation', *International Journal of Disability, Development and Education* 40: 23–44.

—— (1993b) 'Teaching students to use process-based learning and problem solving strategies in mainstream class', *Learning and Instruction* 3: 73–92.

—— (1993c) *Using Cognitive Methods in the Classroom*, London: Routledge.

Ashman, A.F. and Gillies, R. (in press) 'Children's cooperative behavior and interactions in trained and untrained work groups in regular classes', *Journal of School Psychology*.

Ashman, A.F., Gillies, R. and Beavers, S. (1993) 'Counsellor roles and perceptions of training', *Australian Journal of Guidance and Counselling* 3: 1–14.

Ashman, A.F., Wright, S.K. and Conway, R.N.F. (1994) 'Developing the meta-cognitive skills of academically gifted students in mainstream classrooms', *Roeper Review* 16: 198–204.

Atkinson, R. and Shiffrin, R. (1968) 'Human memory: a proposed system and its control processes', in K. Spence and J. Spence (eds) *The Psychology of Learning and Motivation: Advance in Research and Theory*, vol. 2 (pp. 89–195), New York: Academic Press.

Baer, D.M., Wolf, M.M. and Risley, T.R. (1968) 'Some current dimensions of applied behavior analysis', *Journal of Applied Behavior Analysis 1*: 91–7.

Bash, M.S. and Camp, B.W. (1985) *Think Aloud: Increasing Social and Cognitive Skills – A Problem-solving Program for Children in Grades 5–6*, Champaign, IL: Research Press.

Beane, J.A. (1995) 'Curriculum integration and the disciplines of knowledge', *Phi Delta Kappan 76*: 616–22.

Beck, I.L., McKeown, M.G., Sinatra, G.M. and Loxterman, J.A. (1991) 'Revising social studies text from a text-processing perspective: evidence of improved comprehensibility', *Reading Research Quarterly 26*: 251–76.

Beelmann, A., Pfingsten, U. and Losel, F. (1994) 'Effects of training social competence in children: a meta-analysis of recent evaluation studies', *Journal of Clinical Child Psychology 23*: 260–71.

Beery, K.E. (1989) *The Developmental Test of Visual-Motor Integration*, Cleveland, OH: Modern Curriculum Press.

Belmont, J.M. and Mitchell, D.W. (1987) 'The general strategies hypothesis as applied to cognitive theory in mental retardation', *Intelligence 11*: 91–105.

Belmont, J.M., Ferretti, R.P. and Mitchell, D.W. (1982) 'Memorizing: a task of untrained mildly mentally retarded children's problem solving', *American Journal of Mental Deficiency 87*: 197–210.

Bender, L. (1951) *Bender Visual Motor Gestalt Test*, Los Angeles, CA: Western Psychological Services.

Berger, R.M., Guilford, J.P. and Christensen, P.R. (1957) 'A factor analytic study of planning abilities', *Psychological Monographs 71*(435).

Berne, E. (1961) *Transactional Analysis in Psychotherapy*, New York: Grove.

Bethge, H.J., Carlson, J.S. and Wiedl, K.H. (1982) 'Matrices performance, visual search behaviour, test anxiety and test orientation', *Intelligence 6*: 89–105.

Biehler, R.H. and Snowman, J. (1990) *Psychology Applied to Teaching*, 6th edn, Boston, MA: Houghton Mifflin.

Binet, A. and Simon, T. (1905) *A Method of Measuring the Development of the Intelligence of Young Children*, Chicago: Chicago Medical Book.

Blagg, N. (1991) *Can We Teach Intelligence? A Comprehensive Evaluation of Feuerstein's Instrumental Enrichment*, Hillsdale, NJ: Erlbaum.

Block, J.H. (1971) *Mastery Learning: Theory and Practice*, New York: Holt, Rinehart & Winston.

Block, J.H. and Burns, R.B. (1976) 'Master learning', in L.S. Shulman (ed.) *Review of Research in Education*, vol. 4, Itaska, IL: Peacock.

Bloom, B.S. (1976) *Human Characteristics and School Learning*, New York: McGraw-Hill.

Boekarts, M. (1993) 'Being concerned with well being and with learning', *Educational Psychologist 28*: 149–67.

Boersma, F.J. and Chapman, J.W. (1992) *Perception of Ability Scale for Students*, Los Angeles, CA: Western Psychological Services.

Boring, E. (1923) 'Intelligence as the tests test it', *New Republic* 6 June: 35–7.

Borkowski, J.G. and Buchel, F.P. (1983) 'Learning and memory strategies in the mentally retarded', in M. Pressley and J.R. Levin (eds) *Cognitive Strategy Research: Psychological Foundations* (pp. 103–28), New York: Springer-Verlag.

Borkowski, J.G. and Turner, L.A. (1990) 'Transsituational characteristics of meta-cognition', in W. Schneider and F.E. Weinert (eds) *Interactions among Aptitudes, Strategies, and Knowledge in Cognitive Performance* (pp. 159–76), New York: Springer-Verlag.

Borkowski, J.G., Estrada, M.T., Millstead, M. and Hale, C.A. (1989) 'General problem-solving skills: relations between metacognition and strategic processing', *Learning Disability Quarterly 12*: 57–70.

Borkowski, J.G., Carr, M., Rellinger, E. and Pressley, M. (1990) 'Self-regulated cognition: interdependence of metacognition, attributions, and self-esteem', in B.F. Jones and L. Idol (eds) *Dimensions of Thinking and Cognitive Instruction*, Hillsdale, NJ: Erlbaum.

Bowers, G.H. (1991) 'Emotion and social perception', paper presented at the annual meeting of the Southwestern Psychological Association, New Orleans, April.

Boyer, M. and Horne, A. (1989) *Schools and Parents: Partners in Career Equity Guidance for Young Adolescents, Equity Career Guidance Project*, Monograph 2, Terre Haute, IN: Indiana State University Department of Counselling and the Indiana Commission on Vocational and Technical Education.

Brailsford, A. (1981) 'The relationship between cognitive strategy training and performance on tasks of reading comprehension with a learning disabled group of children', unpublished doctoral thesis, University of Alberta, Edmonton, Canada.

Brailsford, A., Snart, F. and Das, J.P. (1984) 'Strategy training and reading comprehension', *Journal of Learning Disabilities 17*: 287–90.

Bransford, J.D., Stein, B.S., Arbitman-Smith, R. and Vye, N.J. (1985) 'Improving thinking and learning skills: an analysis of three approaches', in J. Segal, S.F. Chipman and R. Glaser (eds) *Thinking and Learning Skills: Relating Instruction to Research*, vol. 1 (pp. 133–208), Hillsdale, NJ: Erlbaum.

Bransford, J., Sherwood, R., Vye, N. and Rieser, J. (1986) 'Teaching thinking and problem-solving: research foundations', *American Psychologist 41*: 1078–89.

Braselton, S. and Decker, B.C. (1994) 'Using graphic organizers to improve the reading of mathematics', *The Reading Teacher 48*: 276–81.

Brown, A.L. and Barclay, C.R. (1976) 'The effects of training specific mnemonics on the metamnemonic efficiency of retarded children', *Child Development 47*: 71–80.

Brown, A.L. and Palincsar, A.S. (1982) *Inducing Strategic Learning from Texts by Means of Informed, Self-control Training*, Technical Report 262, Champaign, IL: University of Illinois at Urbana Champaign, Center for the Study of Reading.

Brown, A.L., Campione, J.C. and Barclay, C.R. (1979) 'Training self-checking routines for estimating test readiness: generalization from list learning to prose recall', *Child Development 50*: 501–12.

Brown, A.L., Bransford, J.D., Ferrera, R.A. and Campione, J.C. (1983) 'Learning, remembering, and understanding', in J.H. Flavell and E.M. Markman (eds) *Handbook of Child Psychology*, vol. 3, *Cognitive Development* (pp. 77–166), New York: John Wiley.

Brown, J.S., Collins, A. and Duguid, P. (1989) 'Situated cognition and the culture of learning', *Educational Researcher 18*(1): 32–42.

Bruer, J.T. (1993) *Schools for Thought: A Science of Learning in the Classroom*, Cambridge, MA: MIT Press.

Bryant, P. (1985) 'The distinction between knowing when to do a sum and knowing how to do it', *Educational Psychology 5*: 207–15.

Bryant, P. and Bradley, L. (1985) *Children's Reading Problems*, Oxford: Blackwell.

Budoff, M. (1967) 'Learning potential among institutionalized young adult retardates', *American Journal of Mental Deficiency 72*: 404–11.

——— (1987) 'The validity of learning potential assessment', in C.S. Lidz (ed.) *Dynamic Assessment: An Interactional Approach to Evaluating Learning Potential* (pp. 52–81), New York: Guilford.

Budoff, M. and Corman, L. (1974) 'Demographic and psychometric factors related to improved performance on the Kohs learning potential procedure', *American Journal of Mental Deficiency 78*: 578–85.

Budoff, M. and Friedman, M. (1964) '"Learning potential" as an assessment approach to the adolescent mentally retarded', *Journal of Consulting Psychology 28*: 434–9.

Butterfield, E.C., Wambold, C. and Belmont, J.B. (1973) 'On the theory and practice of improving short-term memory', *American Journal of Mental Deficiency 77*: 654–69.

Byrd, D.E. (1990) 'Peer tutoring with the learning disabled: a critical review', *Journal of Educational Research 84*: 115–18.

Byrne, R.W. (1979) 'The form and use of knowledge in a decor-design task', unpublished manuscript, University of St Andrews, Scotland.

—— (1981) 'Mental cookery: an illustration of fact retrieval from plans', *Quarterly Journal of Experimental Psychology 33A*: 31–7.

Byrnes, M. and Spitz, H. (1977) 'Performance of retarded adolescents and non retarded children on the Tower of Hanoi problem', *American Journal of Mental Deficiency 81*: 561–9.

Campione, J.C. (1989) 'Assisted assessment: a taxonomy of approaches and an outline of strengths and weaknesses', *Journal of Learning Disabilities 22*: 151–65.

Campione, J.C., Brown, A.L. and Bryant, N.R. (1985a) 'Individual differences in learning and memory', in R.J. Sternberg (ed.) *Human Abilities: An Information Processing Approach* (pp. 103–26), New York: W.H. Freeman.

Campione, J.C., Brown, A.L., Ferrara, R.A., Jones, R.S. and Steinberg, E. (1985b) 'Differences between retarded and non-retarded children in transfer following equivalent learning performances: breakdowns in flexible use of information', *Intelligence 9*: 297–315.

Carlo, G., Knight, G.P., Eisenberg, N. and Rotenberg, K.J. (1991) 'Cognitive processes and prosocial behaviors among children: the role of affective attributions and reconciliations',. *Developmental Psychology 27*: 456–61.

Carlson, J.S. and Das, J.P. (1992) *The Cognitive Assessment and Reading Remediation of Chapter 1 Students*, Riverside, CA: California Educational Research Cooperative of University of California, Riverside.

Carlson, J.S. and Wiedl, K.H. (1978) 'The use of testing-the-limits procedures in the assessment of intellectual capabilities in children with learning difficulties', *American Journal of Mental Deficiency 82*: 559–64.

—— (1979) 'Toward a differential testing approach: testing-the-limits employing the Raven matrices', *Intelligence 3*: 323–44.

—— (1992) 'The dynamic assessment of intelligence', in H.C. Haywood and D. Tzuriel (eds) *Interactive Assessment* (pp. 167–86), New York: Springer-Verlag.

Cattell, R.B. (1957) *Personality and Motivation Structure and Measurement*, Yonkers-on-Hudson, NY: World Book.

Chandler, L.K., Lubeck, R.C. and Fowler, S.A. (1992) 'Generalization and maintenance of preschool children's social skills: a critical review and analysis', *Journal of Applied Behavior Analysis 25*: 415–28.

Chi, M.T.H., De Leeuw, N., Chiu, M-H. and LaVancher, C. (1994) 'Eliciting self-explanations improves understanding', *Cognitive Science 18*: 439–77.

COGNET (1995) 'An in-depth description of the cognitive enrichment network educational model COGNET: a comprehensive educational approach approved by the national division network's program effectiveness panel', unpublished manuscript, University of Tennessee, Knoxville, TN.

Cohen, R.L. and Nealon, J. (1979) 'An analysis of short-term memory differences between retardates and nonretardates', *Intelligence 3*: 65–72.

Cole, P.G. and Chan, L.K.S. (1990) *Methods and Strategies for Special Education*, Sydney: Prentice Hall.

Collins, A., Brown, J.S. and Newman, S.E. (1989) 'Cognitive apprenticeship: teaching the crafts of reading, writing, and mathematics', in L.B. Resnick (ed.) *Knowing, Learning and Instruction: Essays in Honor of Robert Glaser* (pp. 453–94), Hillsdale, NJ: Erlbaum.

Collins, A., Hawkins, J. and Carver, S.M. (1991) 'A cognitive apprenticeship for disadvantaged students', in B. Means, C. Chelemer and M.S. Knapp (eds) *Teaching Advanced Skills to At-risk Students* (pp. 216–43), San Francisco, CA: Jossey-Bass.

Conoley, J.C. and Impara, J.C. (eds) (1992) *Mental Measurement Yearbook*, Lincoln, NB: Buros Institute of Mental Measurement, University of Nebraska, Lincoln.

Conte, R. and Andrews, J. (1993) 'Social skills in the context of learning disability definitions: a reply to Gresham and Elliott and future directions', *Journal of Learning Disabilities* 26: 146–53.

Conte, R., Andrews, J.J.W., Loomer, M. and Hutton, G. (1995) 'A classroom-based social skills intervention for children with learning disabilities', *Alberta Journal of Educational Research* 41: 84–102.

Conway, R.N.F. (1985) 'The information processing model and the mildly developmentally delayed child: assessment and training', unpublished doctoral thesis, Macquarie University, North Ryde, NSW, Australia.

—— (1994) 'Students with behavioural and emotional problems', in A.F. Ashman and J. Elkins (eds) *Educating Students with Special Needs*, 2nd edn (pp. 291–344), Sydney: Prentice Hall.

—— (1996) 'Curriculum adaptations', in P. Foreman (ed.) *Integration and Inclusion in Action*, Sydney: Harcourt Brace Jovanovich.

Conway, R.N.F. and Ashman, A.F. (1992) 'Teaching students to accept responsibility for their behaviour through planning skills', in B. Willis and J. Izard (eds) *Student Behaviour Problems: Directions, Perspectives, Expectations*, Melbourne: Australian Council for Educational Research.

Conway, R.N.F. and Hopton, L.J. (1997) 'Application of a school-wide metacognitive strategy training model: effects on academic and planning performance', *Journal of Cognitive Education*.

Conway, R.N.F., Schofield, N.J. and Tierney, J.T. (1991) *The Fair Discipline Code: A Review of the Fair Discipline Code in NSW Secondary Schools*, Newcastle, NSW: Report to the NSW Department of Education.

Cooper, C.R. and Cooper, R.G. (1984) 'Skill in peer learning discourse: what develops?', in S.A. Kucaj II (ed.) *Discourse Development* (pp. 77–98), New York: Springer-Verlag.

Coopersmith, S. (1967) *The Antecedents of Self-esteem*, San Francisco, CA: Freeman.

Cormier, P., Carlson, J.S. and Das, J.P. (1990) 'Planning ability and cognitive performance: the compensatory effects of a dynamic assessment approach', *Learning and Individual Differences* 2: 437–49.

Costa, A.L. (1991) *Developing Minds*, rev. edn, Alexandria, VA: Association for Supervision and Curriculum.

Craik, F.I.M. and Lockhart, R.S. (1972) 'Levels of processing: a framework for memory research', *Journal of Verbal Learning and Verbal Behavior* 11: 671–84.

Craven, R.G., Marsh, H.W. and Debus, R.L. (1991) 'Effects of internally focused feedback and attributional feedback on enhancement of academic self-concept', *Journal of Educational Psychology* 83: 17–27.

Cronbach, L.J. (1975) 'Five decades of public controversy over mental testing', *American Psychologist* 30: 1–14.

Curtis, M.J. and Meyers, J. (1988) 'Consultation: a foundation for alternative services in the schools', in J.L. Graden, J.E. Zins and M.J. Curtis (eds) *Alternative Educational Delivery Systems: Enhancing the Instructional Options for all Students* (pp. 35–48),

Washington, DC: National Association of School Psychologists.

Danoff, B., Harris, K.R. and Graham, S. (1993) 'Incorporating strategy instruction within the writing process in the regular classroom: effects on the writing of students with and without learning disabilities', *Journal of Reading Behavior 25*: 295–322.

Das, J.P. (1985) 'Remedial training for the amelioration of cognitive deficits in children', in A.F. Ashman and R.S. Laura (eds) *The Education and Training of the Mentally Retarded: Recent Advances* (pp. 215–44), London: Croom Helm.

Das, J.P. and Conway, R.N.F. (1992) 'Reflections on remediation and transfer: a Vygotskian perspective', in H.C. Haywood and D. Tzuriel (eds) *Interactive Assessment* (pp. 94–115), New York: Springer-Verlag.

Das, J.P. and Naglieri, J.A. (1992) 'Assessment of attention, simultaneous-successive coding and planning', in H.C. Haywood and D. Tzuriel (eds) *Interactive Assessment* (pp. 207–32), New York: Springer-Verlag.

——— (1996) *Das•Naglieri Cognitive Assessment System Administration and Scoring Manual*, Riverside, CA: Psychological Corporation.

Das, J.P., Kirby, J. and Jarman, R.F. (1975) 'Simultaneous and successive synthesis: an alternative model of cognitive abilities', *Psychological Review 82*: 87–103.

——— (1979) *Simultaneous and Successive Cognitive Processes*, New York: Academic Press.

Das, J.P., Mensink, D. and Janzen, H. (1990) 'The K-ABC, coding, and planning: an investigation of cognitive processes', *Journal of School Psychology 28*: 1–11.

Das, J.P., Naglieri, J.A. and Kirby, J.R. (1994) *Assessment of Cognitive Processes: The PASS Theory of Intelligence*, Boston, MA: Allyn & Bacon.

Das, J.P., Mishra, R.K. and Pool, J. (1995) 'An experiment on cognitive remediation of word-reading difficulty', *Journal of Learning Disabilities 28*: 66–79.

Das, J.P., Carlson, J., Davidson, M.B. and Longe, K. (1997) *PREP: PASS Remedial Program*, Seattle, WA: Hogrefe.

Davis, W.E. (1991) 'Promoting effective communication between schools and parents of disadvantaged students', paper presented at the 99th Annual Convention of the American Psychological Association, San Francisco, CA, August.

Davison, J. (1990) 'The process of school consultation: give and take', in E. Cole and J.A. Siegel (eds) *Effective Consultation in School Psychology* (pp. 53–71). Toronto: Hogrefe & Huber.

Deffenbacher, J.L., Thwaites, G.A., Wallace, T.L. and Oetting, E.R. (1994) 'Social skills and cognitive-relaxation approaches to general anger reduction', *Journal of Counseling Psychology 41*: 386–96.

de Jong, F.P.C.M. (1990) 'Executive control, self-regulation trained in mathematics', in J.M. Pieters, K. Breuer and P.R.J. Simons (eds) *Learning Environments: Contributions from Dutch and German Research*, New York: Springer-Verlag.

Derry, S.J., Hawkes, L.W. and Tsai, C. (1987) 'A theory for remediating problem-solving skills of older children and adults', *Educational Psychologist 22*: 55–87.

Deshler, D.D. and Schumaker, J.B. (1986) 'Learning strategies: an instructional alternative for low-achieving adolescents', *Exceptional Children 53*: 583–90.

Dinwiddie, S.A. (1993) 'Playing in the gutters: enhancing children's cognitive and social play', *Young Children 48*: 70–3.

Dixon, P. (1987) 'The structure of mental plans for following directions', *Journal of Experimental Psychology: Learning, Memory and Cognition 13*: 18–26.

Dole, J.A., Duffy, G.C., Roehler, L.R. and Pearson, P.D. (1991) 'Moving from the old to the new: research on reading comprehension instruction', *Review of Educational Research 61*: 239–64.

Dole, J.A., Brown, K.J. and Trathern, W. (1996) 'The effects of strategy instruction on the comprehension performance of at-risk students', *Reading Research Quarterly* *31*(1): 62–88.

Dougherty, A.M., Dougherty, L.P. and Purcell, D. (1991) 'The sources and management of resistance to consultation', *The School Counselor 38*: 178–87.

Doyle, W. (1983) 'Academic work', *Review of Educational Research 53*: 159–99.

Doyle, W. and Ponder, G.A. (1975) 'Classroom ecology: some concerns about a neglected dimension of research on teaching', *Contemporary Education 46*: 183–90.

Dubow, E.F., Tisak, J., Causey, D., Hryshko, A. and Reid, G. (1991) 'A two-year longitudinal study of stressful life events, social support, and social problem-solving skills: contributions to children's behavioral and academic adjustment', *Child Development 62*: 583–99.

Duffy, G.C. (1993) 'Teachers' progress towards becoming expert strategy teachers', *The Elementary School Journal 94*: 111–20.

Dunn, L.M. and Dunn, L. (1981) *Peabody Picture Vocabulary Test–Revised*, Circle Pines, MN: American Guidance Service.

Dupper, D.R. and Krishef, C.H. (1993) 'School-based social-cognitive skills training for middle school students with school behavior problems', *Children and Youth Services Review 15*: 131–42.

Ebbinghaus, H. (1913) *Memory, a Contribution to Experimental Psychology*, New York: Columbia University Press.

Elias, M.J., Gara, M., Urbriaco, M., Rothman, P.A., Clabby, J.F. and Schuyler, T. (1986) 'Impact of a preventative social problem solving intervention on children's coping with middle school stressors', *American Journal of Community Psychology 14*: 259–76.

Elliott, C.D. (1990) *Differential Ability Scales*, San Antonio, TX: Psychological Corporation.

Elliott, C.D., Murray, D.J. and Pearson, L.S. (1983) *British Ability Scale*, 2nd edn, Slough: NFER-Nelson.

Ellis, E.S. (1993) 'Integrative strategy instruction: a potential model for teaching content area subjects to adolescents with learning disabilities', *Journal of Learning Disabilities 26*(6): 358–83.

Ellis, E.S., Deshler, D.D., Lenz, K., Schumaker, J.B. and Clark, F.L. (1991) 'An instructional model for teaching learning strategies', *Focus on Exceptional Children 23*: 1–24.

Englert, C.S., Calatta, B.E. and Horn, D.G. (1987) 'Influence of irrelevant information in addition word problems on problem-solving', *Learning Disability Quarterly 10*: 29–36.

Englert, C.S., Tarrant, K.L., Mariage, T.V. and Oxer, T. (1994) 'Lesson talk as the work of reading groups: the effectiveness of two interventions', *Journal of Learning Disabilities 27*: 165–85.

Eyde, D.R. and Altman, R. (1978) *An Exploration of Metamemory Processes in Mildly and Moderately Retarded Children* (final report), Columbia, MO: Department of Special Education, University of Missouri, Columbia.

Eysenck, H.J. (1967) 'Intelligence assessment: a theoretical and experimental approach', *British Journal of Educational Psychology 37*: 81–98.

Fad, K.S., Ross, M. and Boston, J. (1995) 'We're better together: using cooperative learning to teach social skills to young children', *Teaching Exceptional Children 27*: 28–34.

Ferinden, W.R. and Jacobson, S. (1969) *Educational Interpretation of the Wechsler Intelligence Scale for Children*, Linden, NJ: Remediation Associates.

Feuerstein, R. (1970) 'A dynamic approach to causation, prevention, and alleviation of retarded performance', in H.C. Haywood (ed.) *Social-cultural Aspects of Mental Retardation* (pp. 341–77), New York: Appleton-Century-Crofts.

Feuerstein, R., Rand, Y. and Hoffman, M.B. (1979) *The Dynamic Assessment of Retarded Performers: The Learning Potential Assessment Device   Theory, Instruments, and Techniques*, Baltimore, MD: University Park Press.

Feuerstein, R., Rand, Y., Hoffman, M.B. and Miller, R. (1980) *Instrumental Enrichment*, Baltimore, MD: University Park Press.

Feuerstein, R., Rand, Y., Jensen, M.R., Kaniel, S. and Tzuriel, D. (1987) 'Prerequisites for assessment of learning potential: the LPAD model', in C.S. Lidz (ed.) *Dynamic Assessment* (pp. 35–51), New York: Guilford.

Filson, A. (1991) *The Theory of Structural Cognitive Modifiability and its Applied Aspects*, London: Sankofa Institute.

Finch, A.J., Nelson, W.M. and Ott, E.S. (1993) *Cognitive-Behavioral Procedures with Children and Adolescents: A Practical Guide*, Boston, MA: Allyn & Bacon.

Fine, M.J., Grantham, V.L. and Wright, J.G. (1979) 'Person variables that facilitate or impede consultation', *Psychology in the Schools 16*: 533–9.

Fitzgerald, J. and Markman, L.R. (1987) 'Teaching children about revision in writing', *Cognition and Instruction 4*: 3–24.

Flavell, J.H. (1976) 'Metacognitive aspects of problem solving', in L.B. Resnick (ed.) *The Nature of Intelligence* (pp. 231–5), Hillsdale, NJ: Erlbaum.

Flavell, J.H., Fredericks, A.B. and Hoyt, J.D. (1970) 'Developmental changes in memorization processes', *Cognitive Psychology 1*: 324–40.

Fogarty, R. and Bellanca, J. (1993) *Patterns for Thinking: Patterns for Transfer: A Cooperative Team Approach for Critical and Creative Thinking in the Classroom*, Palatine, IL: Skylight.

Foot, H., Morgan, M. and Shute, R. (1990) *Children Helping Children*, Chichester: John Wiley.

Fredericksen, N. (1984) 'Implications of cognitive theory for instruction in problem-solving', *Review of Educational Research 54*: 363–407.

Frisby, C.L. and Braden, J.P. (1992) 'Feuerstein's dynamic assessment approach: a semantic, logical, and empirical critique', *Journal of Special Education 26*: 281–301.

Gallagher, J.J. (1994) 'Teaching and learning: new models', *Annual Review of Psychology 45*: 171–95.

Gamoran, A. (1993) 'Alternate uses of ability grouping in secondary schools: can we bring high-quality instruction to low-ability classes?' *American Journal of Education 102*: 1 22.

Gamoran, A. and Berends, M. (1988) *The Effects of Stratification in Secondary Schools: Synthesis of Survey and Ethnographic Research*, Madison, WI: National Centre of Effective Secondary Schools, University of Wisconsin at Madison.

Gardner, H. (1983) *Frames of Mind: The Theory of Multiple Intelligences*, New York: Basic Books.

—— (1990) 'The difficulty of school: probable causes, probable cures', *Daedalus 119*: 85–113.

Gazzaniga, M.S. (1975) 'Brain mechanisms and behaviour', in M.S. Gazzaniga and C. Blakemore (eds) *Handbook of Psychobiology* (pp. 565–90), New York: Academic Press.

Gerber, M. (1983) 'Learning disabilities and cognitive strategies: a case for training or containing problem-solving', *Journal of Learning Disabilities 16*: 255–60.

Gersten, R. and Carnine, D. (1986) 'Direct instruction in reading comprehension', *Educational Leadership 43*(7): 70 8.

Gillies, R.M. (1994) 'The effects of structured and unstructured cooperative learning groups on students' behaviours, interactions, and learning outcomes', unpublished doctoral dissertation, University of Queensland.

Glidden, L.M. and Warner, D.A. (1983) 'Semantic processing and recall improvement of EMR adolescents', *American Journal of Mental Deficiency* 88: 96–105.

Glyshaw, K., Cohen, L.H. and Towbes, L.C. (1989) 'Coping strategies and psychological distress: prospective analyses of early and middle adolescents', *American Journal of Community Psychology* 17: 607–23.

Gold, A., Bowe, R. and Ball, S.J. (1993) 'Special educational needs in a new context: micropolitics, money and "education for all"', in R. Slee (ed.) *Is There a Desk with My Name on it? The Politics of Integration* (pp. 51–64), London: Falmer.

Golden, C.J. (1987) *Luria-Nebraska Neuropsychological Battery: Children's Revision*, Los Angeles, CA: Western Psychological Services.

Golden, C.J., Purisch, A.D. and Hammeke, T.A. (1985) *Luria-Nebraska Neuropsychological Battery: Forms I and II*, Los Angeles, CA: Western Psychological Services.

Good, T.L. and Brophy, J.E. (1987) *Looking in Classrooms*, 4th edn, New York: Harper & Row.

Goor, M.B. and Schwenn, J.O. (1993) 'Accommodating diversity and disability with cooperative learning', *Intervention in School and Clinic* 29(1): 6–16.

Gordon, C., Arthur, M. and Butterfield, N. (1996) *Promoting Positive Behaviour*, Melbourne: Nelson.

Gould, S.J. (1981) *The Mismeasure of Man*, New York: W.W. Norton.

Graham, S. and Harris, K.R. (1988) 'Instructional recommendations for teaching writing to exceptional children', *Exceptional Children* 54: 506–12.

Greenberg, K.H. (1989) *Cognitive Enrichment Network Follow Through Project: Manual and Mini-lessons*, Knoxville, KY: University of Tennessee.

—— (1990) 'Combining research and theoretical application: the COGNET project', *International Journal of Cognitive Education and Mediated Learning* 1: 237–44.

—— (1995) *The Cognitive Enrichment Network Educational Model COGNET: Evidence of Effectiveness*, Knoxville, KY: COGNET Follow Through Project.

Gregg, V. (1986) *Introduction to Human Memory*, London: Routledge and Kegan Paul.

Groteluschen, A.K., Borkowski, J.G. and Hale, C. (1990) 'Strategy instruction is often insufficient: addressing the interdependency of executive and attributional processes', in T.E. Scruggs and B.Y.L. Wong (eds) *Intervention Research in Learning Disabilities* (pp. 82–101), New York: Springer-Verlag.

Guerra, N.G. and Slaby, R.G. (1990) 'Cognitive mediators of aggression in adolescent offenders: 2. Intervention', *Experimental Psychology* 26: 269–77.

Guilford, J.P. (1959) 'Three faces of intellect', *American Psychologist* 14: 469–79.

Guilford, J.P. and Lacey, J.I. (eds) (1947) *Army Air Force Aviation Psychological Research Report* (no. 5), Washington, DC: US Government Printing Office.

Gupta, R.M. and Coxhead, P. (eds) (1988) *Cultural Diversity and Learning Efficiency: Recent Developments*, New York: St Martin's Press.

Guskey, T.R. and Gates, S.L. (1986) 'Synthesis of research on the effects of mastery learning in elementary and secondary classrooms', *Educational Leadership* 43: 73–80.

Guthke, J. and Wingenfeld, S. (1992) 'The learning test concept: origins, state of the art, and trends', in H.C. Haywood and D. Tzuriel (eds) *Interactive Assessment* (pp. 64–93), New York: Springer-Verlag.

Haeussermann, E. (1958) *Developmental Potential of Preschool Children*, New York: Grune and Stratton.

Hains, A.A. (1992) 'Comparison of cognitive-behavioral stress management techniques with adolescent boys', *Journal of Counseling and Development 70*: 600–5.

Hains, A.A. and Hains, A.H. (1987) 'The effects of a cognitive strategy intervention on the problem-solving abilities of delinquent youths', *Journal of Adolescence 10*: 399–413.

Hains, A.A. and Herrman, L.P. (1989) 'Social cognitive skills and behavioural adjustment of delinquent adolescents in treatment', *Journal of Adolescence 12*: 323–8.

Hains, A.A. and Szyjakowski, M. (1990) 'A cognitive stress-reduction intervention program for adolescents', *Journal of Counseling Psychology 37*: 79–84.

Halstead, W.C. (1947) *Brain and Intelligence*, Chicago, IL: University of Chicago Press.

Harlow, J.M. (1848) 'Passage of an iron rod through the head', *Boston Medical and Surgical Journal 39*: 389–93.

—— (1868) 'Recovery from the passage of an iron rod through the head', *Massachusetts Medical Society 2*: 327–46.

Harris, K.R. (1990) 'Developing self-regulated learners: the role of private speech and self-instructions', *Educational Psychologist 25*: 35–49.

Harris, K.R. and Graham, S. (1992) *Helping Young Writers Master the Craft: Strategy Instruction and Self-regulation in the Writing Process*, Cambridge, MA: Brookline.

Harter, S. (1982) 'The perceived competence scale for children', *Child Development 53*: 87–97.

Hartman, H.J. (1994) 'From reciprocal teaching to reciprocal education', *Journal of Developmental Education 18*(1): 3–8, 32.

Hawkins, R.P., Pingree, S. and Adler, I. (1987) 'Searching for cognitive processes in the cultivation effect: adult and adolescent samples in the United States and Australia', *Human Communication Research 13*: 553–77.

Hayes-Roth, B. and Hayes-Roth, F. (1979) 'A cognitive model of planning', *Cognitive Science 3*: 275–310.

Haywood, H.C. (1988) 'Bridging: a special technique of mediation', *The Thinking Teacher 4*(2): 4–5.

—— (1989) 'Multidimensional treatment of mental retardation', *Psychology in Mental Retardation and Developmental Disabilities 15*(1): 1–10.

—— (1990) 'A total cognitive approach in education: enough bits and pieces!', *The Thinking Teacher 5*(3): 1–6.

—— (1992a) 'Book review of evaluation of instrumental enrichment in England', *Contemporary Psychology 37*: 206–7.

—— (1992b) 'New educational techniques, instructional methods and curriculum organization', paper presented at international seminar to observe twentieth anniversary of the National Institute of Special Education, Tokyo, October.

—— (1993) 'A mediational teaching style', *International Journal of Cognitive Education and Mediated Learning 3*(1): 27–38.

—— (1995) 'Follow-up evaluation of cognitive education programs', paper presented at the fifth conference of the International Association for Cognitive Education, Monticello, New York, July.

Haywood, H.C. and Brown, A.L. (1990) 'Behavior management in cognitive early education', *European Journal of Psychology of Education 5*: 243–52.

Haywood, H.C. and Tzuriel, D. (eds) (1992) *Interactive Assessment*, New York: Springer-Verlag.

Haywood, H.C., Brooks, P.H. and Burns, S. (1986) 'Stimulating cognitive development at developmental level: a tested, non-remedial preschool curriculum for preschoolers and older retarded children', in M. Schwebel and C. Maher (eds) *Facilitating Cognitive Development: Principles, Practices, and Programs* (pp. 127–47), New York: Haworth.

Haywood, H.C., Brown, A.L. and Wingenfeld, S. (1990) 'Dynamic approaches to psychoeducational assessment', *School Psychology Review 19*: 411–22.

Haywood, H.C., Brooks, P. H. and Burns, S. (1992a) *Bright Start: Cognitive Curriculum for Young Children*, Waterton, MA: Charlesbridge.

Haywood, H.C., Tzuriel, D. and Vaught, S. (1992b) 'Psychoeducational assessment from a transactional perspective', in H.C. Haywood and D. Tzuriel (eds) *Interactive Assessment* (pp. 38–63), New York: Springer-Verlag.

Hoffman, R., Bringman, W., Bamberg, M. and Klein, R. (1987) 'Some historical observations of Ebbinghaus', in D. Gorlein and R. Hoffman (eds) *Memory and Learning: The Ebbinghaus Centennial Conference* (pp. 57–75), Hillsdale, NJ: Erlbaum.

Houck, C.K. (1993) 'Ellis's "potential" integrative strategy instruction model: an appealing extension of previous efforts', *Journal of Learning Disabilities 26*: 399–403.

Hudson, J.A. and Fivush, R. (1991) 'Planning in the preschool years: the emergence of plans from general event knowledge', *Cognitive Development 6*: 393–415.

Hutchinson, N.L. (1987) 'Strategies for teaching learning disabled adolescents algebraic problems', *Reading, Writing and Learning Disabilities 3*: 63–74.

Idol, L. (1983) *Special Educator's Consultation Handbook*, Austin, TX: Pro-ed.

Idol, L. and Baran, S. (1992) 'Elementary school counselors and special educators consulting together: perilous pitfalls or opportunities to collaborate?', *Elementary School Guidance and Counseling 26*: 202–14.

Idol, L., Paolucci-Whitcomb, P. and Nevin, A. (1986) *Collaborative Consultation*, Rockville, MD: Aspen Systems.

Jastak, S. and Wilkinson, G. (1994) *Wide Range Achievement Test – Third Edition*, San Antonio, TX: Psychological Corporation.

Jensen, A.R. (1969) 'How much can we boost I.Q. and scholastic achievement?', *Harvard Educational Review 39*: 1–123.

—— (1973) 'Level I and Level II abilities in three ethnic groups', *American Educational Research Journal 10*: 263–76.

Jones, B.F., Palincsar, A.S., Ogle, D.S. and Carr, E.G. (1987) *Strategic Teaching and Learning: Cognitive Instruction in the Content Areas*, Alexandria, VA: Association for Supervision and Curriculum Development.

Kamann, M.P. and Wong, B.Y.L. (1993) 'Inducing adaptive coping self-statements in children with learning disabilities through self-instruction training', *Journal of Learning Disabilities 29*: 630–8.

Kaniel, S. (1994) 'Strategies for improving the function of working memory', *Journal of Cognitive Education 4*: 57–67.

Kar, B.C., Dash, U.N., Das, J.P. and Carlson, J.S. (1992) 'Two experiments on the dynamic assessment of planning', *Learning and Individual Differences 5*: 13–29.

Kaufman, A. and Kaufman, N. (1983) *Kaufman Assessment Battery for Children*, Circle Pines, MN: American Guidance Service.

Kaufman, A.S., Kaufman, N.L. and Goldsmith, B.Z. (1983) *K-SOS: Kaufman-Sequential or Simultaneous*, Circle Pines, MN: American Guidance Service.

Kaufman, D. (1978) 'The relationship of academic performance to strategy training and remedial techniques: an information processing approach', unpublished doctoral thesis, University of Alberta, Edmonton, Canada.

Kaufman, D. and Kaufman, P. (1979) 'Strategy training and remedial techniques', *Journal of Learning Disabilities 12*: 63–6.

Kearins, J. (1986) 'Visual spatial memory in Aboriginal and white Australian children', *Australian Journal of Psychology* 38: 203–14.

Kelly, M., Moore, D.W. and Tuck, B.F. (1994) 'Reciprocal teaching in a regular primary school classroom', *Journal of Educational Research* 88. 53–61.

Kendall, C.R., Borkowski, J.G. and Cavanaugh, J.C. (1980) 'Metamemory and the transfer of an interrogative strategy by EMR children', *Intelligence 4*: 255–70.

Kendall, P.C. (ed.) (1991) *Child and Adolescent Therapy: Cognitive-behavioral Procedures*, New York: Guilford.

Kennedy, M.M. (1991) *An Agenda for Research on Teacher Learning* (special report), East Lansing, MI: National Centre for Research on Teacher Learning.

Kennedy, R.E. (1984) 'Cognitive behavioral interventions with delinquents', in A.W. Meyers and W.E. Craighead (eds) *Cognitive Behavior Therapy with Children*, New York: Plenum.

Kirby, J.R. and Ashman, A.F. (1984) 'Planning skills and mathematics achievement: implications regarding learning disabilities', *Journal of Psychoeducational Assessment 2*: 9–22.

Kirby, J.R. and Williams, N. (1991) *Learning Problems: A Cognitive Approach*, Toronto, ON: Kagan & Woo.

Klebanoff, S.G. (1945) 'Psychological changes in organic brain lesions and ablations', *Psychological Bulletin 42*: 585–623.

Klich, L.Z. and Davidson, G.R. (1984) 'Toward a recognition of Australian Aboriginal competence in cognitive functions', in J.R. Kirby (ed.) *Cognitive Strategies and Educational Performance* (pp. 155–202), New York: Academic Press.

Kolko, D.J., Loar, L.L. and Sturnick, D. (1990) 'Inpatient social-cognitive skills training groups with conduct disordered and attention deficit disordered children', *Journal of Child Psychology and Psychiatry 31*: 737–48.

Kormann, A. and Sporer, S.L. (1983) 'Learning tests – concepts and critical evaluation', *Studies in Educational Evaluation 9*: 1679–84.

Kornhaber, M., Krechevsky, M. and Gardner, H. (1990) 'Engaging intelligence', *Educational Psychologist 25*: 177–99.

Kramer, J.J. and Engle, R.W. (1981) 'Teaching awareness of strategic behavior in combination with strategy training: effects on children's memory performance', *Journal of Experimental Child Psychology 32*: 513–30.

Kramer, J.J., Nagle, R.J. and Engle, R.W. (1980) 'Recent advances in mnemonic strategy training with mentally retarded persons: implications for educational practice', *American Journal of Mental Deficiency 85*: 306–14.

Kreitler, S. and Kreitler, H. (1986) 'Individuality in planning: meaning patterns of planning styles', *International Journal of Psychology 21*: 565–87.

Kreutzer, M.A., Leonard, C. and Flavell, J.H. (1975) 'An interview study of children's knowledge about memory', *Monographs of the Society for Research in Child Development* (serial no. 159, no. 1).

Krywaniuk, L.W. (1974) 'Patterns of cognitive abilities of high and low achieving school children', unpublished doctoral thesis, University of Alberta, Edmonton, Canada.

Krywaniuk, L.W. and Das, J. P. (1976) 'Cognitive strategies in native children: analysis and intervention', *Alberta Journal of Educational Research 22*: 271–80.

Kulieke, M.J. and Jones, B.F. (1993) 'Cognitive instructional techniques in relation to whole language approaches', *Remedial and Special Education 14*(4): 26–9.

Kulik, C-L.C., Kulik, J.A. and Bangert-Drowns, R.L. (1990) 'Effectiveness of mastery learning programs: a meta-analysis', *Review of Educational Research 60*: 265–99.

Langer, J.A. and Applebee, A.N. (1986) 'Reading and writing instruction: toward a theory of teaching and learning', in E. Rothkopf (ed.) *Review of Research in Education*, vol. 13 (pp. 171–94), Washington, DC: American Educational Research Association.

Lashley, K.S. (1933) 'Integrative functions of the cerebral cortex', *Physiological Review 13*: 1–42.

Lee, C.D. (1995) 'A culturally based cognitive apprenticeship: teaching African American high school students skills in literary interpretation', *Reading Research Quarterly 30*(4): 608–30.

Lee, V. (ed.) (1990) *Children's Learning in School*, London: Hodder and Stoughton.

Lenz, B.K., Bulgren, J. and Hudson, P. (1990) 'Content enhancement: a model for promoting the acquisition of content by individuals with learning disabilities', in T.E. Scruggs and B.Y.L. Wong (eds) *Intervention Research in Learning Disabilities* (pp. 122–65), New York: Springer-Verlag.

Lewis, A.B. (1989) 'Training students to represent arithmetic word problems', *Journal of Educational Psychology 81*: 521–31.

Lezak, M.D. ([1976] 1995) *Neuropsychological Assessment*, 3rd edn, New York: Oxford University Press.

Lidz, C.S. (ed.) (1987a) *Dynamic Assessment: An Interactional Approach to Evaluating Learning Potential*, New York: Guilford.

—— (1987b) 'Historical perspectives', in C.S. Lidz (ed.) *Dynamic Assessment: An Interactional Approach to Evaluating Learning Potential* (pp. 3–32), New York: Guilford.

—— (1991) *Practitioner's Guide to Dynamic Assessment*, New York: Guilford.

Lindner, R.W. and Harris, B. (1992) 'Self-regulated learning: its assessment and instructional implications', *Educational Research Quarterly 16*: 29–37.

Lockhart, J. and Hay, I. (1995) 'Enhancing the self-concept of at-risk adolescent girls using reflective thinking and a challenge-based program', *Journal of Cognitive Education 5*: 55–70.

Lombano, J.H. and Lombano, A.E. (1982) 'The home–school partnership: a model for counselors', *Personnel Guidance Journal 61*: 35–9.

Lundeberg, M.A. and Fawver, J.E. (1994) 'Thinking like a teacher: encouraging cognitive growth in case analysis', *Journal of Teacher Education 45*: 289–97.

Luria, A.R. (1966) *Higher Cortical Functions in Man*, New York: Basic Books.

—— (1973) *The Working Brain*, Harmondsworth: Penguin.

MacArthur, C.A., Graham, S., Schwartz, S.S. and Schafer, W.D. (1995) 'Evaluation of a writing instruction model that integrated a process approach, strategy instruction, and word processing', *Learning Disability Quarterly 18*: 278–91.

McCarthy, D. (1972) *McCarthy Scales of Children's Ability*, San Antonio, TX: Psychological Corporation.

McInerney, D. and McInerney, V. (1994) *Educational Psychology*, Sydney: Prentice Hall.

McIntosh, R., Vaughn, S. and Zaragoze, N. (1991) 'A review of social interventions for students with learning disabilities', *Journal of Learning Disabilities 8*: 451–8.

McLaughlin, T.F. (1991) 'Use of a personalized system of instruction with and without a same day retake contingency on spelling performance of behaviorally disordered children', *Behavioral Disorders 16*: 127–32.

McLeod, D.B. and Adams, V.M. (1989) *Affect and Mathematical Problem Solving: A New Perspective*, New York: Springer-Verlag.

Mager, R.F. (1990) *Preparing Instructional Objectives*, 2nd edn, London: Kogan Page.

Magnusson, S.J. and Palincsar, A.S. (1995) 'The learning environment as a site of science education reform', *Theory and Practice 34*: 43–50.

Magoun, H.W. (1963) *The Waking Brain*, 2nd edn, Springfield, IL: C.C. Thomas.

Marsh, H.W. (1990a) 'Confirmatory factor analysis of multitrait-multimethod data: the construct validation of multidimensional self concept responses', *Journal of Personality 58*: 661–92.

—— (1990b) *Self-Description Questionnaire-II: Manual*, San Antonio, TX: Psychological Corporation.

Martin, P., Connolly, J., Kutcher, S. and Korenblum, M. (1993) 'Cognitive social skills and social self-appraisal in depressed adolescents', *Journal of the American Academy of Child and Adolescent Psychiatry 32*: 739–44.

Martin, R.P. (1994) 'Child temperament and common problems in schooling: hypotheses about causal connections', *Journal of School Psychology 32*: 119–34.

Marzano, R., Brandt, R.S., Hughes, C., Jones, B.F., Presseisen, B.Z., Rankin, S. and Suhor, C. (1988) *Dimensions of Thinking*, Alexandria, VA: Association for Supervision and Curriculum Development.

Maultsby, M.C. (1990) *Rational Behavior Therapy*, Appleton: Rational Self-Help Books/I'ACT.

Mayer, R.E. (1992) 'Cognition and instruction: their historic meeting within educational psychology', *Journal of Educational Psychology 84*: 405–12.

Meichenbaum, D. (1977) *Cognitive-behavior Modification: An Integrative Approach*, New York: Plenum.

Meichenbaum, D. and Asarnow, J. (1978) 'Cognitive-behavioral modification and metacognitive development: implications for the classroom', in P. Kendall and S. Hollon (eds) *Cognitive-behavioral Interventions: Theory, Research and Procedure* (pp. 11–36), New York: Academic Press.

Meichenbaum, D. and Goodman, J. (1971) 'Training impulsive children to talk to themselves: a means of developing self-control', *Journal of Abnormal Psychology 77*: 115–26.

Miles, D.M. and Forcht, J.P. (1995) 'Mathematics strategies for secondary students with learning disabilities or mathematical deficiencies: a cognitive approach', *Intervention in School and Clinic 31*: 91–6.

Miller, G.A., Galanter, E.H. and Pribram, K.H. (1960) *Plans and the Structure of Behavior*, New York: Holt, Rinehart and Winston.

Milner, J.S., Robertson, K.R. and Rogers, D.L. (1990) 'Childhood history of abuse and adult child abuse potential', *Journal of Family Violence 5*: 15–34.

Minick, N. (1987) 'Implications of Vygotsky's theories for dynamic assessment', in C.S. Lidz (ed.) *Dynamic Assessment* (pp. 116–40), New York: Guilford.

Missiuna, C. and Samuels, M. (1988) 'Dynamic assessment: review and critique', *Special Services in the Schools 5*: 1–22.

Moll, L.C. (ed.) (1990) *Vygotsky and Education: Instructional Implications and Applications of Sociohistorical Psychology*, Cambridge: Cambridge University Press.

Montague, M. and Applegate, B. (1993) 'Mathematical problem-solving characteristics of middle school children with learning disabilities', *Journal of Special Education 27*: 175–201.

Montgomery, J.R. (1994) 'Global trend in education: shifting from a teaching-focus to a learning-focus', paper presented at the International Experiential Learning Conference, Washington, DC, November.

Naglieri, J.A. (1988) *Draw-a-Person: A Quantitative Scoring System*, San Antonio, TX: Psychological Corporation.

Naglieri, J.A. and Das, J.P. (1996) *The Das•Naglieri Cognitive Assessment System Administration and Scoring Manual*, Chicago, IL: Riverside.

Naglieri, J.A. and Gottling, S.H. (1995) 'A cognitive education approach to math instruction for the learning disabled: an individual study', *Psychological Reports* 76: 1343–54

—— (1996) 'Mathematics instruction and PASS cognitive processes: an intervention study', *Journal of Learning Disabilities.*

National Board of Employment, Education and Training (NBEET) (1992) *Curriculum Initiatives*, Commissioned report no. 12, Canberra: Australian Government Publishing Service.

Naveh-Benjamin, M. (1990) 'The acquisition and retention of knowledge: exploring mutual benefits to memory research and the educational setting', *Applied Cognitive Psychology* 4: 295–320.

Nebes, R.D. (1974) 'Hemispheric specialization in commissurotomized man', *Psychological Bulletin* 81: 1–14.

Neisser, U. (1967) *Cognitive Psychology*, New York: Appleton-Century-Crofts.

Nevin, A., Thousand, J.S. and Villa, R.A. (1993) 'Establishing collaborative ethics and practices', *Journal of Educational and Psychological Consultation* 4: 293–304.

Olson, J. and Platt, J. (1993) *Teaching Children and Adolescents with Special Needs*, New York: Merrill.

Orth, L.C. and Martin, R.P. (1994) 'Interactive effects of student temperament and instruction method on classroom behaviour and achievement', *Journal of School Psychology* 32: 149–66.

Palincsar, A.S. (1991) 'Scaffolded instruction of listening comprehension with first graders at risk for academic difficulty', in A. McKeough and J.L. Lupart (eds) *Towards the Practice of Theory-based Instruction: Current Cognitive Theories and their Educational Promise* (pp. 50–65), Hillsdale, NJ: Erlbaum.

Palincsar, A.S. and Brown, A.L. (1984) 'Reciprocal teaching of comprehension-fostering and comprehension-monitoring activities', *Cognition and Instruction 1*: 117–75.

—— (1986) 'Interactive teaching to promote independent learning from text', *The Reading Teacher 39*: 771–7.

Palincsar, A.S. Ranson, K. and Derber, S. (1988) 'Collaborative research and the development of reciprocal teaching', *Educational Leadership 46*: 37–40.

Paour, J.L., Ccbc, S., Lagarrigue, P. and Luiu, D. (1993) 'A partial evaluation of Bright Start with pupils at risk of school failure', *The Thinking Teacher 8*(2): 1–7.

Paris, S.G. (1988) 'Models and metaphors of learning strategies', in C.E. Weinstein, E.T. Goetz and P.A. Alexander (eds) *Learning and Study Strategies: Issues in Assessment, Instruction, and Evaluation* (pp. 299–321), San Diego, CA: Academic Press.

—— (1993) 'Fixed effect fallacies and the perils of instructional research', invited paper presented at Schonell Special Education Research Centre, University of Queensland, Brisbane, Australia.

—— (1995) 'Children's learning outside of school settings in cultural contexts', paper presented at the fifth conference of the International Association for Cognitive Education, Monticello, New York, July.

Paris, S.G. and Newman, R.S. (1990) 'Developmental aspects of self-regulated learning', *Educational Psychologist 25*: 87–102.

Paris, S.G. and Winograd, P. (1990) 'How metacognition can promote academic learning and instruction', in B.F. Jones and L. Idol (eds) *Dimensions of Thinking and Cognitive Instruction* (pp. 15–51), Hillsdale, NJ: Erlbaum.

Parmenter, T.R. (1984) 'An investigation of the strategic behaviour of mildly intellectually handicapped adolescents in acquiring reading skills', unpublished doctoral thesis, Macquarie University, North Ryde, NSW, Australia.

Partington, G. (1995) 'Human diversity and schools: culture and gender', in F. Maltby, N.L. Gage and D.C. Berliner (eds) *Educational Psychology: An Australian Perspective* (pp. 154–91), Brisbane: John Wiley.

Patton, P.L. (1995) 'Rational behavior skills: a teaching sequence for students with emotional disabilities', *The School Counselor 43*: 133–41.

Pavlov, I.P. (1927) *Conditional Reflexes*, London: Oxford University Press.

Pearson, P.D. and Dole, J. (1988) 'Explicit comprehension instruction: a review of research and a new conceptualization of instruction', *Elementary School Journal 88*: 151–65.

Pearson, P.D. and Raphael, T.E. (1990) 'Reading comprehension as a dimension of thinking', in B.F. Jones and L. Idol (eds) *Dimensions of Thinking and Cognitive Instruction* (pp. 209–40), Hillsdale, NJ: Erlbaum.

Pellegrini, D.S. and Urbain, E.S. (1985) 'An evaluation of interpersonal cognitive problem solving training with children' *Journal of Child Psychology and Psychiatry 26*: 17–41.

Penfield, W. and Evans, J. (1934) 'Function deficits produced by cerebral lobectomies. Association for research in nervous and mental disease', *Localization of Function in the Cerebral Cortex* (pp. 352–77; Research Publication XIII), Baltimore, MD: Williams & Williams.

Petersen, L. and Gannoni, L. (1989) 'Stop, Think, Do: manual for social skills training in young people, with parent and teacher programs', Melbourne: Australian Council for Educational Research.

Phillips, V. and McCullough, L. (1990) 'Consultation-based programming: instituting the collaborative ethic in schools', *Exceptional Children 56*: 291–304.

Piaget, J. (1952) *The Origins of Intelligence in Children*, New York and Paris: International Universities Press.

—— (1960) *The Language and Thought of the Child*, London: Routledge & Kegan Paul.

Piersel, W.C. and Gutkin, T.B. (1983) 'Resistance to school-based consultation: a behavioral analysis of the problem', *Psychology in the Schools 20*: 311–20.

Popham, W.J. (1993) *Educational Evaluation*, 3rd edn, Boston, MA: Allyn & Bacon.

Porteus, S.D. (1965) *Porteus Maze Test: Fifty Years Application*, Palo Alto, CA: Pacific.

Pressley, M. (1994) *Transactional Instruction of Reading Comprehension Strategies*, National Reading Research Centre, Perspectives on Reading Research Report, no. 5,. Universities of Georgia and Maryland.

Pressley, M. and Woloshyn, V. (1995) *Cognitive Strategy Instruction that Really Improves Children's Academic Performance*, 2nd edn, Cambridge, MA: Brookline.

Pressley, M., Levin, J.R. and Bryant, S.L. (1983) 'Memory strategy instruction during adolescence: when is explicit instruction needed?', in M. Pressley and J.R. Levin (eds) *Cognitive Strategy Research: Psychological Foundations* (pp. 25–49), New York: Springer-Verlag.

Pressley, M., Borkowski, J.G. and Schneider, W. (1989a) 'Good information processing: what it is and how education can promote it', *International Journal of Educational Research 13*: 857–66.

Pressley, M., Goodchild, F., Fleet, J., Zajchowski, R. and Evans, E.D. (1989b) 'The challenges of classroom strategy instruction', *Elementary School Journal 89*: 301–42.

Pressley, M., Johnson, C.J., Symons, S., McGoldrick, J.A. and Kurita, J.A. (1989c) 'Strategies that improve children's memory and comprehension of text', *Elementary School Journal 90*: 3–32.

Pribram, K.H. (1986) 'The cognitive revolution and mind/brain issues', *American Psychologist 41*: 507–20.

Raven, J.C. (1962) *Coloured Progressive Matrices*, London: H.K. Lewis.

Reid, G. (1980) 'Overt and covert rehearsal in short-term memory of mentally retarded and nonretarded persons', *American Journal of Mental Deficiency 85*: 377–82.

Reid, R. and Harris, K.S. (1993) 'Self-monitoring of attention versus self-monitoring of performance: effects on attention and academic performance', *Exceptional Children 60*: 29–40.

Reitan, R.M. and Davidson, L.A. (1974) *Clinical Neuropsychology: Current Status and Applications*, New York: Winston/Wiley.

Reitan, R.M. and Wolfson, D. (1993) *Halstead-Reitan Battery*, Tucson, AZ: Reitan Neuropsychology Laboratory, University of Arizona, Tucson.

Resnick, L.B. (1987) *Education and Learning to Think*, Washington, DC: National Academic Press.

Rey, A. (1934) 'D'un procédé pour évalyuer l'educabilité (quelques applications en psychopathogie)', *Archives de Psycholgie 24*: 297–337.

Rey, A. and Dupont, J.B. (1953) 'Organization de groupes de points en figures géométriques simples', *Monographies de Psychologies Appliquée*, 3.

Rich, R. and Gentle, M. (1995) 'Integrating content and strategy instruction at the college level: a collaborative model', *Intervention in School and Clinic 31*: 97–100.

Rogoff, B. and Gardner, W. (1984) 'Adult guidance of cognitive developmen', in B. Rogoff and J. Lake (eds) *Everyday Cognition: Its Development in Social Contexts,*. Cambridge, MA: Harvard University Press.

Rohwer, W.D. and Thomas, J.W. (1989) 'Domain-specific knowledge, metacognition, and the promise of instructional reform', in C.B. McCormick, G.E. Miller and M. Pressley (eds) *Cognitive Strategy Research: From Basic Research to Educational Application* (pp. 104–32), New York: Springer-Verlag.

Rojewski, J.W. and Schell, J.W. (1994) 'Cognitive apprenticeship for learners with special needs: an alternative framework for teaching and learning', *Remedial and Special Education 15*(4): 234–43.

Rooney, E.F., Poe, E., Drescher, D. and Frantz, S.C. (1993) 'I can problem solve: an interpersonal cognitive problem-solving program', *Journal of School Psychology 31*: 335–9.

Roos, P. (1985) 'Parents of mentally retarded children: misunderstood and mistreated', in H.R. Turnbull III and A.P. Turnbull (eds) *Parents Speak Out: Then and Now* (pp. 245–60), Columbus, OH: Charles E. Merrill.

Rutland, A. and Campbell, R. (1995) 'The validity of dynamic assessment methods for children with learning difficulties and nondisabled children', *Journal of Cognitive Education 5*: 81–94.

Saariluoma, P. and Hohlfeld, M. (1994) 'Apperception in chess players' long-range planning', *European Journal of Cognitive Psychology 6*: 1–22.

Salvia, J. and Hritcko, T. (1984) 'The K-ABC and ability training', *Journal of Special Education 18*: 345–56.

Salvia, J. and Ysseldyke, J.E. (1995) *Assessment*, 6th edn, Boston, MA: Houghton Mifflin.

Samuels, M. (1995) 'Must our paradigms shift? Cognitive education in the 21st century', *Journal of Cognitive Education 4*: 1–16.

Sapp, M. (1993) *Text Anxiety: Applied Research, Assessment and Treatment Interventions*, Lanham: University Press of America.

Sapp, M. and Farrell, W. (1994) 'Cognitive-behavioral interventions: applications for academically at-risk and special education students', *Preventing School Failure* *38*(2): 19–24.

Sattler, J.M. (1992) *Assessment of Children*, 3rd edn, San Diego, CA: Jerome M. Sattler.

Schlesinger, B. (1962) *Higher Cortical Functions and their Clinical Disorders*, New York: Grune & Stratton.

Schmeck, R.R. (1988) 'Individual differences and learning strategies', in C.E. Weinstein, E.T. Goetz and P.A. Alexander (eds) *Learning and Study Strategies: Issues in Assessment, Instruction and Evaluation* (pp. 171–91), San Diego, CA: Academic Press.

Schneider, W. and Weinert, F.E. (1990) 'The role of knowledge, strategies and aptitudes in cognitive performance: concluding comments', in W. Schneider and F.E. Weinert (eds) *Interactions among Aptitudes, Strategies and Knowledge in Cognitive Performance* (pp. 286–302), New York: Springer-Verlag.

Scholnick, E.K. and Friedman, S.L. (1990) 'The planning construct in the psychological literature', in S.L. Friedman, E.K. Scholnick and R.R. Cocking (eds) *Blueprints for Thinking: The Role of Planning in Cognitive Development* (pp. 3–38), Cambridge: Cambridge University Press.

Schucman, H. (1960) 'Evaluating the educability of the severely mentally retarded child', *Psychological Monographs 74*(14): whole no. 501.

Schunk, D.L. (1990) 'Self-efficacy and cognitive achievement: implications for students with learning problems', in J.K. Torgesen (ed.) *Cognitive and Behavior Characteristics of Children with Learning Difficulties*, Austin, TX: ProEd.

Scruggs, T.T. and Ritcher, L. (1988) 'Tutoring learning disabled students: a critical review', *Learning Disability Quarterly 11*: 274–86.

Shachar, H. and Sharan, S. (1994) 'Talking, relating and achieving: effects of cooperative learning and whole-class instruction', *Cognition and Instruction 12*: 313–53.

Sharan, S. (ed.) (1990) *Cooperative Learning Theory and Research*, New York: Praeger.

Sheinker, J. and Sheinker, A. (1988) *A Metacognitive Approach to Social Skills Training*, Rockville, MD: Aspen.

Sheridan, S.M., Kratochwill, T.R. and Elliott, S.N. (1990) 'Behavioral consultation with parents and teachers: delivering treatment for socially withdrawn children at home and school', *School Psychology Review 19*: 33–52.

Sherrington, C.S. (1933) *The Brain and its Mechanisms*, London: Cambridge University Press.

Shif, Z.I. (1969) 'Development of children in schools for the mentally retarded', in M. Cole and I. Maltzman (eds) *A Handbook of Contemporary Soviet Psychology* (pp 326–53), New York: Basic Books.

Short, E.J. and Weissberg-Benchell, J.A. (1989) 'The triple alliance for learning: cognition, metacognition and motivation', in C.B. McCormick, G.E. Miller and M. Pressley (eds) *Cognitive Strategy Research: From Basic Research to Educational Application* (pp. 33–64), New York: Springer-Verlag.

Short, E.J., Schatschneider, C.W. and Friebert, S.E. (1993) 'Relationship between memory and metamemory performance: a comparison of specific and general strategy knowledge', *Journal of Educational Psychology 85*: 412–23.

Shure, M.B. (1992) *I Can Problem Solve: An Interpersonal Cognitive Problem-solving Program*, Champaign, IL: Research Press.

Simpson, M.L. (1995) 'Talk throughs: a strategy for encouraging active learning across the content areas', *Journal of Reading 38*: 296–304.

Skinner, B.F. (1968) *The Technology of Teaching*, New York: Appleton-Century-Crofts.

——— (1971) *Beyond Freedom and Dignity*, New York: Alfred A. Knopf.

Skrtic, T.M. (1991) 'The special education paradox: equity as the way to excellence', *Harvard Educational Review 61*: 148–206.

Slavin, R.E. (1990) 'Mastery learning re-reconsidered', *Review of Educational Research 60*: 300–2.

Snow, R.E. (1989) 'Aptitude-treatment interaction as a framework for research on individual differences in learning', in P.A. Ackerman, R.J. Sternberg and R. Glaser (eds) *Learning and Individual Differences* (pp. 13–59), New York: W.H. Freeman.

Spearman, C. (1904) '"General intelligence" objectively defined and measured', *American Journal of Psychology 15*: 201–93.

Sternberg, R.J. (1977) *Intelligence, Information Processing, and Analogical Reasoning: The Componential Analysis of Human Abilities*, Hillsdale, NJ: Erlbaum.

——— (1980) 'Sketch of a componential subtheory of human intelligence', *Behavior and Brain Science 3*: 573–614.

——— (1985) *Beyond IQ: A Triarchic Theory of Human Intelligence*, Cambridge: Cambridge University Press.

Stevens, K.B., Blackhurst, A. E. and Slaton, D. (1991) 'Teaching memorized spelling with a micro-computer: time delay and computer-assisted instruction', *Journal of Applied Behavior Analysis 24*: 153–60.

Stokes, T.F. and Baer, D.M. (1977) 'An implicit technology of generalization', *Journal of Applied Behavior Analysis 10*: 349–67.

Swanson, H.L. and Hill, G. (1993) 'Metacognitive aspects of moral reasoning and behavior', *Adolescence 28*: 711–35.

Sweller, J. (1990) 'On the limited evidence for the effectiveness of teaching general problem-solving strategies', *Journal of Research in Mathematics Education 21*: 411–15.

Szepkouski, G.M., Gauvain, M. and Carberry, M. (1994) 'The development of planning skills in children with and without mental retardation', *Journal of Applied Developmental Psychology 15*: 187–206.

Taffe, R. and Smith, I.D. (1994) 'Behavioural and cognitive approaches to social skills training with young children', *Australasian Journal of Special Education 18*: 26–35.

Terman, L.M. (1916) *The Measurement of Intelligence*, Boston, MA: Houghton Mifflin.

Terman, L. and Merrill, M. (1973) *Stanford-Binet Intelligence Scale*, Chicago, IL: Riverside.

Tharp, R.G. and Gallimore, R. (1985) 'The logical status of metacognitive training', *Journal of Abnormal Child Psychology 13*: 455–66.

Thorndike, E.L. (1913) *The Psychology of Learning*, New York: Macmillan.

——— (1931) *Human Learning*, New York: Appleton-Century-Crofts.

Thorndike, R.L., Hagen, E. and Sattler, J. (1985) *Stanford-Binet Intelligence Scale*, Chicago, IL: Riverside.

Thurstone, L.L. (1938) 'Primary mental abilities', *Psychological Monographs 1*.

Todman, J. and McBeth, J. (1994) 'Optimal mismatch for transfer of planning skills by slow learners', *British Journal of Developmental Psychology 12*: 195–208.

Tolan, S.S. (1987) 'Parents and "professionals": a question of priorities', *Roeper Review 9*: 184–7.

Towers, J.M. (1992) 'Outcome-based education: friend or foe?', *Educational Research Quarterly 15*: 5–20.

Turner, L.A. and Bray, N.W. (1985) 'Spontaneous rehearsal by mildly mentally retarded children and adolescents', *American Journal of Mental Deficiency 90*: 57–63.

Tzuriel, D. (1992) 'The dynamic assessment approach: a reply to Frisby and Braden', *Journal of Special Education* 26: 302–24.

Tzuriel, D. and Haywood, H.C. (1992) 'The development of interactive-dynamic approaches to assessment of learning potential', in H.C. Haywood and D. Tzuriel (eds) *Interactive Assessment* (pp. 3–37), New York: Springer-Verlag.

Tzuriel, D. and Kaniel, S. (1992) 'Evaluation of CCYC (Cognitive Curriculum for Young Children) in Israel', paper given at the Third International Congress of the Association for Cognitive Education, Riverside, CA, February.

Valletutti, P.J. and Dummett, L. (1992) *Cognitive Development: A Functional Approach*, San Diego, CA: Singular.

van den Wijngaert, R. (1991) 'Cognitive education with speech and language disordered children', *The Thinking Teacher* 6(3): 1–5.

Vaughn, S., Schumm, J.S. and Gordon, J. (1993) 'Which motoric condition is most effective for teaching spelling to students with and without learning disabilities?', *Journal of Learning Disabilities* 26(3): 191–8.

Vernon, P.E. (1969) *Intelligence and Cultural Environment*, London: Methuen.

Vosler-Hunter, R.W. (1989) *Changing Roles, Changing Relationships: Parent–Professional Collaboration on Behalf of Children with Emotional Disabilities*, Portland, OR: Portland State University, Research and Training Center on Family Support and Children's Mental Health.

Vygotsky, L.S. (1962) *Thought and Language*, Cambridge, MA: MIT Press.

—— (1978) *Mind in Society: The Development of Higher Psychological Processes*, edited and translated by M. Cole, V. John-Steiner, S. Scribner and E. Souberman, Cambridge, MA: Harvard University Press.

Warnez, J. (1991) 'Implementation of the CCYC in a therapeutic center', *The Thinking Teacher* 6(1): 7–9.

Watson, J.B. (1913) 'Psychology as the behaviorist views it', *Psychological Review* 20: 157–8.

—— (1930) *Behaviorism*, 2nd edn, Chicago: University of Chicago Press.

Watson, J.B. and Raynor, R. (1920) 'Conditional emotional reactions', *Journal of Experimental Psychology* 3: 1–4.

Waugh, R. (1995) 'Assessment and standardised testing', in F. Malty, N.L. Gage and D.C. Berliner (eds) *Educational Psychology: An Australian Perspective* (pp. 555–80), Brisbane: John Wiley.

Wechsler, D. (1949) *The Wechsler Intelligence Scale for Children*, Cleveland, OH: Psychological Corporation.

—— (1955) *The Wechsler Adult Intelligence Scale*, Cleveland, OH: Psychological Corporation.

—— (1967) *The Wechsler Preschool and Primary Scale of Intelligence*, Cleveland, OH: Psychological Corporation.

Weinert, F.E. and Perlmutter, M. (eds) (1988) *Memory Development: Universal Changes and Individual Differences*, Hillsdale, NJ: Erlbaum.

West, J.F. and Cannon, G.S. (1988) 'Essential collaborative consultation competencies for regular and special educators', *Journal of Learning Disabilities* 21: 56–63.

West, J.F. and Idol, L. (1987) 'School consultation (Part 1): an interdisciplinary perspective on theory, models, and research', *Journal of Learning Disabilities* 20: 388–408.

Westwood, P. (1993) *Commonsense Methods for Children with Special Needs*, 2nd edn, London: Routledge.

Wheldall, K. and Merrett, F. (1984) *Positive Teaching: The Behavioural Approach*, London: Allen & Unwin.

Whitaker, P. (1995) *Managing to Learn*, London: Cassell.

Wilson, D. (1996) 'The school psychologist as co-teacher: an example using the COGNET program as a means of teaching thinking skills', *Journal of Cognitive Education 5*: 171–83.

Wilson, M.S. and Reschly, D.J. (1996) 'Assessment in school psychology: training and practice', *School Psychology Review 25*: 9–23.

Witt, J.C. (1990) 'Collaboration in school-based consultation: myth in need of data', *Journal of Educational and Psychological Consultation 1*: 367–70.

Wittrock, M.C. (1988) 'A constructive review of research on learning strategies', in C.E. Weinstein, E.T. Goetz and P.A. Alexander (eds) *Learning and Study Strategies: Issues in Assessment, Instruction and Evaluation* (pp. 287–98), San Diego, CA: Academic Press.

Wolfgram, C. and Goldstein, M.L. (1987) 'The search for the physical basis of memory', *Bulletin of the Psychonomic Society 25*: 65–8.

Wong, B.Y.L. (1993) 'Pursuing an elusive goal: molding strategic teachers and learners', *Journal of Learning Disabilities 26*: 354–7.

Wong, B.Y.L., Harris, K.S. and Graham, S. (1991) 'Academic applications of cognitive-behavioral programs with learning disabled students', in P.C. Kendall (ed.) *Child and Adolescent Therapy: Cognitive-behavioral Procedures* (pp. 245–75), New York: Guilford.

Woodcock, R.W. and Johnson, M.B. (1989) *Woodcock-Johnson Psycho-Educational Battery – Revised*, Riverside, CA: DML Teaching Resources.

Yates, F.A. (1969) *The Art of Memory*, Harmondsworth: Penguin.

Yerkes, R.M. (1921) 'Psychological examining in the army', in *Memoirs of the National Academy of Sciences* (vol. 15), Washington, DC: US Government Printing Office.

York, J., Doyle, M.B. and Kronberg, R. (1992) 'A curriculum development process for inclusive classrooms', *Focus on Exceptional Children 25*(4): 1–16.

Zimmerman, B.J. (1989) 'Models of self-regulated learning and academic achievement', in B. Zimmerman and D. Schunk (eds) *Self-regulated Learning and Academic Achievement: Theory, Research and Practice* (pp. 1–25), New York: Springer-Verlag.

—— (1990) 'Self-regulated learning and academic achievement: an overview', *Educational Psychologist 25*: 3–17.

Zimmerman, B.J. and Martinez-Pons, M. (1988) 'Construct validation of a strategy model of student self-regulated learning', *Journal of Educational Psychology 80*: 284–90.

Zinkin, L. (1987) 'The hologram as a model for analytical psychology', *Journal of Analytical Psychology 32*: 1–21.

Author index

Subject index

Note: page numbers in italics refer to figures or diagrams